Richard Bickerton Pemell Lyons

Correspondence Relating to the Civil War in the United States of North America

Richard Bickerton Pemell Lyons

Correspondence Relating to the Civil War in the United States of North America

ISBN/EAN: 9783337410759

Printed in Europe, USA, Canada, Australia, Japan

Cover: Foto ©ninafisch / pixelio.de

More available books at **www.hansebooks.com**

NORTH AMERICA.
No. 1.

CORRESPONDENCE

RELATING TO THE

CIVIL WAR

IN THE

UNITED STATES

OF

NORTH AMERICA.

Presented to both Houses of Parliament by Command of Her Majesty.
1862.

LONDON:
PRINTED BY HARRISON AND SONS.

TABLE OF CONTENTS.

No.		Date.	Subject.	Page
1.	Lord Lyons	Nov. 12, 1860	Election of Mr. Lincoln as President. Dissatisfaction in Southern States. Apprehensions of danger to Union	1
2.	To Lord Lyons	29,	Concern of Her Majesty's Government on learning that Secession of States from the Union is apprehended	2
3.	Lord Lyons	Dec. 4,	Inclosing copy of letter from Mr. Porcher Miles, Member of Congress of South Carolina, alluding to probable Secession of Southern States, and inclosing Pamphlet on nature of the Federative system	2
4.	,, ,,	4,	Probability of South Carolina immediately declaring herself an independent State	3
5.	,, ,,	10,	Tenour of President's Message. Reception of, by Congress. Tone of Southern Members. Alarm of North	3
6.	To Lord Lyons	26,	Views of Her Majesty's Government. Observations on President's Message	4
7.	Lord Lyons	18,	Progress of events. Hopes of preserving the Union not strengthened. Little moderation to be expected from cotton-growing States. Overweening notion their own importance	5
8.	,, ,,	18,	Resignation of General Cass, Secretary of State, Mr. Howell Cobb, Secretary of the Treasury, and Mr. Trescott, Assistant Secretary of State	6
9.	To Lord Lyons	Jan. 5, 1861	Instructions in the event of being asked advice by Mr. Lincoln's Cabinet	7
10.	Lord Lyons	Dec. 24, 1860	Ordinance passed at Charleston declaring Secession of South Carolina. Effect produced	7
11.	,, ,,	31,	Progress of events unfavourable to maintenance of Union. Speech of Mr. Benjamin, Senator for Louisiana	7
12.	,, ,,	Jan. 15, 1861	Rapid progress of disunion. Formal secession of Mississippi, Florida, and Alabama. Appeal of President to Congress. Speech from Mr. Seward	8
13.	,, ,,	21,	Progress of events unfavourable to solution of difficulties. Secession of Georgia. Proceedings of Legislature of Virginia	10
14.	,, ,,	29,	Secession of Louisiana. Policy of Federal Government. Expectations entertained from Convention of Commissioners of non-Slave-holding and Slave-holding States summoned by State of Virginia on 4th of February	11
15.	To Lord Lyons	Feb. 12,	Hopes of Her Majesty's Government from steps taken by Legislature of Virginia	12
16.	Lord Lyons	4,	First meeting of Convention of Commissioners. Hopes of a compromise. Further speech of Mr. Seward. His views on state of the country	12
17.	To Lord Lyons	20,	Policy of Her Majesty's Government in the event of Mr. Lincoln raising questions with Great Britain	13
18.	Lord Lyons	12,	Results of elections in Virginia and Tennessee. Hopes of Unionists raised thereby. Proceedings of Congress of Montgomery. Sittings of Commissioners of Slave-holding States. Plan of Northern politicians	13
19.	To Mr. Dallas	Mar. 21,	Inclosing draft of despatch of March 22 to Lord Lyons. As to whether purport of despatch from Judge Black is correctly represented therein	14
20.	Mr. Dallas	21,	Returning draft of despatch to Lord Lyons of March 22, approved	14
21.	To Lord Lyons	22,	Substance of Judge Black's despatch of February 28. As to whether Great Britain would recognize Seceded States. Substance of reply to Mr. Dallas	14

TABLE OF CONTENTS.

No.		Date.	Subject.	Page
22.	Lord Lyons	Mar. 12, 1861	Closing of thirty-sixth Congress of United States. Special session of thirty-seventh Congress. Proceedings of. Observations on Inaugural Address. Appointment of Cabinet	14
23.	,, ,,	18,	Intentions of new Administration obscure. Probable evacuation of Fort Sumter	16
24.	To Lord Lyons	Apr. 6,	To recommend conciliation if opinion is asked; but not to obtrude advice unasked	17
25.	Mr. Seward to Mr. Dallas	Mar. 9,	To take measures to prevent the success of efforts which may be made to procure recognition of Southern States by Great Britain. Inclosing Address of President for communication	17
26.	To Lord Lyons	Apr. 12,	Inclosing copy of Mr. Seward's despatch of March 9, and reporting substance of conversation with Mr. Dallas	19
27.	Lord Lyons	15,	Surrender of Fort Sumter. Adoption of coercive measures against the South. Apprehensions of an attack on Washington	19
28.	To the Lords Commissioners of the Admiralty	May 1,	Necessity of reinforcing Her Majesty's squadron on the North American and West India Station	20
29.	Lord Lyons	Apr. 22,	Inclosing letter to Sir E. Head relative to report that secret Agents had been sent from the United States to Canada	21
30.	,, ,,	22,	Progress of events leading to civil war. Military movements	22
31.	,, ,,	22,	Proclamation of President of Southern Confederacy inviting application for letters of marque. Proclamation of President Lincoln declaring Southern privateers pirates, and announcing blockade of Southern ports	23
32.	,, ,,	23,	Inclosing copy of letter from Mr. Seward to Governor of Maryland rejecting proposal made by latter that Lord Lyons should act as mediator between contending parties	25
33.	To Lord Lyons	May 11,	Reporting substance of conversation with Messrs. Yancey, Rost, and Mann	26
34.	Lord Lyons	Apr. 27,	Military operations. Virginian Convention has decreed union of the State with Southern Confederacy	26
35.	To Lord Lyons	May 15,	Inclosing Her Majesty's Proclamation of Neutrality	27
36.	,, ,,	16,	Impression produced on Her Majesty's Government by Mr. Seward's explanations respecting secret Agents sent to Canada	30
37.	Lord Lyons	2,	Calling out of Militia. Raising of volunteers and military preparations	30
38.	,, ,,	2,	Representations of Mr. Seward respecting the steamer "Peerless," a vessel under British colours. Protest of Lord Lyons against intended seizure of	31
39.	To Lord Lyons	18,	Approving course adopted by Lord Lyons with regard to the "Peerless"	33
40.	Lord Lyons	4,	Agents sent by United States' Government to England and France to purchase arms	33
41.	To Lord Lyons	21,	Conversation with Mr. Adams respecting the Secession. As to recognition of the Confederate States	34
42.	Lord Lyons	11,	Southern Congress has declared war against the United States, and has authorized issue of letters of marque	35
43.	,, ,,	11,	Copy of despatch from Sir E. Head relative to Agent sent by Mr. Seward to Canada	35
44.	,, ,,	12,	Progress of events. Probable period of war. Secession of Tennessee and Arkansas	37
45.	To Lord Commissioners of the Admiralty	June 1,	Interdiction to armed ships and privateers from carrying prizes into British ports, harbours, &c.	38
46.	To Lord Lyons	1,	Inclosing copy of the above	38
47.	Lord Lyons	May 21,	Further intelligence. No collision as yet between North and South	38
48.	,, ,,	23,	Tone of Northern Press on learning that England and France acknowledge the South as a belligerent	39
49.	,, ,,	23,	Renewal of plan for declaring Southern ports not ports of entry. Proposal to collect Customs duties on board ship	39
50.	,, ,,	23,	No military operations of importance. Southern Congress adjourned, and will meet again at Richmond on July 20. North Carolina has passed Ordinance of Secession	40

No.		Date.	Subject.	Page
51. Lord Lyons	..	May 25, 1861	Inclosing circular addressed to Collectors, &c., on the Northern and North-Western waters of the United States respecting vessels attempting to convey munitions of war ..	40
52. To Lord Lyons	..	June 21,	Position assumed by Her Majesty's Government. Conversation with Mr. Adams with reference to the Queen's Proclamation	42
53. Lord Lyons	..	8,	Inclosing Act of Southern Congress prohibiting export of cotton, except through ports of Confederate States	43
54. ,, ,,	..	8,	Case of the "Winifred." Apparent recognition by Federal Government of Article 3 of Declaration of Paris ..	44
55. To Lord Lyons	..	29,	Conversation with Mr. Adams relative to the Confederate vessel "Peter Marcy" which has arrived in the Thames. Copies of correspondence with Treasury, respecting ..	45
56. Lord Lyons	..	17,	Communication to Mr. Seward of interdiction respecting taking prizes into British ports ..	46
57. ,, ,,	..	17,	Secret Agent in Canada. Communication to Mr. Seward of dissatisfaction of Her Majesty's Government	47
58. Earl Cowley	..	July 4,	Closing of Southern ports. French Government will not admit legality of the Decree	47
59. To Lord Lyons	..	6,	Closing Southern ports. Concur with French Government. Lord Lyons to act with M. Mercier	47
60. Lord Lyons	..	1,	Merchandize for Seceded States. Circular prohibiting export of. Requests instructions	48
61. To Lord Lyons	..	19,	Judge Dunlop's decision in case of the "Tropic Wind." Argument against right of closing Southern ports ..	49
62. Lord Lyons	..	8,	Inclosing President's Message. Temper of Congress. Military movements ..	54
63. ,, ,,	..	12,	Inclosing copy of Bill further to provide for the collection of duties on imports, &c.	55
64. ,, ,,	..	12,	Inclosing copy of a Joint Resolution to approve acts of President for suppressing insurrection and rebellion.	57
65. ,, ,,	..	15,	Act closing ports of entry, and for collecting of duties on shipboard, passed both Houses of Congress	58
66. ,, ,,	..	16,	Proceedings of Congress	58
67. ,, ,,	..	19,	Inclosing copy of Act of Congress respecting the collection of duties on board ship and closing Southern ports	58
68. ,, ,,	..	20,	Act closing Southern ports. Steps taken in conjunction with M. Mercier	59
69. ,, ,,	..	22,	Defeat of Federal army at Bull's Run	60
70. To Lord Lyons	..	Aug. 8,	Bill for regulating Customs duties and Act closing Southern ports. Observations and instructions respecting	61
71. ,, ,,	..	9,	Lord Lyons to use his discretion as to communicating the preceding despatch	62
72. Lord Lyons	..	July 29,	Mr. Seward declines to produce correspondence with foreign Powers relative to "maritime rights" and "existing insurrection"	62
73. ,, ,,	..	30,	Loans voted by Congress. Steps taken for increasing the revenue. Progress of affairs ..	63
74. Messrs. Yancey, Rost, and Mann		Aug. 14,	Giving history of the Secession, and stating grounds on which they urge recognition of Confederate States	63
75. Mr. Adams	..	15,	Steamer fitting out at Hartlepool for hostile purposes. Requests steps may be taken	69
76. To Mr. Adams	..	15,	Answer to the above. Proper Department has been informed	70
77. ,, ,,	..	22,	Steamer fitting out at Hartlepool. Not evidence enough to warrant interference of Her Majesty's Government ..	70
78. To Messrs. Yancey, Rost, and Mann		24,	Receipt of their letter of August 14. Her Majesty's Government intend to observe a strict neutrality between contending parties ..	70
79. Lord Lyons	..	12,	Inclosing copy of Act of Congress for protection of commerce, and for punishment of the crime of piracy	71
80. ,, ,,	..	12,	Congress, adjournment of. Legalization of blockade ..	71
81. ,, ,,	..	12,	Closing the Southern ports. Has informed Mr. Seward that British Government will not recognize the Decree	72
82. To Lord Lyons	..	27,	Approving steps taken, as reported in preceding despatch	73

TABLE OF CONTENTS.

No.		Date.	Subject.	Page
83. Lord Lyons		Aug. 19, 1861	Commercial intercourse with the Southern States. Inclosing copy of Proclamation prohibiting	73
84. ,, ,,		19,	Arrangement for raising money on Treasury bonds	74
85. ,, ,,		27,	Intends to consult M. Mercier before communicating instructions to Mr. Seward respecting closing of Southern ports	76
86. To Lord Lyons		19,	The intervention of Her Majesty's Government not necessary as regards the Act passed by Congress for protection of commerce and punishment of piracy	76
87. Lord Lyons		Sept. 6,	Relative to arrest of Mr. Patrick. Inclosing correspondence on the subject, and calling attention to the system of arbitrary arrest	76
88. ,, ,,		6,	Relative to illegal arrest and imprisonment of Mr. John C. Rahming. Officers of army decline to make any return to writs of *habeas corpus*	79
89. To Lord Lyons		28,	Receipt of the two preceding despatches. To remonstrate against arbitrary arrests of British subjects	81
90. Lord Lyons		16,	General report on the state of affairs	81
91. Mr. Adams		30,	Southern privateer "Sumter" at Trinidad. Complaint against authorities of that island for violation of the Queen's Proclamation	82
92. ,, ,,		Oct. 1,	Representation respecting alleged violation of the Queen's Proclamation by Mr. Adderley, of Nassau, New Providence	83
93. To Lord Lyons		3,	Prohibition of commerce with the South. Opinion respecting Proclamation	84
94. To Mr. Adams		4,	Governor of Trinidad has not violated the Queen's Proclamation as regards the "Sumter"	85
95. Lord Lyons		Sept. 23,	Inclosing copy of circular addressed to Marshals and District Attorneys of United States relative to confiscating property belonging to inhabitants of Southern States	85
96. To Mr. Adams		Oct. 8,	Relative to alleged violation of neutrality. Proclamation at Nassau. Inquiries will be instituted	86
97. Lord Lyons		Sept. 30,	Information respecting the loan. Weekly amount of regular expenditure	86
98. ,, ,,		Oct. 8,	Expedition on large scale to act on coasts of Southern States. Question of opening a port for the exportation of cotton	87
99. ,, ,,		12,	Copy of a despatch from Sir E. Head relative to a violation of British territory by United States' soldiers	88
100. ,, ,,		14,	Inclosing copy of note to Mr. Seward remonstrating against arbitrary arrests of British subjects	89
101. ,, ,,		17,	Inclosing copy of further despatch from Governor-General of Canada respecting violation of British territory	90
102. ,, ,,		17,	Inclosing copy of a despatch from Sir E. Head relative to attempt to enlist men in Canada for the United States' army	92
103. ,, ,,		18,	Copy of note from Mr. Seward respecting arbitrary arrests of British subjects. As to power of the President to suspend writ of *habeas corpus*	93
104. To Lord Lyons		Nov. 5,	Approving note to Mr. Seward respecting violation of Canadian territory	96
105. Lord Lyons		Oct. 24,	Inclosing copy of note from Mr. Seward respecting attempt of Federal Government to raise troops in Canada	96
106. ,, ,,		24,	Inclosing newspaper extract containing case of arrest of Judge Merrick with reference to suspension of writ of *habeas corpus*	97
107. To Lord Lyons		Nov. 9,	Relative to indemnification to Mr. Rahming for his imprisonment. Useless, at present, to renew discussion on the subject	99
108. Lord Lyons		4,	Inclosing correspondence with Mr. Seward respecting violation of Canadian territory	100
109. ,, ,,		4,	Conversation with Mr. Seward respecting reception of privateer "Sumter" in British and Dutch ports	101
110. ,, ,,		4,	Conversation with Mr. Seward relative to communications between the British and French Government and the *de facto* Government in the South, and to the arbitrary arrests of British subjects	102
111. ,, ,,		4,	Mr. Seward requests to be informed whether anything has passed between British and French Governments respecting the cotton supply	103
112. To Lord Lyons		22,	Instruction respecting reception of Confederate vessels in British ports	103

No.		Date.	Subject.	Page
113.	To Lord Lyons	Nov. 22, 1861	Instructions relative to the arbitrary arrests of Messrs. Patrick and Rahming, and to the suspension of the writ of *habeas corpus*	103
114.	Lord Lyons	9,	Mr. Seward urges non-admission of Confederate vessels into British ports	104
115.	Messrs. Yancey, Rost, and Mann	30,	Calling attention to the ineffective nature of the blockade of the Southern ports, and inclosing list of vessels which have broken it..	105
116.	Lord Lyons	15,	Proceedings of the great naval expedition against the Southern Coast	107
117.	,, ,,	18,	Inclosing copy of a despatch from Viscount Monck accepting the explanation given by Mr. Seward of the violation of Canadian territory	107
118.	,, ,,	18,	Inclosing copy of a despatch from Mr. Consul Cridland, reporting proceedings taken under the Sequestration Act of the Confederate States	108
119.	To Acting Consul Cridland	Dec. 6,	Instructing him to remonstrate against the Sequestration Act of the Confederate States	108
120.	To Her Majesty's Consuls in the Confederate States	6,	Instructions to protest, if necessary, against the Sequestration Act of the Confederate States	109
121.	To Admiralty	6,	To cause the preceding instructions to be conveyed to their respective destinations	110
122.	To Lord Lyons	6,	Inclosing copies of the instructions to Her Majesty's Consuls in the Confederate States respecting the Sequestration Act	110
123.	Lord Lyons	Nov. 22,	Inclosing copy of circular to Collectors and other officers of the United States' Customs relative to the seizure of vessels under the 6th section of the Act of Congress of July 13, 1861	110
124.	To Messrs. Yancey, Rost, and Mann	Dec. 7,	Receipt of letter of November 30. Declining to enter into any official communication with them	111
125.	Lord Lyons	Nov. 25,	Progress of military and naval operations	112
126.	,, ,,	29,	Inclosing extracts from newspapers relative to preparations made by Federal Government to obstruct harbours and inlets of the South by sinking ships laden with stones	113
127.	To Lord Lyons	Dec. 20,	View of Her Majesty's Government in regard to intention of the President to block up harbours of the South	114
128.	,, ,,	20,	Great Britain prepared to abolish privateering in the event of war, if United States will agree	114
129.	,, ,,	20,	Instructions relative to the circular issued by United States' Treasury with regard to the seizure of ships	114
130.	Lord Lyons	6,	Inclosing copy of the Papers relating to Foreign Affairs which have been laid before Congress. Observations thereon	115
131.	,, ,,	13,	Estimate of the expenditure of the Federal Government for the year ending June 30, 1862	116
132.	To Mr. Adams	Jan. 8, 1862	Explanation respecting the alleged shipments of warlike stores through Nassau for the Confederate States	117
133.	Mr. Adams	10,	Satisfaction at the above	118
134.	Lord Lyons	Dec. 31, 1861	Restoration of the persons taken from the "Eugenia Smith"	118
135.	,, ,,	31,	Suspension of specie payments	119
136.	,, ,,	31,	Oath exacted from three seamen of the "Adeline." Mr. Seward releases them from their obligation	119
137.	,, ,,	31,	Insult to the British flag in the case of the "James Campbell." The act disavowed by the United States' Government	121
138.	,, ,,	Jan. 2, 1862	Bill introduced into Congress to declare the Southern ports closed	123
139.	,, ,,	2,	Measures adopted to stop up the Southern ports by sinking vessels laden with stones	126
140.	,, ,,	3,	Projected naval and military movements	127
141.	The Liverpool Shipowners' Association	13,	Representation as to the stoppage of Charleston harbour by sinking vessels laden with stones	128
142.	To Liverpool Shipowners' Association	15,	Answer to the above. Instructions sent to Lord Lyons	128
143.	To Lord Lyons	16,	Instructions to remonstrate with the United States' Government as to the stoppage of Southern harbours	129
144.	,, ,,	16,	Satisfaction at the seamen of the "Adeline" having been released from their oath	129
145.	,, ,,	17,	Receipt of despatch of 2nd instant as to stoppage of Southern ports by sinking stones. Instructions already sent	129
146.	,, ,,	17,	Satisfaction at the release of the persons taken from the "Eugenia Smith"	130

No.		Date.	Subject.	Page
147.	To Lord Lyons	Jan. 17, 1862	Satisfaction at the course pursued regarding the "James Campbell"	130
148.	Lord Lyons	4,	Treatment of Southern privateersmen. Letter in the "New York Tribune"	130
149.	,, ,,	4,	Official receptions on New Year's Day	133
150.	,, ,,	9,	Correspondence respecting the "James Campbell"	134
151.	,, ,,	9,	Correspondence respecting the seamen of the "Adeline"	135
152.	To Lord Lyons	24,	Treatment of Southern privateersmen. Prisoners taken should be regarded as prisoners of war	137
153.	Lord Lyons	14,	Explanation offered by Mr. Seward as to the obstruction of Southern harbours	137
154.	,, ,,	14,	Note from Mr. Seward respecting the arrests of British subjects	138
155.	,, ,,	14,	Interview with Mr. Seward. Postal communication with the South	139
156.	To Lord Lyons	Feb. 1,	Inclosing a copy of the instructions issued for the preservation of neutrality in all places within British jurisdiction	139

Correspondence relating to the Civil War in the United States of North America.

No. 1.

Lord Lyons to Lord J. Russell.—(Received November 27.)

My Lord, *Washington, November* 12, 1860.

THE result of the primary elections has been to ensure to Mr. Lincoln a larger number of votes in the Electoral College than is necessary to place him in the Presidential Chair. He is therefore virtually elected President for the term beginning on the 4th of March next, and ending on the 4th of March, 1865.

This transfer of the executive power from the South to the North, from the Pro-Slavery to the Anti-Slavery party, has caused an explosion of dissatisfaction in some of the Southern States, even more violent than was anticipated. In South Carolina especially the excitement has carried men of all classes beyond the bounds of reason and common sense. In the Federal Court of that State the Grand Jury declined to proceed with their presentments on the ground that "the verdict of the Northern section of the Confederacy, solemnly announced to the people through the ballot-box, had swept away the last hope for the permanence, for the stability, of the Federal Government." In reply, the Judge announced from the Bench his own resignation, and declared that, "so far as he was concerned, the temple of justice raised under the Constitution of the United States was closed." The United States' District Attorney followed the example of the Judge, and threw up his office on the spot. Other Federal officers have also resigned their appointments. Mr. Chesnut, one of the two Members for South Carolina of the United States' Senate, has given up his seat in that body. The Legislature of the State has passed unanimously a Resolution calling a Convention of the people to decide the question of secession from the Union. Preparations have been made for organising and arming military bodies to resist the Federal troops in case the Government of the Confederation should attempt to enforce the execution of the constitution and laws of the United States. A separate flag for the State, bearing a "lone" star, has been devised and hoisted. In Georgia and some other States proceedings of less violence, but of the same character, have been resorted to.

These ill-judged measures are the fruits of passion and resentment rather than of any real apprehension of danger from the passing of the Executive power into the hands of the Republican party. All this violence is, to say the least, premature. Mr. Lincoln is himself very little known, and he has not hitherto made any announcement of his intentions with regard to the composition of his Cabinet. It is generally expected that he will endeavour to conciliate the South by forming an eminently Conservative Administration. At any rate, his means of interfering with the institution of slavery or injuring the interests of the South will be but small. For the party which has placed him in power will be in a minority in both Houses of the Legislature for the next two years at least, unless, indeed, some of the Southern States withdraw their Members.

It is, indeed, by thus declining to send Senators and Representatives to Congress that the smaller Southern States may be able to bring the Union into danger. There seems to be little doubt that a Conservative majority has the preponderance in the South, and that the bulk of the Southern people desire to cling to the Union, so long, at all events, as their influence in Congress is sufficient to protect them from all attacks from the Anti-Slavery party. But if, by the withdrawal of the Members for South Carolina and three or four more of the violent little States, the Anti-Slavery Party should be placed in possession of a permanent working majority in the Congress, then the whole South may be brought to consider it necessary in self-defence to secede from the Confederation.

So far as I can judge, the opinion of the most sagacious politicians of this country is that the Union is really in danger, certainly in much greater danger than it has ever been before, but that it will nevertheless weather this storm. Confidence, however, in its absolute permanence is very much shaken. If the passions and supposed interests of North and South continue to be so conflicting that parties in the Confederation are divided by a geographical line, all the voters from one side of which are invariably opposed to all the voters from the other side, then, indeed, it will be impossible to maintain the Union. But it is hoped that the present parties may disappear under Mr. Lincoln's Administration, and that a Union party may be formed on such principles as may rally to it men of Conservative principles from both North and South.

In the meantime alarm and agitation are beginning to produce the injury to trade and industry which ever follows them. A considerable depreciation of public securities has already taken place, and other evil consequences are seriously apprehended.

I have, &c.
(Signed)   LYONS.

No. 2.

Lord J. Russell to Lord Lyons.

My Lord,   *Foreign Office, November* 29, 1860.
I HAVE received your Lordship's despatch of the 12th instant, reporting the excitement in some of the Southern States caused by the selection of the Republican candidate for the office of President of the United States.

I have in reply to state to you that Her Majesty's Government learn with concern that there is danger of secession from the great Confederacy of States which form the North American Union; but Her Majesty's Government trust that the prudence and good sense of the new President and his Administration will preserve that Union.

I am, &c.
(Signed)   J. RUSSELL.

No. 3.

Lord Lyons to Lord J. Russell.—(*Received December* 18.)

My Lord,   *Washington, December* 4, 1860.
I HAVE the honour to inclose a copy of a letter which has been addressed to me by Mr. William Porcher Miles, one of the Members of Congress for South Carolina. A similar letter has been addressed by Mr. Miles to the other Representatives of Foreign Powers at Washington.

I should not have troubled your Lordship with a copy of the letter, had I not heard that it had been represented as an overture from South Carolina for the recognition of her independence. It does not, however, appear to me to bear that construction. I have no intention of making any answer to it.

I have not been able to obtain more than one copy for your Lordship of each of the pamphlets which accompanied it. They do not appear to contain any new arguments on the well-worn themes to which they relate.

I have, &c.
(Signed)   LYONS.

Inclosure in No. 3.

Mr. Miles to Lord Lyons.

My Lord,   *Charleston, South Carolina, November* 15, 1860.
I TAKE the liberty of sending your Lordship a pamphlet upon the relations of the States composing the Confederacy to the "General" or United States' Government.

At a time when there is almost a certainty that several of the Southern States will secede from the present Union, and form a new Confederacy among themselves, it is desirable that the Representatives of foreign nations at Washington, who must watch with deep interest such a movement, should be correctly informed of the nature of our Federative system. This is the more important in view of the fact that foreign Powers may soon be called upon to form Treaties with the Seceding States.

The Southern States which may determine that their security and interest require them to withdraw from the present Confederacy, it must constantly be borne in mind, commit by such withdrawal no act of rebellion. All the States are sovereign, and have a perfect constitutional right to sever their connection with the United States.

But this feature of our Federative system (which perhaps has scarcely hitherto attracted the attention of foreign nations) is so ably expounded and enforced in the pamphlet alluded to as to make it unnecessary for me to do more than commend it to your careful consideration.

It is written by one of the most eminent and influential citizens of South Carolina, the Honourable W. D. Porter, the President of the State Senate.

It has been at the request of many of my constituents, of the highest standing and position, that I have forwarded the pamphlet and addressed this letter to your Lordship.

With assurances, &c.
(Signed) W. PORCHER MILES, M.C.

No. 4.

Lord Lyons to Lord J. Russell.—(Received December 18.)

(Extract.) *Washington, December 4, 1860.*

THE despatches of Mr. Bunch, Her Majesty's Consul at Charleston, will have made your Lordship fully acquainted with the details of what has passed in South Carolina with regard to secession from the Confederation of the United States. Your Lordship is aware that a Convention is to meet in that State on the 17th instant, and that the result generally expected is that South Carolina will immediately declare itself a sovereign, independent State, and renounce all the obligations to which it is subject under the Constitution of the United States.

No. 5.

Lord Lyons to Lord J. Russell.—(Received December 24.)

(Extract.) *Washington, December 10, 1860*

IT was hoped that when the leading politicians from the Northern and Southern States met here, on the opening of Congress, it might appear that the violent language used by the newspapers in both divisions of the country did not faithfully portray the state of public feeling. It was thought that Senators and Representatives of Conservative principles from the South, as well as from the North, would be numerous, and disposed to agree upon a compromise for the sake of saving the Union. It was even expected by some that the President's Message might not be without effect towards allaying the strife. If the first week of the session be taken as a criterion, the result is directly contrary to these hopes.

Congress met on the 3rd of this month. On the following day the President sent down his Message.

Those parts of the Message which speak of foreign relations have attracted little attention. The paragraph concerning Great Britain is, probably, the most cordial which has appeared in any President's Message since the foundation of the Republic. It mentions, in appropriate terms, the visit of His Royal Highness the Prince of Wales. Very friendly language is used of other foreign Powers. Pains even seem to have been taken to make the reiteration of the recommendation to purchase Cuba as little offensive to Spain as possible. No mention is made of Peru, between which and the United States there is a serious misunderstanding.

In fact, however, as is natural in the present perilous state of affairs at home, little or no thought is bestowed by the American people upon foreign affairs. The part of the Message which relates to the state of the Union alone occupies men's minds. It may be said to have pleased nobody. The President holds that no State has a right to secede from the Union without the consent of the others. He holds also that the other States have no right to use force against a seceding State. He proposes, as a compromise between the North and the South, the introduction of three Articles confirming the extreme pretensions of the slave-owning States.

I suppose that, at least, as much might be said against the President's doctrines regarding secession as he has said in favour of them in his Message. But the only immediate interest which they possess is as being an indication of what he will do, if, or (as people now say) when, South Carolina secedes from the Union. He will, of course, not make any attempt to bring her back by force. This would be in contradiction to his own doctrines, and would be deprecated by all parties at the present moment. Indeed, he has already acquiesced in the suspension of the administration of the Federal laws in South Carolina. He has not appointed any Judge or other officers of the United States' District Court, in the room of those who threw up their offices last month. This much being already conceded, two practical questions alone remain : What is to be done with the United States' forts at the entrance of Charleston harbour? What course is to be taken with regard to the collection of the United States' Customs duties? The President informs Congress that he has directed the officer in command of the forts to act strictly on the defensive. It is observed, however, that no measures have hitherto been taken to increase the garrisons of the forts, or to put them in a more efficient state for defence. With regard to the Customs duties, the President seems to anticipate that he shall be able to collect them; and it is supposed, therefore, that he intends, in case of need, to make use of a United States' ship of war for that purpose.

The Message was very far from being well received by Congress. In fact, the tone of the Southern Members has gone far to produce the conviction that the party now dominant in almost all the Southern States desire disunion for disunion's sake; that they look upon Mr. Lincoln's election, not as the reason for dissolving the Union, but as the favourable opportunity for carrying into execution a foregone determination. This has taken the North quite by surprise. The denunciations of the Union were looked upon by the North as mere electioneering manœuvres. It was expected that as soon as Mr. Lincoln's election became an ascertained fact, excitement would subside at once. No doubt many of the Southern political leaders did countenance the agitation without any other intention than than that of deterring the North from electing Mr. Lincoln. But the movement is now beyond control. The disunion party has for the moment completely the upper hand. The Conservative element, which undoubtedly exists in the South, is not allowed to appear. The hope of preserving the Union consists in gaining time to enable this element to work its way to the surface. The dominant party are well aware of this, and are using every effort to precipitate matters. They feel confident that South Carolina will secede before the end of this month; they have strong hopes that the other Cotton States will follow immediately, and they think that then the remainder of the Slave States, being left in a helpless minority in Congress, will have no other resource than to join the seceders.

The North is now seriously alarmed, and everywhere, except perhaps in New England, a disposition is manifesting itself to make any reasonable concessions for the sake of maintaining the Union. It is difficult, however, for such men as Mr. Seward and Mr. Sumner, and other leaders of the Republican party, to act in opposition to the declarations so forcibly and so recently made by them in the course of the election. Time is required for the organisation of a Conservative party, while the violent disunion party of the South is ready and eager for action. The House of Representatives has appointed a Committee of one Member from each State to consider " so much of the President's Message as relates to the present perilous condition of the country;" but very little benefit to the cause of union seems at present to be expected from their labours. In short, judging from present appearances, it is at least as probable that this Confederation will be dissolved as that it will be maintained.

The uncertainty has already produced its natural ill-effects upon commercial and manufacturing interests. Had the crisis not occurred at a time when the country was at an unexampled pitch of material prosperity and after an abundant harvest, the consequences would even now have been disastrous.

No. 6.

Lord J. Russell to Lord Lyons.

My Lord, *Foreign Office, December* 26, 1860.

IN the present critical state of affairs in the United States, Her Majesty's Government are disposed to avoid, as much as possible, giving opinions which events may contradict, and, above all, to refrain from any action which may seem to favour one party rather than the other.

It was with some surprise, I confess, that I read the Message of the President. The Message laid down certain conditions as those upon which alone the great Confederacy of the United States could be preserved from disruption. In so doing, the President appeared to be preparing beforehand an apology for the Secession. Had the conditions, indeed, been such as the Northern States would be likely to accept, the Message might have been considered one of peace. But it seems very improbable that the Northern States should now, at the moment of their triumph, and with large majorities of Republicans in their Assemblies, submit to conditions which, during many years of struggle, they have rejected or evaded.

The best chance of preserving the Union, and at the same time the best hope of preserving amity among the States in case of disunion, lies in the abstinence from any act of violence. Her Majesty's Government are happy to see that the President is, in this respect, very cautious. Your Lordship and Her Majesty's Consuls, if asked for advice by any State Government, will advise them, above all, to refrain from violence, and to prevent bloodshed. A single collision might give rise to civil war; and civil war once commenced, the negro population would not fail to help those whom they look upon as their friends.

If separation is to take place, the interests of humanity and civilization demand that it should be a peaceable separation.

But perhaps the South may be finally satisfied with a promise not to interfere with slavery in the Slave States. That the North will go beyond this, and actually favour slavery by new laws and new declarations, is not to be expected; nor if they were to do so, could a people so free as the American people be expected to gag their press and their Assemblies on a topic which so warmly excites religious and moral sympathies as the topic of slavery.

I am, &c.
(Signed) J. RUSSELL.

No. 7.

Lord Lyons to Lord J. Russell.—(Received January 2, 1861.)

My Lord, *Washington, December* 18, 1860.

VERY little change has taken place in the state of things in this country since I had the honour to address to your Lordship my despatch of the 10th instant. The occurrences of the week supply few materials for forming an opinion as to the extent and consequences of the endeavours of a Party in the South to break up the Confederation. The hopes of preserving the Union have certainly not been strengthened by the speeches which have been made in Congress. Perhaps the most favourable symptom is the extreme anxiety of the Southern Leaders to hurry on the Secession; for this anxiety no doubt proceeds from misgivings concerning the real strength of their Party, and fears as to the consequences of time being given for reflection. In the meantime commerce and manufactures are suffering, and the increasing distress of the poorer classes, both in the North and in the South, is beginning to give rise to very serious alarm.

Large meetings, in favour of union and conciliation, have been held in several of the great Northern cities, but no response to their overtures has yet come from the South.

The Convention which is to decide the question of the Secession of South Carolina met at Columbia (the capital of the State), yesterday, but in consequence of the prevalence of small-pox at that place adjourned to meet, to-day, at Charleston. Little doubt seems to be entertained that it will decree the immediate withdrawal of the State from the Union. It is thought very probable that the Cotton States will follow very soon, and that then the larger Slave-holding States will have to decide whether they shall join the seceders at once or endeavour to act as mediators, with a view to re-constituting the Confederation.

I am afraid very little moderation is to be expected from the people of the cotton-growing States. Great as is the real importance of their staple, their own notions of the influence it will secure to them have become so much exaggerated as to be preposterous. They seem to think that the necessity of obtaining a sufficient supply of this commodity will oblige all Europe, and especially Great Britain, to treat with them upon any terms which they may dictate. They talk of withholding their cotton, as a means of coercion, forgetting that their own prosperity depends much more upon selling it than that of the Northern States and of Europe can ever depend upon buying it. They do not choose to remember the lesson so often taught by experience, that stopping the supply of a commodity from the ordinary sources results in stimulating and giving success to endeavours to produce it elsewhere, and to provide a substitute for it. In answer to all arguments they are apt to repeat their senseless cry that "Cotton is King."

This overweening notion of their own importance may lead to very serious inconvenience if they should succeed in establishing their independence. Our need of their cotton is quite great enough to render it extremely desirable that we should be on good terms with them, and encourage any disposition which they may show to place their commercial relations with us on a mutually advantageous footing. We might be willing to consider that a quarrel with them would give us no means of ameliorating the condition of their slaves, while it would bring a great deal of hardship and suffering upon vast numbers of our own working people. But still it must ever be repugnant to our feelings to be in intimate relations with a Confederation formed on the avowed principle of perpetuating, if not of extending, slavery. Unless the Seceding States can be induced to act with moderation upon the question of slavery, they may rouse a feeling of indignation and horror in Great Britain which will overpower all consideration of material interest. Of this many of their leading men in the present movement do not seem to be aware. Some of them even talk openly of reviving the African Slave Trade. An attempt actually to do this would, it may be supposed, be at once put down by the united force of the Northern States, of Great Britain, and of civilised Europe. But, on the other hand, it might be extremely difficult to bring any of the slave-holding States to renounce, in principle, the right of trading in negroes, or to induce them to enter into any treaty engagement on the subject. Any such engagement would be regarded by them as an admission that they were in the wrong on the question on which their contest with the North has so inflamed their passions that they have lost sight of all reason. How could they bind themselves not to extend to larger numbers of Africans the blessings of the institution of American slavery, which they hold to be ordained of God for the happiness and improvement of the negro race. It is to be apprehended that we shall have very considerable difficulty in placing our relations, commercial or political, on a satisfactory footing with a people imbued with such sentiments, immense as is the importance to us of procuring a cheap and abundant supply of their staple commodity.

I have, &c.
(Signed) LYONS.

No. 8.

Lord Lyons to Lord J. Russell.—(Received January 2, 1861.)

(Extract.) *Washington, December* 18, 1860.

THE two principal members of Mr. Buchanan's Cabinet, General Cass, the Secretary of State, and Mr. Howell Cobb, the Secretary of the Treasury, have resigned their offices. Mr. Trescot, the Assistant Secretary of State, has done the same thing. The Southern men who still remain in the Cabinet appear to take an unlimited license both in their language and personal conduct regarding the questions which are distracting the country.

Mr. Cobb sent in his resignation on the 8th instant, and immediately issued a long address to the people of Georgia urging them to quit the Union. He has left Washington with the intention, it is understood, of placing himself at the head of the Secession movement.

General Cass withdrew from the Cabinet on the 14th. He differed with the President concerning the propriety of sending reinforcements to the garrison of the Federal fortresses at Charleston. General Cass thought that a naval and military force should be despatched thither immediately. The President was of opinion that there was no necessity for any such measure in order to secure the forts against attack, and he would not sanction it lest it should lead to collision and bloodshed.

The Secretary of the Interior, Mr. Thompson, still holds his office, but it is stated in the papers this morning that he is gone to North Carolina, having been appointed Commissioner for Mississippi to that State to consult on the means of obtaining its co-operation in "measures rendered necessary by Mr. Lincoln's election to the Presidency."

Mr. Trescot gave in his resignation of the post of Assistant Secretary of State some days ago, but remained until yesterday at the Department to carry on the business until a Secretary of State should be appointed. He is, I believe, to be the Commissioner or Plenipotentiary to be sent by South Carolina to announce its secession from the Union to the Federal Government.

Mr. P. F. Thomas of Maryland has been appointed by the President Secretary of the Treasury in the room of Mr. Cobb; and Mr. Binck, the Attorney-General, has been appointed Secretary of State in the room of General Cass.

No. 9.

Lord J. Russell to Lord Lyons.

(Extract.)   *Foreign Office, January* 5, 1861.

YOUR Lordship may be asked by President Buchanan, or one of his Cabinet, or by one of the friends of Mr. Lincoln, to give advice respecting the lamentable state of the Union. In such case you will reply that you are not authorized to give any advice, nor will Her Majesty's Government do so unless both parties should apply to Her Majesty for counsel.

No. 10.

Lord Lyons to Lord J. Russell.—(*Received January* 8, 1861.)

(Extract.)   *Washington, December* 24, 1860.

ON the 20th instant the Convention at Charleston passed unanimously an Ordinance declaring that the "union now subsisting between South Carolina and other States, under the name of the 'United States of America,' is dissolved."

The secession of South Carolina has been for some time regarded as certain. The formal accomplishment of it has, therefore, not in itself produced much sensation. It will, perhaps, have the effect of bringing the perilous state of the country home to the minds of the people in the North and North-West, who are even now hardly aware of it. The Northern politicians were before sufficiently alarmed, and were endeavouring to devise the means of effecting a compromise with the South with as little damage as possible to their own credit and political position. The Central States, such as New York and Pennsylvania, are willing to make great concessions to maintain, or rather to restore, the Union. So, probably, will the great majority of the people throughout the North be, when they become thoroughly convinced of the reality of the danger. Time is, above all things, required by the supporters of the Union; their hopes depend upon preventing other States from following the example of South Carolina, without waiting to consider the conciliatory proposals which the North will probably ere long be ready to bring forward. Great efforts are being made to elicit at once some declaration satisfactory to the South from the President elect, Mr. Lincoln, and from the Leader of the Republican party, Mr. Seward.

But while on the side of the Union party all is doubt and perplexity, the leaders of the Secession movement are fixed in purpose, and, reckless of consequences, are eagerly urging the Southern States to quit the Confederation at once. They desire disunion, for its own sake and at any price, and have for the present succeeded in silencing almost all opposition in the South.

The written intelligence of the secession of South Carolina having reached Washington only this morning, nothing has transpired as to the intentions of the President. It is thought probable, however, that he may in the course of the day send a Message on the subject to Congress. The practical difficulties regarding the Post-office, the Custom-house, and the Federal forts at Charleston, must almost immediately present themselves, unless the Convention and the Legislature of South Carolina act with more prudence and moderation than their recent conduct gives reason to expect.

No. 11.

Lord Lyons to Lord J. Russell.—(*Received January* 16, 1861.)

(Extract.)   *Washington, December* 31, 1860.

THE events of the last week have not been encouraging to those who desire to maintain the Union. The President-elect has as yet made no sign. The Committee of the Senate "on the perilous state of the country" have reported that they have not been able to agree upon any general plan of adjustment. The Committee of the House of Representatives appears to be still less harmonious. A very remarkable and eloquent disunion speech has been made to-day in the Senate by Mr. Benjamin, Senator for Louisiana, who has hitherto been considered rather a moderate advocate of secession.

"Next week," Mr. Benjamin said, "three States will go out of the Union; in the week after that three more will secede; of the secession of several others I have strong hopes. I desire, and hope it is no stain upon the honour of my State, that we part in peace; but if the issue be forced upon us, we will endeavour to meet it like men, and, trusting to the God of Battles, strive to merit victory. The fortune of war may be adverse; you may fill our land with bloodshed and ruin; you may desolate us with fire and sword; you may, in emulation of those who incited the savages in the Revolution, loose upon us those who are so eager for dissolution, and add to our miseries all the horrors of a servile insurrection; you may do all this, but you can never break the spirit of a free people; you can never subjugate us—never, never, never!"

While such is the language and such the attitude of the partisans of Secession, the friends of the Union are almost silent, under the pressure of fear in the South, of perplexity in the North. The leaders of the Republican party have abstained from irritating speeches, but they have done no more. Some of the less distinguished members of that party have equalled the Secessionists in violence of language.

The temporising policy which President Buchanan has hitherto followed may, perhaps, be the best for the country. It certainly does not appear to be answering the purpose of carrying him to the end of his term of office with ease or credit. The practical difficulties of persevering in it become every day more evident. He appeared by his Message to calculate upon being able to collect the Customs revenue in South Carolina. In this, as your Lordship is aware, he has been signally disappointed, and he can hardly avoid taking some measures, if not to assert at home the authority of the Government of which he is the head, at all events to cover its responsibility with foreign Powers. He trusted that by a private arrangement with the South Carolinians, he should be enabled to hold the Charleston Forts during the remainder of his term of office. This plan has been frustrated by an act of the officer in command, who has withdrawn from the larger and less defensible fort in which he was stationed, to Fort Sumter, a stronger and more commanding position.

To add to the perplexity of the President, and to the discredit of the Government, it has been discovered that a sum of 830,000 dollars has disappeared from a chest in the office of the Interior Department. To so great a degree has the financial credit of the United States been shaken, that so much, I am told, as 36 per cent. interest has been demanded by purchasers of Treasury bonds. These bonds are sold at par, and the interest they are to bear is agreed upon between the Treasurer and the purchaser.

No. 12.

Lord Lyons to Lord J. Russell.—(*Received January* 28.)

(Extract.) *Washington, January* 15, 1861.

THE events which have actually occurred during the last eight days would seem to indicate a rapid progress in disunion.

Three more States, Mississippi, Florida, and Alabama, have formally seceded.

Forts, arsenals, and other Federal property, have been seized by the State authorities in States which are still nominally members of the Confederation.

A steam-vessel (the "Star of the West"), despatched by the Federal Government with reinforcements to Major Anderson at Fort Sumter, has been fired into from the batteries in the hands of the South Carolinians, and has retreated to New York.

The President has shown a laudable desire to avoid shedding blood, but recent events have neither increased his reputation nor improved his position. Acting under the influence of General Scott, he has consented to the concentration of some Federal troops at Washington and its neighbourhood. He has also, it is understood, sanctioned the sending Federal troops to endeavour to secure some of the forts and arsenals of the Confederation in the South. The result, however, of these measures seems hitherto to have been only to incite the State authorities to seize the United States' property before the Federal troops have arrived. The expedition of the "Star of the West" to Charleston, and her return without landing the reinforcements, tend to make the Government and the army the objects of ridicule. The failure of this attempt appears to have put an end, for the moment, to the intention to collect the Customs duties at Charleston by force.

By his original refusal to send reinforcements to Charleston, the President lost the head of his Cabinet, General Cass. By the recent attempt to send them, he has lost his Secretary of the Interior, Mr. Jacob Thompson. Like Mr. Floyd (the late Secretary of War), Mr. Thompson accuses the President of having broken faith with him. The newly appointed Secretary of the Treasury, Mr. Thomas, has also withdrawn from the Cabinet. He has been succeeded by General Dix, of New York, whose appointment is looked on with favour by bankers and commercial men at New York. I do not think it necessary to occupy your Lordship's time by stating numerous other particulars, showing the extreme difficulties with which President Buchanan is beset.

The President, in his perplexity, has addressed an almost despairing Message to Congress, throwing upon them all responsibility. He has not made any definite request for additional powers to enforce the Federal Laws, but has left the whole matter in the hands of Congress. He recommends one special measure as a settlement of the differences between North and South. "The proposition," he says, "to compromise by letting the North have exclusive control of the territory above a certain line, and to give Southern institutions protection below that line, ought to receive universal approbation."

Hitherto Congress has made little response to the President's appeal to save the country. It has, however, elicited a speech from Mr. Seward, which occupies all thoughts, as he has spoken with the authority belonging to the Secretary of State, or Chief Member, of the incoming Administration.

In this speech Mr. Seward does distinctly say that "so far as the abstract question whether, by the Constitution of the United States, the bondsman who is made such by the laws of a State is still a man, or only property, he answers that within that State its laws on the subject are supreme; that when he has escaped from that State into another, the Constitution regards him as a bondsman, who may not by any law or regulation of that State be discharged from his service, but shall be delivered up on claim to the party to whom his service is due."

Mr. Seward further declares that "he agrees that all laws of the States, whether Free States or Slave States, which relate to this class of persons, or any others recently coming from or resident in other States, and which laws contravene the Constitution of the United States, or any law of Congress passed in conformity thereto, ought to be repealed."

He goes on to say, "If misapprehension of my position needs so strong a remedy, I am willing to vote for an amendment of the Constitution, declaring that it shall not by any future amendment be so altered as to confer on Congress a power to abolish or interfere with slavery in any State."

He announces that "when the angry excitement of the hour shall have subsided, and calmness shall have resumed its sway over the public mind, then, and not until then, one, or two, or three years hence, he should cheerfully advise a Convention of the people, to consider and decide whether any and what amendments of the Organic National Law ought to be made."

It is thought that by these declarations Mr. Seward will have alienated some of the more ardent Abolitionists, but that he will have rallied by them to Mr. Lincoln's Administration a very great amount of support from the Conservative and Union-loving men of the North and North-West. He has by no means succeeded in satisfying the Southern Leaders. To them the test of his intentions is whether or not he will vote at once for the division of the remainder of the vast tracts of country called "territory" into two States, into one of which slavery shall be admissible, while it shall be for ever excluded from the other. The language of the speech on this point is not clear. I am told that on the questions being put distinctly to Mr. Seward, yesterday, by a Senator, he answered that he would not vote at once for a Bill to divide the territory in the manner proposed. If this be so, his speech will have little or no effect towards calming the South.

The hope of preserving, or rather of immediately reconstructing the Union, appears now to be in the Border States being able to come to an agreement upon terms to propose to both North and South, and expressing their determination to unite with and support whichever side will accept them. I do not think that confidence is felt in the possibility of carrying this scheme into execution.

On the other hand, the plans of the Secessionists are settled: they intend to have a Southern Confederacy fully established, with a President and Congress duly installed in some Southern city before the 3rd of March; they declare that they shall then be prepared to negotiate on equal terms with the United States for a Union of the two Confederacies. Such a Union, they say, they should be prepared to form, provided the Constitutional arrangements were such as would prevent the vastly larger population of the Northern Confederacy having power to overwhelm by the number of their votes the influence of the South in the General Government.

No. 13.

Lord Lyons to Lord J. Russell.—(*Received February* 6.)

(Extract.) *Washington, January* 21, 1861.

THERE seems to be an undefined impression that the prospects of this country are rather less gloomy than they were a week ago; it has probably been occasioned by some appearances of hesitation in various Southern States, and by symptoms that even in those States which have already seceded the people are neither so enthusiastic nor so unanimous in favour of disunion as they were represented to be by the party leaders.

It can hardly, however, be thought that the actual events of the week are calculated to inspire increased confidence.

The State of Georgia has formally seceded; the Ordinance was passed by the Convention, the day before yesterday, by 208 votes to 89.

The proceedings of the Legislature in Virginia, the most important of the slave-holding border States, are less reassuring than was expected. The House of Delegates in that State has, indeed, passed a Resolution inviting all the States, slave-holding or not slave-holding, which "are willing to unite with Virginia in an earnest effort to adjust the present unhappy controversies . . . . so as to afford to the people of the slave-holding States adequate guarantees for the security of their rights, to appoint Commissioners to meet on the 4th day of February next, at Washington, similar Commissioners appointed by Virginia to consider, and if practicable, to agree upon some suitable adjustment." It is to be feared, however, that the Legislature of Virginia will not consider anything to be an adequate security for the rights of the slave-holding States, which does not amount to a complete surrender by the North of all the points in dispute on the question of slavery. In the Senate of Virginia a Resolution has been passed unanimously that "if all efforts to reconcile the unhappy differences between sections of our country shall prove abortive, then every consideration of honour and interest demands that Virginia shall unite her destinies with her sister slave-holding States."

The occurrences of the week in the Congress of the United States do not tend to increase the hope that the adjustment of the difficulties will come from that quarter. Your Lordship is aware that the Southern Senators had to a certain extent agreed that the Resolutions proposed by Mr. Crittenden, Senator for Kentucky, should be held to embody the minimum of the concessions required by the South. These Resolutions provide for taking the sense of the people immediately upon certain amendments to the Constitution. The Senate on the 16th instant adopted, by a vote of twenty-five to twenty-three, an Amendment to Mr. Crittenden's Resolutions, moved by Mr. Clark, of New Hampshire, and declaring, in substance, that the Constitution needs to be obeyed, not to be amended. Mr. Seward and all his party voted for Mr. Clark's amendment. On the 18th, however, a motion to reconsider the adoption of the Amendment was carried by a majority of twenty-seven to twenty-four. Mr. Seward and his friends voted against the reconsideration. The vote of Mr. Seward, as the representative of the President Elect, is regarded as the important matter. It was evident that he could not vote in favour of Mr. Crittenden's Resolutions. He had, indeed, recorded votes against them in the Committee of Thirteen, but it was thought he might hesitate to adhere to a declaration that no Amendments should be made to the Constitution. The question is to be brought before the Senate again to-day. The result will probably be communicated by telegraph to the New York papers before the departure of the packet which will bring this despatch to England.

I mentioned in a previous despatch that the Senate Committee of Thirteen "on the perilous state of the country" had reported that they had not been able to agree upon any general plan of adjustment. The Committee of the House of Representatives on the same subject have not been more harmonious. They have presented to the House one Report of the majority, and two from different minorities. The majority Report itself is only that of a majority of a quorum, not that of a majority of the whole Committee.

The Executive branch of the Government appears to be waiting for some answer from Congress to the President's recent Message. Its hands have been in some degree strengthened by the Senate's having confirmed the appointment of Mr. Holt as Secretary of War. Mr. Holt was Postmaster-General, and on the retirement of Mr. Floyd took charge temporarily of the War Department. He is a man of character and energy, and is understood to support General Scott's views as to the defence of the Federal fortresses. On this account his appointment will not be regarded as conciliatory by the South.

The new Commissioner from South Carolina has been for some days in communication with the Cabinet. The object of his mission is understood to be to make some temporary arrangement respecting the occupation of the forts at Charleston, and the trade and Customs duties of that harbour.

No. 14.

Lord Lyons to Lord J. Russell.—(Received February 11.)

My Lord,   *Washington, January 29, 1861.*
 ON the 26th instant the State of Louisiana formally withdrew from the Confederation. The Convention of that State passed, simultaneously with the Ordinance of Secession, a Resolution declaring the navigation of the Mississippi to be free to all friendly States.
 Thus six States, South Carolina, Georgia, Florida, Alabama, Mississsipi, and Louisiana, have quitted the Union.
 The Executive branch of the Federal Government holds, in theory, that the relations of these States to the General Government has been in nothing changed by the acts of Secession. This theoretical principle seems to prevent the President from taking any effectual means either to remedy the daily increasing inconveniences of this anomalous state of things or to avoid the risk of a collision between the United States' troops and the forces of the several States. By good luck more than by good management, the shedding of blood has hitherto been avoided. The small United States' garrisons in the Federal forts and arsenals in the South have in most cases surrendered immediately on being summoned to do so.
 Since the failure of the attempt to smuggle reinforcements into Fort Sumter, the Administration appear to have resorted to their old policy. They seem to be unwilling either to authorize the abandonment of the posts, or to place the garrisons in a situation to maintain them. Happily the desire to avoid bloodshed seems at present to be strong on all sides. If a collision take place under President Buchanan's administration, it will undoubtedly be in opposition to his earnest wishes and endeavours. But as long as he keeps the garrisons at Fort Sumter and other points, with orders to defend themselves, and without sufficient force to deter the Secessionists from attacking them, there must be a daily risk of bloodshed.
 From the present Administration little can be looked for, either towards effecting a peaceful separation, or towards re-constructing the Union. President Buchanan can bring no personal influence or popularity to the aid of the very small powers entrusted by the Constitution to the Executive branch of the Government.
 From Congress not much more is expected. The Committee of the Senate on the perilous state of the country reported that it could not agree upon a report. The Committee of the House of Representatives has at last presented one so-called majority report, and no less than seven minority reports; besides which, as the Senators and Representatives of the Seceding States have withdrawn from Congress, it can no longer be held to represent the whole nation.
 Under these circumstances the hopes of the country are turned to the Convention of Commissioners from non-slave-holding as well as slave-holding States, which the Legislature of the State of Virginia has invited to meet in this city on the 4th of next month. The object of the State of Virginia, as explained yesterday in the Senate by Mr. Mason, Senator from that State, is to offer herself as a mediator between the Northern and Southern States; to heal the rupture if possible, by obtaining guarantees and provisions of safety for the South; to induce the President to refrain from any act which may bring the public force of the United States into collision with the public force of the Seceding States, and to prevent Congress from taking any step which may complicate the present state of affairs; in short, to preserve the public peace *ad interim,* and see if the Northern States will adopt amendments of the Constitution and furnish guarantees acceptable to all the Southern States; and if that should not be done, then to provide that the Confederation be broken up and peace still be maintained.
 The proposal of Virginia was recommended by the President to Congress in a Message which he sent to that Body yesterday.
                              I have, &c.
                        (Signed)   LYONS.

No. 15.

Lord J. Russell to Lord Lyons.

My Lord,　　　　　　　　　　　　　　*Foreign Office, February* 12, 1861.

I HAVE received and laid before the Queen your despatch of the 29th ultimo.

The step taken by the Legislature of Virginia, as reported in your Lordship's despatch, viz., the summoning a Convention of Commissioners from slave-holding and non-slave-holding States, appears highly judicious; and Her Majesty's Government hope that it may be successful either in averting disunion, or in providing for a peaceable and friendly separation.

I am, &c.
(Signed)　　J. RUSSELL.

No. 16.

Lord Lyons to Lord J. Russell.—(Received February 18.)

(Extract.)　　　　　　　　　　　　　　*Washington, February* 4, 1861.

THE Convention of Commissioners from slave-holding and non-slave-holding States, which was invited by the Legislature of Virginia to meet at Washington, is to hold its first sitting to-day in this city. A considerable number of States, both Northern and Southern, have sent Commissioners. Great hopes are entertained by some people that a compromise may be devised by this Convention, which will satisfy both North and South, keep the Border States in the Confederation, and bring the seceding States back to it. Less sanguine men trust that the Convention will at least have the effect of preventing the risk of bloodshed for the moment, and of giving time for angry passions, both in the North and South, to cool.

Great efforts are made, with a view to settling the terms of the compromise, to elicit a declaration of the intentions of the Administration which is to come into power. But Mr. Lincoln says nothing, and Mr. Seward speaks vaguely.

Mr. Seward made another speech in the Senate on the 2nd instant. It was accepted as conciliatory by the friends of Union of all parties, although it was scarcely less indefinite than the former speech. He expressed perfect confidence that the Union would be preserved (he would not admit that it was already impaired and required to be restored); and he pointed out, with considerable effect, the unpractical character of the question which is (nominally, at all events) the cause of the dispute. This question is that of Slavery in the "territories" of the United States.

"What," Mr. Seward asked, "is the extent of the territories which remain after the admission of California, of Oregon, of Kansas? One million, sixty-three thousand, five hundred and seven square miles, an area twenty-four times that of the State of New York, the largest of the old and fully-developed States. How many Slaves are there in it? How many have been brought into it during the twelve years in which it has been not only relinquished to slavery, but in which the Supreme Court and the Legislature, and the Administration, have maintained, protected, defended, and guaranteed slavery there? Twenty-four African slaves; one slave for every 24,000 square miles."

Mr. Seward's real view of the state of the country appears to be, that, if bloodshed can be avoided until the new Government is installed, the Seceding States will in no long time return to the Confederation. He seems to think that in a few months the evils and hardships produced by Secession will become intolerably grievous to the Southern States; that they will be completely reassured as to the intentions of the Administration; and that the Conservative element, which is now kept under the surface by the violent pressure of the Secessionists, will emerge with irresistible force. From all these causes he confidently expects that when the elections for the State Legislatures are held in the Southern States in November next, the Union Party will have a clear majority, and will bring the Seceding States back into the Confederation. He then hopes to place himself at the head of a strong Union Party, having extensive ramifications both in the North and in the South, and to make "Union" or "Disunion," not "Freedom" or "Slavery," the watchwords of Political Parties.

No. 17.

Lord J. Russell to Lord Lyons.

(Extract.) *Foreign Office, February* 20, 1861.

THE success or failure of Mr. Seward's plans to prevent the disruption of the North American Union is a matter of deep interest to Her Majesty's Government. But they can only expect and hope. They are not called upon, nor would they be acting prudently were they to obtrude their advice on the dissentient parties in the United States.

Supposing, however, that Mr. Lincoln, acting under bad advice, should endeavour to provide excitement for the public mind by raising questions with Great Britain, Her Majesty's Government feel no hesitation as to the policy they would pursue. They would, in the first place, be very forbearing. They would show by their acts how highly they value the relations of peace and amity with the United States. But they would take care to let the Government which multiplied provocations and sought for quarrels, understand that their forbearance sprung from the consciousness of strength, and not from the timidity of weakness. They would warn a Government which was making political capital out of blustering demonstrations, that our patience might be tried too far.

If this tone is taken, when necessary, and only when necessary, I have no fears that the American Republic will seek a quarrel with a nation sprung from the same parents, and united by language as well as by ties of kindred, and a long period of friendly intercourse.

No. 18.

Lord Lyons to Lord J. Russell.—(Received February 25.)

(Extract.) *Washington, February* 12, 1861.

THE hopes of the supporters of the Union are very much raised by the results of the elections in Virginia and Tennessee. But it must not be forgotten that the success of the "Union" Party in those States means no more than that men in favour of consideration and consultation have been returned in opposition to partisans of instantaneous action. It is still doubtful whether any concessions which the North can or will make, will satisfy even the most moderate of the men elected in the two States. Time has, nevertheless, been gained; and, at all events Mr. Lincoln's inauguration is not now likely to be interrupted by an attack upon this capital.

The "Congress" of the Seceding States at Montgomery appears to be disposed to bid for European support by the insertion of an article in its Constitution, to prohibit for ever the African Slave Trade, and by the immediate promulgation of a comparatively low tariff of import duties.

The Commissioners from slave-holding States, who have assembled here by the invitation of Virginia, hold their sittings with closed doors. Commissioners have been appointed by the States of Maine, New Hampshire, Vermont, Massachusetts, Rhode Island, Connecticut, New York, New Jersey, Pennsylvania, Delaware, Maryland, Virginia, North Carolina, Tennessee, Kentucky, Missouri, Ohio, Indiana, Illinois, Iowa, Wisconsin. It is considered very doubtful whether these Commissioners will be able to agree upon any plan to recommend to Congress; it is considered still more doubtful whether Congress would accept any such plan. The States which have already seceded have not sent Commissioners, and loudly declare that their own secession is final and irrevocable; that upon no terms whatever will they consent to a reunion.

The present plan of the Northern politicians appears to be to avoid coming into actual collision with the Seceding States, but to force them back into the Union by subjecting them to such inconveniences as shall make secession unpopular, if not intolerable. The principal engines to be employed are, cutting off postal communication and stopping foreign trade. It seems to be taken for granted that all foreign Powers will acquiesce in the exclusion of their merchant-vessels from the ports of the South.

No. 19.

Lord J. Russell to Mr. Dallas.

Foreign Office, March 21, 1861.

LORD JOHN RUSSELL presents his compliments to Mr. Dallas, and has the honour to transmit to him herewith a draft of a despatch which he proposes to address to Lord Lyons, Her Majesty's Minister at Washington,* with reference to their conversation of yesterday, and to request that Mr. Dallas will be good enough to inform him whether he has correctly represented the purport of the despatch from Judge Black.

No. 20.

Mr. Dallas to Lord J. Russell.—(*Received March* 22.)

Legation of the United States, London, March 21, 1861.

MR. DALLAS presents his compliments to Lord John Russell, and, returning the draft of a proposed despatch to Lord Lyons, begs, in answer to the question put to him, to express his opinion that the purport of the note from Judge Black, read to his Lordship yesterday, is correctly represented in that despatch.

No. 21.

Lord J. Russell to Lord Lyons.

My Lord, *Foreign Office, March* 22, 1861.

THE American Minister called upon me yesterday afternoon, and read to me a despatch of Judge Black, dated the 28th of February.

In this despatch Judge Black expresses his conviction that States which have separated from the United States without any legal or constitutional right to do so will not be acknowledged as independent States by Great Britain. Her Majesty's Government have shown, he said, so friendly an interest in the welfare of the United States, that it is due to them to state that the United States have not acknowledged the right of the Seceding States to claim independence, and do not design to do so.

I replied to Mr. Dallas shortly and verbally, stating that, even if the Government of the United States had been willing to acknowledge the separation of the Seceding States as founded in right, Her Majesty's Government would have seen with great concern the dissolution of the Union which bound together the members of the American Republic. That the opposition of the Government of the United States to any such separation, and the denial by them of its legality, would make Her Majesty's Government very reluctant to take any step which might encourage or sanction the separation. That, however, it was impossible to state, at the present moment, in what shape the question might present itself; nor was it in my power to bind the British Government to any particular course of conduct in cases of which the circumstances and the significance were at present unknown to us.

I am, &c.
(Signed) J. RUSSELL.

No. 22.

Lord Lyons to Lord J. Russell.—(*Received March* 24.)

(Extract.) *Washington, March* 12, 1861.

THE thirty-sixth Congress of the United States came to an end at noon on the 4th instant.

The only step taken by it towards a pacification of the country was the passing a Resolution, by a majority of two-thirds of each House, for proposing in Constitutional form to the several States the following amendment of the Constitution:—

* No. 21.

"No amendment shall be made to the Constitution which will authorize or give to Congress the power to abolish or interfere, within any State, with the domestic institutions thereof, including that of persons held to labour or service by the laws of said State."

Such an amendment does not appear to be regarded by the Southern States as likely to afford them any additional security to that which they already have under the Constitution as it stands. Congress is accordingly held by them to have done nothing towards satisfying their demands. It may be doubted whether they would have accepted, as sufficient, anything less than the Crittenden Propositions. Even the plan of the Peace Conference was regarded as inadequate in several of the Border States. The States which had already quitted the Confederation declined to take any proposals into consideration, declaring their own secession to be final and irrevocable.

So soon as the clock announced the end of the thirty-sixth Congress, a Special Session of the Senate of the thirty-seventh Congress was held in virtue of a summons issued some days previously, according to custom, by the President. Having received the President and President Elect, the Senate accompanied them to the portico of the Capitol, where Mr. Abraham Lincoln read his inaugural Address, and was sworn in as President for four years, in the usual form. The ceremony passed off with perfect order and tranquillity. There was a display of Regular troops, not customary in this country, but no necessity for their presence was apparent.

I have the honour to inclose two copies of the Inaugural Address. It very much disappointed those who expected to find in it a clear and detailed exposition of the intentions of the incoming Administration. The violent party in the South denounce it as a declaration of war; the violent party in the North, as an abandonment of principle. Calmer men look upon it as a skilfully-worded document by which the President has avoided making inconvenient pledges concerning his own conduct, without giving cause for any great irritation either to his own party or to the South. Like his predecessor, he declares, "that in view of the Constitution and the Laws, the Union is unbroken; and that, to the extent of his ability, he shall take care that the laws of the Union be faithfully executed in all the States." He goes on to say, "that the power confided to him will be used to hold, occupy, and possess the property and places belonging to the Government, and to collect the duties and imposts." He deprecates bloodshed, but he does not declare, as Mr. Buchanan did, that the Government has absolutely no right to use force to bring a State back into the Union.

So little having been declared by the Address, public opinion became more than ever excited on the subject of the first acts of the new Government. By these it was thought that the correct interpretation of the President's cautious words would be immediately manifested.

Mr. Lincoln's first step was, of course, to appoint the members of his Cabinet. The list was sent by him to the Senate on the day after the inauguration, and was immediately confirmed. The Departments are distributed as follows:—

State	Mr. William H. Seward.
Treasury	Mr. Salmon P. Chase.
Navy	Mr. Gideon Welles.
Interior	Mr. Caleb B. Smith.
Postmaster-General	Mr. Montgomery Blair.
Attorney-General	Mr. Edward Bates.

The greater part of last week appears to have been spent by the President and his advisers in considering the minor appointments. A Mr. Judd, who was very useful in the Presidential canvass, has been appointed Minister to Prussia. A Mr. Kriesman, a German, who emigrated when young from Rudolstadt, accompanies Mr. Judd as Secretary of Legation. A refugee from Prussia, Mr. Carl Schurz, will, it is understood, be sent as Minister to Turin. No other diplomatic appointments have, so far as I know, yet been definitively settled. It seems to be taken for granted that none of the present Representatives of the United States abroad will be allowed to retain their places.

Among the numerous receptions with which the time of the President appears to have been chiefly occupied was that of the Diplomatic Body. A short address was made to him by the Portuguese Minister as senior member of the body, and a short answer was returned. Neither contained anything beyond the usual insignificant compliments.

The Senate continues in Session, as its consent is required in order to give effect to the President's appointments. The Standing Committees have been remodelled in consequence of the change in the relative strength of parties occasioned by the withdrawal of the Southern Members. The Chairman and the majority of Members of each Committee are now taken from the Republican Party. Mr. Charles Sumner, the well-known Senator for Massachusetts, has been placed in the Chair of the Committee of Foreign Relations.

In the meantime the state of the Union has undergone little change. The formal secession of Texas is announced by the telegraph, but that State has been for some time considered to be virtually out of the Union. The forts and property of the Government were given up to the State authorities by Major-General Twiggs, the Commander of the United States' troops before the Secession. For these "acts of treachery to the flag of his country" he was summarily dismissed from the army by President Buchanan. When last heard of he was receiving an ovation at New Orleans.

The Border States without lowering their pretensions still cling to the Union; their reluctance to quit it is manifest: but if the separation of the other Slave States should be permanently established it will be very difficult for the Border States to reconcile themselves to the inferior position, both with regard to votes and influence, in which they will stand in a Confederation composed mainly of the Northern States. An attack made by this Government or any part of the Southern Confederacy might drive the Border States to immediate secession.

It is hoped, however, that prudent counsels have prevailed with Mr. Lincoln. The critical question of the moment is that concerning Fort Sumter, the fort at the entrance of Charleston harbour, which is still held by United States' troops. Either the fort must be abandoned, or reinforcements and provisions must be sent to it almost immediately. It is stated that the people of Charleston have succeeded in rendering the approach to the fort so difficult that to reinforce it would entail a large loss of life, and to require a larger number of troops and ships of war than the Government have at this moment at their disposal; in fact, the question of peace or immediate civil war is generally considered to depend upon the President's decision concerning this fort. A considerable sensation was consequently excited last night by an article in the "National Republican," a journal regarded as the organ of the Administration, stating that it had been determined in a Cabinet Council that the fort should be evacuated.

The article states, indeed, that this measure, by satisfying the country generally of the pacific policy of the Administration, will enable it without the appearance of coercion to be more stringent in the enforcement of the Revenue laws. It appears, nevertheless, to be hoped by the lovers of peace that if there appear to be any great risk of bloodshed, or any considerable difficulty in collecting the Customs duties in the seceding States, that point also will be given up by the President; in fact, the decision concerning Fort Sumter appears to be very generally taken as an indication that the Administration will in the end withdraw their troops from such of the remaining fortresses in the South as cannot be held without the risk of fighting—in fact, that they will, without recognizing the independence of the Southern Confederacy, make no attempt to assert their own authority in it for the present.

Whether so great a departure from the professions of their party will be agreed to by all the Members of the present Cabinet, or even by the President himself, can hardly be considered beyond question. That such is the policy advocated by many of the most wise and prudent statesmen in the country is certain. These men say that a short time will show whether the Southern Confederacy does or does not possess the elements necessary to constitute an independent nation. If it does not possess them, the several States will, in all probability, drop off from it and return of their own accord to the Union. If, on the other hand, it does possess the spirit and the material resources requisite for a separate national existence, it may indeed be subdued by force, after a bloody war, but it can never be brought into a condition to be governed by American institutions. To these arguments is added the consideration that an attack from the North would do more towards uniting the Southern States to each other than any possible measures which can be adopted by their new Government, when deprived of the means of keeping up excitement. Above all it is urged that an attempt to coerce the Southern Confederacy would entail, as an immediate consequence, the loss of the Border States.

No. 23.

Lord Lyons to Lord J. Russell.—(Received April 3.)

(Extract.) *Washington, March* 18, 1861.

VERY little light has been thrown on the intentions of the new Administration since I had the honour to address to your Lordship my despatch of the 12th instant.

There seems to be little or no doubt that Fort Sumter is on the point of being evacuated. In fact this seems to have become a matter of necessity, unless Major Anderson and his troops are to be left to surrender themselves to the Southern Confederacy. Their provisions are nearly exhausted. It is understood that General Scott considers it impracticable to throw reinforcements or supplies into the fort without a force of 10,000 men to act against the batteries thrown up by the South Carolinians. With the utmost exertions to concentrate the United States' troops, he is not, it appears, likely to have as many as 3,000 men at his disposal before the month of August.

It is thought, however, that an endeavour will be made to deprive the evacuation of Fort Sumter of political significance, by simultaneously reinforcing Fort Pickens, and other forts in the South, still in the possession of the United States, and accessible to their ships of war. It is thought that such a measure may calm the indignation which has been excited, especially in the North-West, by the announcement that the national flag is to be struck at Fort Sumter. On the other hand, the evacuation thus accompanied, will tend to irritate, instead of to calm, the Southern and Border States; and the occupation, in increased strength, of Southern fortresses will add to the difficulty of maintaining the actual state of things without war, or of effecting a peaceful separation.

It seems almost certain that President Lincoln and his Cabinet have not yet come to any determination even upon the general principles which are to guide their conduct towards the Seceding States.

If the Administration determine to adopt measures of coercion, they will be obliged to call a special session of Congress. The numerous "Force" Bills, as they were called, which were introduced into the late Congress, failed to pass. The President has no authority to use any extraordinary means for enforcing the laws or collecting the Federal revenue. No unusual addition to the regular army or navy, nor any extraordinary votes of money were granted. The naval and military force of the Confederation is so small, and so much dispersed, as to be quite insufficient for acting against the South.

While questions of this fearful importance are to be determined, the President and his advisers are beset night and day by a swarm of office-seekers, who leave them little or no time for deliberation. The disastrous effects of the system under which all the offices under the Government become simultaneously vacant once in four years have never been more conspicuous.

No. 24.

Lord J. Russell to Lord Lyons.

My Lord, *Foreign Office, April* 6, 1861.

I HAVE received your Lordship's despatch of the 18th ultimo, reporting on the policy and probable intentions of the new Administration, and I have to instruct you to recommend conciliation in the event of your Lordship's opinion being requested, but never to obtrude advice unasked.

I am, &c.
(Signed) J. RUSSELL.

No. 25.

Mr. Seward to Mr. Dallas.—(*Communicated to Lord J. Russell by Mr. Dallas, April* 8.)

Sir, *Department of State, Washington, March* 9, 1861.

MY predecessor, in his despatch addressed to you on the 28th of February last, instructed you to use all proper and necessary measures to prevent the success of efforts which may be made by persons claiming to represent those States of this Union in whose name a Provisional Government has been announced, to procure a recognition of their independence by the Empire of Great Britain.

I am now instructed by the President of the United States to inform you that, having assumed the administration of the Government, in pursuance of an unquestioned election, and of the directions of the Constitution, he renews the injunction which I have mentioned, and relies upon the exercise of the greatest possible diligence and fidelity on your part to counteract and prevent the designs of those who would invoke foreign intervention to embarrass or overthrow the Republic.

When you reflect on the novelty of such designs, their unpatriotic and revolutionary character, and the long train of evils which must follow, directly or consequently, from even their partial or temporary success, the President feels assured that you will justly appreciate and cordially approve the caution which prompts this communication.

I transmit herewith a copy of the address pronounced by the President on taking the constitutional oath of office. It sets forth clearly the errors of the misguided partisans who are seeking to dismember the Union, the grounds on which the conduct of those partizans is disallowed, and also the general policy which the Government will pursue with a view to the preservation of domestic peace and order, and the maintenance and preservation of the Federal Union.

You will lose no time in submitting this address to the British Minister for Foreign Affairs, and in assuring him that the President of the United States entertains a full confidence in the speedy restoration of the harmony and unity of the Government, by a firm, yet just and liberal bearing, co-operating with the deliberate and loyal action of the American people.

You will truthfully urge upon the Government of Great Britain the consideration that the present disturbances have had their origin only in popular passions, excited under novel circumstances of very transient character, and that while not one person of well-balanced mind has attempted to show that dismemberment of the Union would be permanently conducive to the safety and welfare of even his own State or Section, much less of all the States and Sections of our country, the people themselves still retain and cherish a profound confidence in our happy constitution, together with a veneration and affection for it, such as no other form of government ever received at the hands of those for whom it was established.

We feel free to assume that it is the general conviction of men, not only here, but in all other countries, that the Federal Union affords a better system than any other that could be contrived to assure the safety, the peace, the prosperity, the welfare, and the happiness, of all the States of which it is composed.

The position of these States, and their mining, agricultural, manufacturing, commercial, political, and social relations and influences, seem to make it permanently the interest of all other nations that our present political system shall be unchanged and undisturbed. Any advantage that any foreign nation might derive from a connection that it might form with any dissatisfied or discontented portion, State, or section, even if not altogether illusory, would be ephemeral, and would be overbalanced by the evils it would suffer from a disseverance of the whole Union, whose manifest policy it must be hereafter, as it has always been heretofore, to maintain peace, liberal commerce, and cordial amity with all other nations, and to favour the establishment of well-ordered government over the whole American Continent.

Nor do we think we exaggerate our national importance when we claim that any political disaster that should befall us, and introduce discord or anarchy among the States that have so long constituted one great, pacific, prosperous nation under a form of government which has approved itself to the respect and confidence of mankind, might tend by its influence to disturb and unsettle the existing systems of government in other parts of the world, and arrest that progress of improvement and civilization which marks the era in which we live.

The United States have had too many assurances and manifestations of the friendship and goodwill of Great Britain to entertain any doubt that these considerations, and such others as your own large experience of the working of our Federal system will suggest, will have their just influence with the British Government, and will prevent that Government from yielding to solicitations to intervene, in any unfriendly way, in the domestic concerns of our country.

The President regrets that the events going on here may be productive of some possible inconvenience to the people and subjects of Her Britannic Majesty, but he is determined that those inconveniences shall be made as light and as transient as possible; and, so far as it may rest with him, that all strangers who may suffer any injury from them shall be amply indemnified.

The President expects that you will be prompt in transmitting to this Department any information you may receive on the subject of the attempts which have suggested this communication.

                    I am, &c.
(Signed)   WILLIAM H. SEWARD.

No. 26.

Lord J. Russell to Lord Lyons.

My Lord, *Foreign Office, April* 12, 1861.

MR. DALLAS called upon me on the 8th instant, in pursuance of an appointment, and communicated to me a despatch which he had received from Mr. Seward, United States' Secretary of State, and of which I inclose a copy.*

There are several passages in this despatch at which I might have taken exception, but I thought it best not to raise unnecessary questions; I therefore confined myself to the following observations:—

I said that it was not the wish or intention of Her Majesty's Government to pronounce any judgment on the causes which had induced seven of the United States to secede from the rest; whether, as to the past, those States had reason to complain that the terms of the compact of Union had not been observed, or whether they had reason to apprehend that, for the future, justice would not be done to them, were questions which Her Majesty's Government did not pretend to decide. They had seen in the United States a free and prosperous community, with which they had been happy to maintain the most amicable relations.

Now that a Secession had taken place, they were in no hurry to recognize the separation as complete and final. But, on the other hand, I could not bind Her Majesty's Government, nor tell how and when circumstances might arise which would make a decision necessary. That I must, therefore, decline to enter into any further discussion at the present moment, and could only assure him of our regret at the events which had recently occurred.

I am, &c.
(Signed) J. RUSSELL.

No. 27.

Lord Lyons to Lord J. Russell.—(*Received April* 30.)

(Extract.) *Washington, April* 15, 1861.

ON the 8th instant a messenger from this Government informed the Governor of South Carolina and the Military Commandant at Charleston, that President Lincoln had determined to supply Fort Sumter with provisions, peaceably if possible, forcibly if necessary.

On the 11th instant the Military Commandant, in obedience to orders from Montgomery, from the Government of the Southern Confederacy, summoned Fort Sumter to surrender.

On the 12th instant, at half-past 4 o'clock in the morning, the batteries prepared by the troops of the Confederate States opened their fire on the fort.

The day before yesterday Fort Sumter was surrendered unconditionally.

At Washington, the day before yesterday, President Lincoln, in answer to questions from Commissioners sent by the Legislature of Virginia, gave an authoritative interpretation of his inaugural address, leaving no doubt that he had resolved to adopt coercive measures against the South.

This morning the President has issued a Proclamation calling out 75,000 men of the Militia, and summoning a special session of Congress for the 4th of July, the anniversary of the Declaration of Independence.

Civil war is now imminent, or rather has already begun. Had Mr. Lincoln adhered to his determination to evacuate Fort Sumter, hostilities might undoubtedly have been deferred for some time longer. A prudent policy consistently pursued might have led to a peaceful separation, possibly even to a peaceful reconstruction of the Union. Mr. Lincoln, however, has decided upon war, and has carried his Cabinet with him.

An expedition was prepared in the utmost haste at New York. Upon being informed of the intentions of this Goverment, the forces of the Southern Confederacy immediately summoned the fort, and after a bombardment of less than forty hours took it.

No more certain intelligence than the telegraphic despatches to the newspapers have yet been received here from Charleston. The most extraordinary statement which they contain is, that no one was killed on either side during the bombardment. The ships

* No. 25.

forming the expedition from New York appear to have been off Charleston harbour, but to have taken no part in the contest. The tempestuous state of the weather is supposed to have rendered their approach impracticable.

The loss of Fort Sumter is not of itself of much importance, in a military point of view, to this Government. As the beginning of civil war it is a most serious and a most unhappy event. It seems calculated to arouse feelings of resentment and humiliation in the North, which will overwhelm the party of peace, and throw the people with bitter eagerness into the war.

The immediate apprehensions of the Government are for this city. The Chiefs of the Southern Confederacy loudly declare their intention of attacking it immediately if the Border States join them. This Government, previously to the issue of the Proclamation this morning, were already making arrangements with the Governors of Northern States to obtain volunteers and militia to defend it.

Probably the best remaining chance of avoiding a fierce war lies in the Government's being able to assemble in time so large a force for the defence of Washington as to deter the South from attacking it. The Confederate States are, however, at this moment believed to be better prepared to attack the city than the Government is to provide in time for its defence.

Mr. Lincoln's plans, as stated in his answer to the Virginia Commissioners, appear to be devised for the purpose of avoiding, if possible, military operations, except on the coast. He says, "I shall not attempt to collect the duties and imposts by any armed invasion of any part of the country—not meaning by this, however, that I may not land a force deemed necessary to relieve a fort upon the border of the country." He says nothing of his intentions with respect to blockading Southern ports, or collecting Customs duties by means of United States' vessels off the harbours. That measures of this kind are in contemplation is, I fear, hardly to be doubted. For the collection of duties on board ships, the sanction of Congress is said to be legally necessary, as it undoubtedly is for a blockade, if the establishment of one be regarded as equivalent to war. But means can no doubt be found to bring either measure within the terms of the Constitution or the law, if it be desired to do so.

In his answer to the Commissioners Mr. Lincoln threatens to cut off postal communication with the Seceded States. In his Proclamation he announces that " the first service assigned to the forces thereby called out will probably be to repossess the forts, places, and property which have been seized from the Union."

In the approaching contest the North has the superiority in numbers and in wealth, and the immense advantage of possessing and of being able to maintain a navy. It has also an organised, though small, regular army; but the advantage of this will be in a great measure neutralised by the retirement of the Southern officers. The South is, if the accounts which reach us are to be trusted, more unanimous; it is more eager, and, as it has more at stake, is more ready to make sacrifices. The taint of slavery will render the cause of the South repugnant to the feelings of the civilised world. On the other hand, commercial intercourse with the Cotton States is of vital importance to manufacturing nations.

The conduct of Virginia and the other Border States is now more than ever the critical question. If they remain true to the Union, the contest may be confined to small dimensions. Unless, however, they abandon their solemn declarations, they must now make common cause with the South. The telegraph may perhaps convey some important information from these States to the New York newspapers before the departure of the packet which will convey this despatch to your Lordship.

I understand that measures have been taken to bring the United States' men-of-war home from foreign stations as soon as possible. The greatest activity is shown in enlisting sailors, and in fitting out ships in the United States' navy-yards.

A telegraphic despatch to the newspapers announces, I know not how truly, that the relief of Fort Pickens, in Florida, has been effected by the vessels sent some time ago by this Government for the purpose.

No. 28.

Lord J. Russell to the Lords Commissioners of the Admiralty.

My Lords, *Foreign Office, May* 1, 1861.

THE intelligence which reached this country by the last mail from the United States gives reason to suppose that a civil war between the Northern and Southern States of that Confederacy was imminent, if indeed it might not be considered to have already begun.

Simultaneously with the arrival of this news, a telegram purporting to have been conveyed to Halifax from the United States was received, which announced that the President of the Southern Confederacy had taken steps for issuing letters of marque against the vessels of the Northern States.

If such is really the case, it is obvious that much inconvenience may be occasioned to the numerous British vessels engaged in trade on the coast of the United States and in the Gulf of Mexico, and that timely provision should be made for their protection against undue molestation by reason of the maritime operations of the hostile parties; and Her Majesty has accordingly commanded me to signify to your Lordships her pleasure that adequate reinforcements should forthwith be sent to Her Majesty's squadron on the North American and West Indian station, so that the Admiral in command may be able duly to provide for the protection of British shipping in any emergency that may occur.

I need scarcely observe to your Lordships that it may be right to apprize the Admiral that, much as Her Majesty regrets the prospect of civil war breaking out in a country in the happiness and peace of which Her Majesty takes the deepest interest, it is Her Majesty's pleasure that nothing should be done by her naval forces which should indicate any partiality or preference for either party in the contest that may ensue.

I am, &c.
(Signed)   J. RUSSELL.

No. 29.

Lord Lyons to Lord J. Russell.—(Received May 10.)

My Lord,   *Washington, April* 22, 1860.

THE inclosed copy of a letter which I addressed on the 19th instant to Governor-General Sir Edmund Head will make your Lordship acquainted with the steps taken by me with regard to a report that secret agents have been sent by this Government to Canada. The Mr. George Ashman who is stated to be one of these agents, was President of the Convention at Chicago, which nominated Mr. Lincoln as the candidate of the Republican Party for the Presidency of the United States.

In one at least of his speeches during the Presidential canvass, Mr. Seward alluded to the eventual acquisition of Canada as a compensation to the Northern States for any loss they might sustain in consequence of the disaffection of the Southern part of the Union.

I suppose, however, that the agents who now appear to have been sent to Canada have been despatched with some definite and practical object. Your Lordship will perceive from my letter to the Governor-General that although Mr. Seward refused to give me any other information on the subject, he did assure me that no agents were employed by this Government for any object affecting the Colonial relations between Canada and the British Crown.

I have, &c.
(Signed)   LYONS.

Inclosure in No. 29.

Lord Lyons to Sir E. Head.

(Extract.)   *Washington, April* 19, 1861.

I INFORMED you in a private letter some days ago, that I had learnt, from what I thought good authority, that this Government had determined to send two secret agents to Canada, and that it was supposed the object was to ascertain the state of feeling in the province with regard to annexing itself to the United States.

I sent you, yesterday morning, a paragraph from the "New York Herald," of the 17th, of which the following is a copy:—

"It is reported that George Ashman has been sent to Canada as a confidential agent of the Administration to explain our political position under the present state of things."

I sent you yesterday, in the afternoon, a message to the effect that I had drawn the attention of Mr. Seward to the paragraph.

I think the best way to enable you to judge of the matter will be to give you as exact an account as I can of what passed between Mr. Seward and me.

I showed him the paragraph in the paper yesterday afternoon at the State Department, and asked him whether there was any truth in it.

"That," he replied, "is a question which I cannot answer."

"It is," I said, "a very irregular proceeding."

I repeated this remark, and then Mr. Seward asked why it was irregular.

I answered that it was an attempt to hold communication otherwise than in the regular official manner, and through the regular recognized channels.

After a pause Mr. Seward went on to say:—"If you suppose that any agent of this Government has been dispatched with any object affecting the present Colonial relations of Canada to Great Britain, you are entirely mistaken."

I said that I was very far from having intended to suggest so grave a charge against the Government of the United States as this.

"After all," observed Mr. Seward, "if we did send an agent to Canada, I suppose it would be no treason."

I replied that "treason" was usually applied to breakers of the obligations between subjects and the Power to which they owed allegiance; that breaches of international obligations were a different matter.

Here the conversation ended. The impression left upon my mind was that undoubtedly an agent or agents had been sent to Canada, and that whatever the object was, it was clearly one which the Secretary of State was unwilling to avow to the British Minister.

No. 30.

Lord Lyons to Lord J. Russell.—(Received May 10.)

(Extract.) *Washington, April* 22, 1861.

THE progress of events in this country appears to tend, with fatal rapidity, towards a fierce civil war.

I have had the honour to transmit to your Lordship a Proclamation issued by the President of the United States for calling out 75,000 men of the Militia, and summoning a session of Congress.

To this the President of the Southern Confederacy replied, on the 17th instant, by a Proclamation inviting those who might desire to aid his Government by service in private armed vessels at sea, to apply for letters of marque.

The President of the United States rejoined, by a Proclamation dated the 19th instant, announcing a blockade of the Southern ports, and declaring, in effect, that privateers with letters of marque from the Southern Confederacy will be treated as pirates.

The Governors of the Border States answered the call of the President of the United States for troops by prompt and positive refusals, couched, in several instances, in very strong language.

In the North, however, the call has been responded to with enthusiasm; and the Government would, at this moment, have no difficulty in obtaining thence any number of men for which it might ask.

The troops are at present wanted chiefly for the defence of Washington, an attack on which from the South is seriously apprehended. Such an attack, if made immediately and with vigour, would, in the opinion of many people, be successful. Unless, however, the town be taken in a few days, by a sudden *coup de main*, it seems difficult to suppose that the Government will not be able to provide means for its defence at least equal to those which the Southern Confederacy possesses for attacking it.

Some of the Militia from the North have already arrived, and the number would be greater had not a conflict which occurred in the streets of Baltimore, on the 19th instant, led to a refusal on the part of the inhabitants to allow troops from the North to pass through the town, and to the destruction of some of the bridges on the railways by which it is connected with the North.

One of the first results of the announcement of coercive measures on the part of the Government here, has been the passing by the Convention of Virginia of an Ordinance of Secession. It is true that, in conformity with the terms on which the Convention was elected, the Ordinance must be ratified by the people of the State before it becomes definitively valid, but in the meantime the Secession appears, in fact, to have taken place. Virginia has not, however, so far as is known here, formally joined the Southern Confederation.

In consequence of the secession of Virginia, and of the predominance at this moment of the Disunion party in Maryland, the little district in which this capital is situated is entirely surrounded by hostile territory. Correspondence with the North, both by mail and telegraph, has been interrupted for the last two days. Troops, however, can be brought up the Potomac, and if the spirit roused at the North be at all what it is represented to be, it must soon be in the power of the Government to reopen the communication through Maryland.

One of the rumours rife here, is that troops are passing from Virginia into Maryland, and that the first battle between the two sections of the country will take place near Baltimore.

No. 31.

Lord Lyons to Lord J. Russell.—(Received May 10.)

(Extract.) *Washington, April* 22, 1861.

I HAVE the honour to inclose copies of a Proclamation of the President of the Southern Confederacy, inviting application for letters of marque, and also a Proclamation of the President of the United States declaring that Southern privateers will be treated as pirates, and announcing a blockade of the Southern ports.

I lost no time in taking measures to communicate the contents of these Proclamations as fast as possible, both by telegraph and post, to Rear-Admiral Sir Alexander Milne. The subsequent interruption of communication with the North has prevented my learning how far my measures were successful.

I am informed that an official notification of the blockade will be sent to the foreign Legations here in the course of the day.

Under ordinary circumstances the season during which British vessels frequent Southern ports closes in May and does not re-open until October.

I understand that some alarm is felt in the North respecting the Southern privateers, but it must be supposed that the navy of the United States will suffice to arrest their operations. If these privateers, however, make any head in the Gulf of Mexico, it may perhaps be advisable that a British squadron should be sent there to insure the safety of British merchant-vessels.

Inclosure 1 in No. 31.

Proclamation by the President of the Confederate States of America.

WHEREAS Abraham Lincoln, President of the United States, has by Proclamation announced the intention of invading the Confederacy with an armed force for the purpose of capturing its fortresses, and thereby subverting its independence, and subjecting the free people thereof to the dominion of a foreign Power : and whereas it has thus become the duty of this Government to repel the threatened invasion, and defend the rights and liberties of the people by all the means which the laws of nations and usages of civilized warfare place at its disposal :

Now, therefore, I, Jefferson Davis, President of the Confederated States of America, do issue this my Proclamation inviting all those who may desire by service in private armed vessels on the high seas to aid this Government in resisting so wanton and wicked an aggression, to make application for commissions or letters of marque and reprisal, to be issued under the seal of these Confederate States ; and I do further notify all persons applying for letters of marque to make a statement in writing giving the name and suitable description of the character, tonnage, and force of the vessel, name of the place of residence of each owner concerned therein, and the intended number of crew, and to sign such statement, and deliver the same to the Secretary of State or Collector of the port of entry of these Confederate States to be by him transmitted to the Secretary of State ; and I do further notify all applicants aforesaid, before any commission or letter of marque is issued to any vessel or the owner or the owners thereof, and the commander for the time being, they will be required to give bond to the Confederate States, with at least two responsible sureties not interested in such vessel, in the penal sum of five thousand dollars, or if such vessel be provided with more than one hundred and fifty men, then in the penal sum of ten thousand dollars, with the condition that the owners, officers, and crew who shall be employed on board such commissioned vessel shall observe the laws of these Confederate States and the instructions given them for the regulation of their conduct, that shall satisfy all damages done contrary to the tenour thereof by such vessel during her commission, and deliver up the same when revoked by the President of the Confederate States; and I do further specially enjoin on all persons holding offices, civil and military, under the authority of the Confederate States, that they be vigilant and zealous in the discharge of the duties incidental thereto; and I do, moreover, exhort the good people of these Confederate States, as they love their country, as they prize the blessings of free government, as they feel the wrongs of the past and those now threatened in an aggravated form by those whose enmity is more implacable because unprovoked, they exert themselves in preserving order, in promoting concord, in maintaining the authority and efficacy of the laws, and in supporting, invigorating all the measures which may be adopted for a common defence, and by which, under the blessing of Divine Providence, we may hope for a speedy, just, and honourable peace.

In witness whereof, I have set my hand and have caused the seal of the Confederate States of America to be attached this seventeenth day of April, in the year of our Lord one thousand eight hundred and sixty-one.

          (Signed) JEFFERSON DAVIS.
(Signed) ROBERT TOOMBS, *Secretary of State.*

Inclosure 2 in No. 31.

Proclamation by the President of the United States of America.

WHEREAS an insurrection against the Government of the United States has broken out in the States of South Carolina, Georgia, Alabama, Florida, Mississippi, Louisiana, and Texas, and the laws of the United States for the collection of the revenue cannot be effectually executed therein conformably to that provision of the Constitution which requires duties to be uniform throughout the United States;

And whereas a combination of persons, engaged in such insurrection, have threatened to grant pretended letters of marque to authorize the bearers thereof to commit assaults on the lives, vessels, and property of good citizens of the country lawfully engaged in commerce on the high seas, and in waters of the United States;

And whereas an Executive Proclamation has been already issued, requiring the persons engaged in these disorderly proceedings to desist therefrom, calling out a militia force for the purpose of repressing the same, and convening Congress in extraordinary session to deliberate and determine thereon:

Now, therefore, I, Abraham Lincoln, President of the United States, with a view to the same purposes before mentioned, and to the protection of the public peace, and the lives and property of quiet and orderly citizens pursuing their lawful occupations, until Congress shall have assembled and deliberated on the said unlawful proceedings, or until the same shall have ceased, have further deemed it advisable to set on foot a blockade of the ports within the States aforesaid, in pursuance of the laws of the United States and of the law of nations in such case provided. For this purpose a competent force will be posted so as to prevent entrance and exit of vessels from the ports aforesaid. If, therefore, with a view to violate such blockade, a vessel shall approach, or shall attempt to leave any of the said ports, she will be duly warned by the Commander of one of the blockading vessels, who will endorse on her register the fact and date of such warning, and if the same vessel shall again attempt to enter or leave the blockaded port, she will be captured and sent to the nearest convenient port, for such proceedings against her and her cargo as prize as may be deemed advisable.

And I hereby proclaim and declare that if any person, under the pretended authority of the said States, or under any other pretence, shall molest a vessel of the United States, or the persons or cargo on board of her, such person will be held amenable to the laws of the United States for the prevention and punishment of piracy.

In witness whereof I have hereunto set my hand, and caused the seal of the United States to be affixed.

Done at the City of Washington, this nineteenth day of April, in the year of our Lord one thousand eight hundred and sixty-one, and of the Independence of the United States the eighty-fifth.

          (Signed) ABRAHAM LINCOLN.
By the President:
(Signed) WILLIAM H. SEWARD, *Secretary of State.*

No. 32.

Lord Lyons to Lord J. Russell.—(Received May 10.)

My Lord,   *Washington, April* 23, 1861.

I HAVE the honour to inclose a copy of a letter dated yesterday from Mr. Seward, the Secretary of State, to Mr. Hicks, the Governor of Maryland, which has appeared in the Washington newspapers this morning.

I learn from it that the Governor proposed to Mr. Seward that I should be requested to act as mediator between the contending parties to prevent the effusion of blood. I had no previous knowledge of this proposal, nor have I had any communication whatever with Governor Hicks or any other of the Maryland authorities.

The proposal is, as might have been foreseen, unhesitatingly rejected by Mr. Seward.

I am convinced that no good effect could be produced at this moment by any offer on the part of the Representatives of the European Powers to mediate between the North and the South.

I have myself strictly conformed in my language and conduct to the instructions given me by your Lordship's despatch of the 5th January last.

I have, &c.
(Signed)   LYONS.

Inclosure in No. 32.

Mr. Seward to Mr. Hicks.

Sir,   *Department of State, Washington, April* 22, 1861.

I HAVE had the honour to receive your communication of this morning, in which you inform me that you have felt it to be your duty to advise the President of the United States to order elsewhere the troops then off Annapolis, and also that no more may be sent through Maryland; and that you have further suggested that Lord Lyons be requested to act as mediator between the contending parties in our country to prevent the effusion of blood.

The President directs me to acknowledge the receipt of that communication, and to assure you that he has weighed the counsels which it contains with the respect which he habitually cherishes for the Chief Magistrates of the several States, and especially for yourself. He regrets, as deeply as any magistrate or citizen of the country can, that demonstrations against the safety of the United States, with very extensive preparations for the effusion of blood, have made it his duty to call out the force to which you allude.

The force now sought to be brought through Maryland is intended for nothing but the defence of this capital. The President has necessarily confided the choice of the national highway which that force shall take in coming to this city to the Lieutenant-General commanding the army of the United States, who, like his only predecessor, is not less distinguished for his humanity than for his loyalty, patriotism, and distinguished public service.

The President instructs me to add that the national highway thus selected by the Lieutenant-General has been chosen by him, upon consultation with prominent magistrates and citizens of Maryland, as the one which, while a route is absolutely necessary, is farthest removed from the populous cities of the State, and with the expectation that it would therefore be the least objectionable one.

The President cannot but remember that there has been a time in the history of our country when a General of the American Union with forces designed for the defence of its capital was not unwelcome anywhere in the State of Maryland, and certainly not at Annapolis, then, as now, the capital of that patriotic State, and then also one of the capitals of the Union.

If eighty years could have obliterated all the other noble sentiments of that age in Maryland, the President would be hopeful, nevertheless, that there is one that would for ever remain there and everywhere. That sentiment is, that no domestic contention whatever that may arise among the parties of this Republic ought in any case to be referred to any foreign arbitrament, least of all to the arbitrament of an European Monarchy.

I have, &c.
(Signed)   WILLIAM H. SEWARD.

No. 33.

Lord J. Russell to Lord Lyons.*

My Lord, *Foreign Office, May* 11, 1861.

ON Saturday last I received at my house Mr. Yancey, Mr. Mann, and Judge Rost, the three gentlemen deputed by the Southern Confederacy to obtain their recognition as an independent State. One of these gentlemen, speaking for the others, dilated on the causes which had induced the Southern States to secede from the Northern. The principal of these causes, he said, was not slavery, but the very high price which, for the sake of protecting the Northern manufacturers, the South were obliged to pay for the manufactured goods which they required. One of the first acts of the Southern Congress was to reduce these duties, and, to prove their sincerity, he gave as an instance that Louisiana had given up altogether that protection on her sugar which she enjoyed by the legislation of the United States.

As a proof of the riches of the South, he stated that of 350,000,000 dollars of exports of produce to foreign countries, 270,000,000 were furnished by the Southern States.

I said that I could hold no official communication with the Delegates of the Southern States. That, however, when the question of recognition came to be formally discussed, there were two points upon which inquiry must be made: first, whether the Body seeking recognition could maintain its position as an independent State; secondly, in what manner it was proposed to maintain relations with foreign States.

After speaking at some length on the first of these points, and alluding to the news of the secession of Virginia and other intelligence favourable to their cause, these gentlemen called my attention to the Article in their Constitution prohibiting the Slave Trade.

I said that it was alleged very currently that if the Slave States found that they could not compete successfully with the cotton of other countries, they would revive the Slave Trade for the purpose of diminishing the cost of production. They said this was a suspicion unsupported by any proof. The fact was, that they had prohibited the Slave Trade, and did not mean to revive it. They pointed to the new Tariff of the United States as a proof that British manufactures would be nearly excluded from the North, and freely admitted in the South.

Other observations were made, but not of very great importance. The Delegates concluded by stating that they should remain in London for the present, in the hope that the recognition of the Southern Confederacy would not be long delayed.

I am, &c.
(Signed) J. RUSSELL.

No. 34.

Lord Lyons to Lord J. Russell.—(*Received May* 14.)

(Extract.) *Washington, April* 27, 1861.

I AM obliged to send the messenger two days before the regular time in consequence of the interruption of railway communication through Maryland; but, in fact, owing to the general interruption of the communication both by railroad and telegraph between this city and both the Northern and Southern States, I have very little detailed intelligence to submit to your Lordship This Government has abandoned the attempt to convey troops through Baltimore. It has also declared its inability to bring soldiers for the defence of this capital up the Potomac river. It has, however, at last succeeded in establishing a route. The Militia from the North are embarked at Perrysville, a ferry on the Susquehanna, brought by water to Annapolis, and thence by railroad to this place. A considerable number arrived yesterday, and very large forces are said to be pouring down from the Northern States. The spirit of animosity against the South appears to have been successfully aroused by the Government, and if the present mood continue, there will be no lack of men or contributions of money on the Northern side.

Troops are also, I understand, coming up rapidly from the South into Virginia.

The statements of the numbers on each side vary so much that no accurate estimate can be formed. All that is plain is the sad fact that both North and South are arraying themselves for civil war. To possess themselves of this capital is supposed to be

* A similar despatch was addressed on the same day to Earl Cowley.

the aim of the South, while the North naturally make it a point of honour to defend it.

This Government sent an expedition to the United States' Navy-yard at Norfolk, and destroyed by fire and gunpowder the ships, buildings, and stores. The result of these and similar measures is apparent. It had been hoped to maintain Virginia in a neutral position, and thus to avoid a collision between the Northern and Southern forces, and to remove the danger of an attack upon Washington. The day before yesterday the Virginia Convention decreed the immediate union of the State with the Southern Confederacy, reserving, however, as their Constitution obliged them to do, the right of the people of the State to reverse the decree. In the meantime, however, the State is placed under the authority of the Southern Confederacy, and its territory is entirely at the disposal of that Confederacy for military operations.

North Carolina has already taken the usual preliminary step to secession, that of seizing the Federal forts, arsenals, and property. This has caused the ports of that State to be comprised in the additional blockade which is to be announced to-morrow.

Maryland was to have been also included in the blockade, but it was deemed advisable after the Proclamation was signed to erase the name of that State. The Assembly summoned to consider the question of Secession has just met. It has probably been thought advisable not to destroy the last hope of keeping in the Union a State the geographical situation of which renders it so important. In fact, as Washington is completely surrounded by Maryland, the questions of maintaining the authority of the North in Maryland and in this city are nearly identical. If Washington is to be held by the North, Maryland must either be persuaded to adhere to the Northern Union or be subdued by force.

In the city there is a kind of panic, but the place has no other importance than that which it derives from its title of capital of the United States, and from two or three fine public buildings.

No. 35.

Lord J. Russell to Lord Lyons.

My Lord, *Foreign Office, May* 15, 1861.

I TRANSMIT to you herewith a copy of a Proclamation which the Queen has been pleased to issue, warning Her Majesty's subjects against taking part in the hostilities which have broken out in the United States.

I have forwarded copies of this Proclamation to Her Majesty's Consuls at the different ports, with instructions to exhibit the same in their respective Consular offices, and to take suitable steps for making known the purport of the same to Her Majesty's subjects residing or entering within their jurisdiction; taking care, however, to do so in the manner best calculated to avoid wounding the susceptibilities of the authorities or people of the place where they reside.

I am, &c.
(Signed) J. RUSSELL.

Inclosure in No. 35.

BY THE QUEEN.

A Proclamation.

VICTORIA R.

WHEREAS We are happily at peace with all Sovereigns, Powers, and States:

And whereas hostilities have unhappily commenced between the Government of the United States of America and certain States styling themselves the Confederate States of America:

And whereas We, being at peace with the Government of the United States, have declared Our Royal determination to maintain a strict and impartial neutrality in the contest between the said contending parties:

We therefore have thought fit, by the advice of Our Privy Council, to issue this Our Royal Proclamation:

And We do hereby strictly charge and command all Our loving subjects to observe a strict neutrality in and during the aforesaid hostilities, and to abstain from violating or contravening either the laws and statutes of the realm in this behalf, or the law of nations in relation thereto, as they will answer to the contrary at their peril:

And whereas in and by a certain Statute made and passed in the fifty-ninth year of His Majesty King George the Third, intituled "An Act to prevent the Enlisting or Engagement of His Majesty's Subjects to serve in a Foreign Service, and the fitting out or equipping, in His Majesty's Dominions, Vessels for Warlike Purposes, without His Majesty's Licence," it is amongst other things declared and enacted as follows:—

"That if any natural-born subject of His Majesty, his heirs and successors, without the leave or licence of His Majesty, his heirs or successors, for that purpose first had and obtained, under the Sign-Manual of His Majesty, his heirs or successors, or signified by Order in Council, or by Proclamation of His Majesty, his heirs or successors, shall take or accept, or shall agree to take or accept, any military commission, or shall otherwise enter into the military service, as a commissioned or non-commissioned officer, or shall enlist or enter himself to enlist, or shall agree to enlist or to enter himself to serve as a soldier, or to be employed or shall serve in any warlike or military operation in the service of or for or under or in aid of any foreign prince, state, potentate, colony, province, or part of any province or people, or of any person or persons exercising or assuming to exercise the powers of government in or over any foreign country, colony, province, or part of any province or people, either as an officer or soldier, or in any other military capacity; or if any natural-born subject of His Majesty shall, without such leave or licence as aforesaid, accept, or agree to take or accept, any commission, warrant, or appointment as an officer, or shall enlist or enter himself, or shall agree to enlist or enter himself, to serve as a sailor or marine, or to be employed, or engaged, or shall serve in and on board any ship or vessel of war, or in and on board any ship or vessel used or fitted out, or equipped or intended to be used for any warlike purpose, in the service of or for or under or in aid of any foreign power, prince, state, potentate, colony, province, or part of any province or people, or of any person or persons exercising or assuming to exercise the powers of government in or over any foreign country, colony, province, or part of any province or people; or if any natural-born subject of His Majesty shall, without such leave and licence as aforesaid, engage, contract, or agree to go, or shall go to any foreign state, country, colony, province, or part of any province, or to any place beyond the seas, with an intent or in order to enlist or enter himself to serve, or with intent to serve in any warlike or military operation whatever, whether by land or by sea, in the service of or for or under or in aid of any foreign prince, state, potentate, colony, province, or part of any province or people, or in the service of or under or in aid of any person or persons exercising or assuming to exercise the powers of government in or over any foreign country, colony, province, or part of any province or people, either as an officer or a soldier, or in any other military capacity, or as an officer or sailor, or marine in any such ship or vessel as aforesaid, although no enlisting money or pay or reward shall have been or shall be in any or either of the cases aforesaid actually paid to or received by him, or by any person to or for his use or benefit; or if any person whatever, within the United Kingdom of Great Britain and Ireland, or in any part of His Majesty's dominions elsewhere, or in any country, colony, settlement, island, or place belonging to or subject to His Majesty, shall hire, retain, engage, or procure, or shall attempt or endeavour to hire, retain, engage, or procure, any person or persons whatever to enlist, or to enter or engage to enlist, or to serve or to be employed in any such service or employment as aforesaid, as an officer, soldier, sailor, or marine, either in land or sea service, for or under or in aid of any foreign prince, state, potentate, colony, province, or part of any province or people, or for or under or in aid of any person or persons exercising or assuming to exercise any powers of government as aforesaid, or to go or to agree to go or embark from any part of His Majesty's dominions, for the purpose or with intent to be so enlisted, entered, engaged, or employed as aforesaid, whether any enlisting money, pay, or reward shall have been or shall be actually given or received, or not; in any or either of such cases, every person so offending shall be deemed guilty of a misdemeanor, and upon being convicted thereof, upon any information or indictment, shall be punishable by fine and imprisonment, or either of them, at the discretion of the Court before which such offender shall be convicted."

And it is in and by the said Act further enacted,—

"That if any person, within any part of the United Kingdom, or in any part of His Majesty's dominions beyond the seas, shall, without the leave and licence of His Majesty for that purpose first had and obtained as aforesaid, equip, furnish, fit out, or arm, or attempt or endeavour to equip, furnish, fit out, or arm, or procure to be equipped, furnished, fitted out, or armed, or shall knowingly aid, assist, or be concerned in the equipping, furnishing, fitting out, or arming of any ship or vessel, with intent or in order that such ship or vessel shall be employed in the service of any foreign prince, state, or potentate, or of any foreign colony, province, or part of any province or people, or of any person or persons exercising or assuming to exercise any powers of government in or over any foreign state, colony, province, or part of any province or people, as a transport or store-ship, or with intent to cruize or commit hostilities against any prince, state, or potentate, or against the subjects or citizens of any prince, state, or potentate, or against the persons exercising or assuming to exercise the powers of government in any colony, province, or part of any province or country, or against the inhabitants of any foreign colony, province, or part of any province or country, with whom His Majesty shall not then be at war; or shall, within the United Kingdom, or any of His Majesty's dominions, or in any settlement, colony, territory, island, or place belonging or subject to His Majesty, issue or deliver any commission for any ship or vessel, to the intent that such ship or vessel shall be employed as aforesaid, every such person so offending shall be deemed guilty of a misdemeanor, and shall, upon conviction thereof upon any information or indictment, be punished by fine and imprisonment, or either of them, at the discretion of the Court in which such offender shall be convicted; and every such ship or vessel, with the tackle, apparel, and furniture, together with all the materials, arms, ammunition, and stores, which may belong to or be on board of any such ship or vessel, shall be forfeited; and it shall be lawful for any officer of His Majesty's Customs or Excise, or any officer of His Majesty's navy, who is by law empowered to make seizures for any forfeiture incurred under any of the laws of customs or excise, or the laws of trade and navigation, to seize such ships and vessels aforesaid, and in such places, and in such manner in which the officers of His Majesty's Customs or Excise and the officers of His Majesty's navy are empowered respectively to make seizures under the laws of customs and excise, or under the laws of trade and navigation; and that every such ship and vessel, with the tackle, apparel, and furniture, together with all the materials, arms, ammunition, and stores which may belong to or be on board of such ship or vessel, may be prosecuted and condemned in the like manner and in such Courts as ships or vessels may be prosecuted and condemned for any breach of the laws made for the protection of the revenues of Customs and Excise, or of the laws of trade and navigation."

And it is in and by the said Act further enacted,—

"That if any person in any part of the United Kingdom of Great Britain and Ireland, or in any part of His Majesty's dominions beyond the seas, without the leave and licence of His Majesty for that purpose first had and obtained as aforesaid, shall, by adding to the number of the guns of such vessel, or by changing those on board for other guns, or by the addition of any equipment for war, increase or augment, or procure to be increased or augmented, or shall be knowingly concerned in increasing or augmenting, the warlike force of any ship or vessel of war, or cruizer, or other armed vessel, which at the time of her arrival in any part of the United Kingdom, or any of His Majesty's dominions, was a ship of war, cruizer, or armed vessel in the service of any foreign prince, state, or potentate, or of any person or persons exercising or assuming to exercise any powers of government in or over any colony, province, or part of any province or people belonging to the subjects of any such prince, state, or potentate, or to the inhabitants of any colony, province, or part of any province or country under the control of any person or persons so exercising or assuming to exercise the powers of government, every such person so offending shall be deemed guilty of a misdemeanor, and shall, upon being convicted thereof upon any information or indictment, be punished by fine and imprisonment, or either of them, at the discretion of the Court before which such offender shall be convicted."

Now, in order that none of Our subjects may unwarily render themselves liable to the penalties imposed by the said statute, We do hereby strictly command, that no person or persons whatsoever do commit any act, matter, or thing whatsoever, contrary to the provisions of the said statute, upon pain of the several penalties by the said statute imposed, and of Our high displeasure.

And We do hereby further warn all Our loving subjects, and all persons whatsoever entitled to Our protection, that if any of them shall presume, in contempt of this Our Royal Proclamation, and of Our high displeasure, to do any acts in derogation of their duty, as subjects of a Neutral Sovereign in the said contest, or in violation or contravention of the Law of Nations in that behalf; as for example, and more especially, by entering into the military service of either of the said contending parties as commissioned or non-commissioned officers or soldiers; or by serving as officers, sailors, or marines on board any ship or vessel of war or transport of or in the service of either of the said contending parties; or by serving as officers, sailors, or marines on board any privateer bearing letters of marque of or from either of the said contending parties; or by engaging to go or going to any place beyond the seas with intent to enlist or engage in any such service, or by procuring or attempting to procure, within Her Majesty's dominions at home or abroad, others to do so; or by fitting out, arming, or equipping any ship or vessel to be employed as a ship of war or privateer or transport by either of the said contending parties; or by breaking or endeavouring to break any blockade lawfully and actually established by or on behalf of either of the said contending parties; or by carrying officers, soldiers, despatches, arms, military stores, or materials, or any article or articles considered and deemed to be contraband of war, according to the law or modern usage of nations, for the use or service of either of the said contending parties, all persons so offending will incur and be liable to the several penalties and penal consequences by the said Statute or by the Law of Nations in that behalf imposed or denounced.

And We do hereby declare, that all Our subjects and persons entitled to Our protection who may misconduct themselves in the premises will do so at their peril and of their own wrong, and that they will in nowise obtain any protection from Us against any liabilities or penal consequences, but will, on the contrary, incur Our high displeasure by such misconduct.

Given at Our Court at the White Lodge, Richmond Park, this thirteenth day of May, in the year of Our Lord one thousand eight hundred and sixty-one, and in the twenty-fourth year of Our Reign.

God save the Queen.

No. 36.

Lord J. Russell to Lord Lyons.

My Lord,   *Foreign Office, May* 16, 1861.

WHATEVER may have been the object with which, as appears from your despatch of the 22nd ultimo, secret agents have been sent by the United States' Government to Canada, Her Majesty's Government have to complain that no previous notice was given to you of the intention to despatch them, and that, in reply to the inquiry which you addressed to Mr. Seward, no frank explanation was afforded respecting the mission with which these agents were charged; and you will not conceal from Mr. Seward the unfavourable impression which this transaction has made on Her Majesty's Government.

I am, &c.
(Signed)   J. RUSSELL.

No. 37.

Lord Lyons to Lord J. Russell.—(Received May 17.)

My Lord,   *Washington, May* 2, 1861.

ABOUT 20,000 troops, furnished almost exclusively by the Militia regiments of the Northern States, are now collected at Washington. Others arrive daily, and it is considered that ample means of defence have been provided for the city. It is hoped, indeed, that the Southern States will now consider that an attack would be fruitless, and not attempt to make one.

Large bodies of Militia are also gathered together at Philadelphia and other points.

The greatest activity prevails in the United States' Navy yards. Vessels are being fitted out with the utmost speed, and many have been purchased, with a view to establish the blockade effectively, and to keep in check Southern privateers.

The President has considered the exigency to be so pressing as to oblige him to call, without waiting for the sanction of Congress, for 40,000 volunteers to serve the United States for three years; 20,000 men to serve in the regular army for five years; and 18,000 sailors to serve in the navy.

Very large contributions of money are offered to the Government by the merchants of New York and other wealthy men.

The North presents, on the surface at all events, complete unanimity. A spirit of bitter animosity against the South has arisen; no word of conciliation is heard; the cry is that the South must be reduced to obedience, at any cost, by force of arms.

In the South, if the accounts which reach us are to be believed, no less unanimity, no less bitterness of feeling, no less eagerness to come to blows, prevail. Large numbers of troops are assembling in Virginia, so that a few hours would suffice to bring the two armies into the presence of each other. A fierce civil war would seem to be almost inevitable.

Happily the circumstance most likely to lead to a collision will probably soon cease to exist. It is believed that the State of Maryland will not withdraw from the Union, nor any longer oppose the passage of Northern troops to this city. Ordinary military prudence will, no doubt, prevent the authorities from exposing troops on the march to the attacks of a hostile population in the town of Baltimore.

It is apprehended that the States of North Carolina, Arkansas, and Tennessee, will join the Southern Confederacy. The course which will be taken by Missouri and Kentucky, is considered to be more doubtful.

I send this and the accompanying despatches to New York, in the hope that they may be in time for the American mail-packet of the day after to-morrow. I purpose to write to your Lordship more fully by the British packet which will sail on the 8th instant.

I have, &c.
(Signed)   LYONS.

No. 38.

Lord Lyons to Lord J. Russell.—(Received May 17.)

My Lord,   *Washington, May 2, 1861.*

MR. SEWARD, the Secretary of State of the United States, sent for me yesterday to the State Department, and told me that he had reason to believe that an iron steamer, the "Peerless," had been sold to the *de facto* Southern Government, and was on her way out of Lake Ontario to be used as a privateer.* He read to me a part of a telegram which stated that the vessel was still at Toronto, and that it was believed she carried the British flag, and had regular British papers.

Mr. Seward proceeded to suggest that perhaps the Governor-General of Canada might be induced to detain the vessel. I said, somewhat doubtfully, that if her papers were in order, and there was no direct proof of her being actually engaged in any unlawful enterprise, the Governor-General might not have legal power to interfere with her. Mr. Seward replied that that might very well be; and, without further allusion to the Canadian authorities, proceeded to read to me a draft of a telegraphic order to the Naval Officers of the United States to seize the "Peerless," "under any flag, and with any papers," if they had probable information that she had been sold to the Southern insurgents. He went on to say, "I suppose you will hardly assent to this."

I replied that, far from assenting, I most positively dissented.

Mr. Seward said that if the seizure was effected, it would be upon the responsibility of this Government, who would be prepared for all the consequences which it might entail. He added, however, that the order had not yet been sanctioned by the President; that he was about to go to the Executive Mansion to attend a Cabinet Council; and that he would inform me of the decision which should be come to.

I said to Mr. Seward, "I not only dissent, but I solemnly protest, as Her Majesty's Minister, against any attempt to seize a vessel under the British flag, and with regular British papers."

I was very much grieved, not so much at the particular fact, though that appeared to me very serious, as at the arrogant spirit and disregard of the rights and feelings of foreign nations with which the American Government seemed to be disposed to conduct the civil war in which they were about to engage. I was most anxious to do all that I could to impress upon Mr. Seward, at the outset, the impolicy and danger of the course upon which he seemed determined to enter. I particularly reminded him of the extreme susceptibility which had at all times been manifested by the Americans themselves on the subject of any interference with vessels under their own flag. I said that even if the "Peerless" should in fact be sold to the Seceded States, she could never cause the United States anything like the inconvenience which would follow a deliberate violation of neutral rights. I concluded by repeating my protest.

Mr. Seward said little more in reply than that he would give due weight to the protest, and that nothing would be done without the sanction of the President, whom he was about to see at a Cabinet Council.

I said to Mr. Seward that I begged that when he submitted the proposed order to the President, he would distinctly say that the British Minister solemnly protested against it.

This Mr. Seward promised to do. Seeing that he was evidently anxious to go to the President's house without further delay, I took my leave, merely observing that I should probably feel it my duty to address him in writing on the subject.

* See page 116.

As soon as I got home, I wrote a note to Mr. Seward repeating my protest. I sent it to the State Department by Mr. Irvine, Her Majesty's Secretary of Legation. Mr. Seward had already left the Department, but Mr. Irvine delivered my note to the Assistant Secretary of State, who promised to send it in to the Cabinet Council which was sitting at the President's house.

In the evening Mr. Seward sent me a note informing me that notwithstanding my protest, the orders had been issued. I felt it my duty to reply by a note maintaining and repeating the protest.

I have the honour to inclose copies of the notes above mentioned.

I send to-day to the Governor-General copies of the inclosures in this despatch.

I have, &c.
(Signed)   LYONS.

Inclosure 1 in No. 38.

Lord Lyons to Mr. Seward.

Sir,   *Washington, May* 1, 1861.

YOU have just done me the honour to inform me verbally that you had under consideration the propriety of issuing orders to the United States' naval forces to seize a vessel under British colours and with regular papers, under the suspicion that she had been purchased, for unlawful purposes, by parties in the Southern States.

I at once stated to you several times, and as emphatically as I could, that I solemnly protested against any such seizure. You were good enough to assure me that you would take note of the protest. I think it, however, necessary, in order to cover my own responsibility, to record in writing, without a moment's delay, that a solemn protest was made by Her Britannic Majesty's Minister against such orders before they were issued.

I have, &c.
(Signed)   LYONS.

Inclosure 2 in No. 38.

Mr. Seward to Lord Lyons.

My Lord,   *Department of State, Washington, May* 1, 1861.

THE so-called Confederate States have waged an insurrectionary war against this Government. They are buying, and even seizing vessels in several places for the purpose of furnishing themselves with a naval force, and they are issuing letters of marque to privateers to be employed in preying upon the commerce of this country.

You are aware that the President has proclaimed a blockade of the ports included within the insurgent States. All these circumstances are known to the world.

The President this morning received information, believed to be authentic, that the iron steamer "Peerless" is in the hands of the enemy on her way out of Lake Ontario, and that she has regular British papers.

Thereupon I did myself the honour to solicit an interview with you. In that interview I suggested that it would be agreeable to the President if the Governor-General of Canada, with or under instructions from you, would direct the vessel to be detained. You did not think that such directions could be given in view of the uncertainties that hang over the matter. I replied that certainly under the circumstances this Government could not require such directions. I further stated, however, that the Government could not tolerate the fitting out and delivery of piratical vessels on the St. Lawrence, and that I should direct the "Peerless" to be seized and detained if the United States' forces should have reliable information that she has been sold, or contracted to be sold, and has been delivered, or is to be delivered to the insurgents to be used against the United States under whatever flag or papers she may bear, and that the parties affected should be referred to this Government.

You thereupon, verbally, protested unequivocally, and without reservation, as your note of this date, now just received, affirms.

I have, nevertheless, and notwithstanding your Lordship's protest, given conditional directions for the seizure of the "Peerless," in the following words :—

"To Commanders of naval or other forces of the United States.

"If you have reliable information that the 'Peerless' has been sold, or contracted for, and has been delivered, or is to be delivered to the insurgents to be used against the United States, seize and bring her into port, and detain her there, under whatever flag or papers she may bear, and refer the parties to this Government."

I hardly need to add that this proceeding is taken with no feelings of hostility against the Government of Great Britain. The President feels satisfied that Her Majesty's Government will not think the seizure unnecessary, or unwarrantable, or injurious, if the information upon which it proceeds shall prove to be correct; and, on the other hand, if it shall prove to be incorrect, full satisfaction will be promptly given to the Government of Her Majesty and the parties aggrieved. The British Government will be satisfied that such proceedings are sometimes indispensable when a flag is abused to cover aggressions upon a friendly nation.

I have, &c.
(Signed) WILLIAM H. SEWARD.

Inclosure 3 in No. 38.

Lord Lyons to Mr. Seward.

Sir, *Washington, May* 1, 1861.

I LEARN, with deep regret, from a note which I have just had the honour to receive from you, that the Government of the United States has given orders to the Commanders of its forces to seize a vessel and bring her into port, and detain her there, "under whatever flag, or whatever papers she may bear."

So far as the British flag and British papers may be affected by this measure, I must, as Her Britannic Majesty's Minister, maintain and repeat the protest which I made to you, both by word of mouth and by written note, before the orders were issued.

I have, &c.
(Signed) LYONS.

No. 39.

Lord J. Russell to Lord Lyons.

(Extract.) *Foreign Office, May* 18, 1861.

HER Majesty's Government approve the course which you took with reference to the declaration made to you by Mr. Seward, as reported in your second despatch of the 2nd instant,* in regard to the course which the United States' Government intended to pursue towards the British steamer "Peerless," suspected to have passed into the possession of the Confederate States, and to be intended to be employed as a privateer against the shipping of the United States.

You were quite right in protesting beforehand against the determination announced by Mr. Seward, that if probable cause of suspicion existed that vessel would be seized, under whatever flag it might be sailing. But Her Majesty's Government, as matters stand, accept the assurance given to you by Mr. Seward, that if the suspicions entertained against the vessel, and on which proceedings might be taken, should prove unfounded, the Government of the United States would be prepared to make suitable reparation for the wrongful act of seizing the vessel.

No. 40.

Lord Lyons to Lord J. Russell.—(*Received May* 21.)

My Lord, *Washington, May* 4, 1861.

MR. SEWARD said to me, on the 1st instant, that perhaps he ought to have told me before, that the United States' Government had sent agents to England to purchase arms. He added, that the agents would go on to France for the same purpose.

I have, &c.
(Signed) LYONS.

---

* No. 38.

No. 41.

Lord J. Russell to Lord Lyons.

My Lord,　　　　　　　　　　　　　　　　　　*Foreign Office, May* 21, 1861.

MR. ADAMS came to me at Pembroke Lodge on the 18th instant. After some general conversation, he said he was instructed to ask me for an explanation of the language I had used to Mr. Dallas. The expressions I had employed had been interpreted in the United States as being of an unfriendly tenour, and as intimating a change of policy on the part of Great Britain. He led me to understand that any such change would put an end to his mission, and unfavourably affect the relations of the two countries.

I repeated to Mr. Adams what I had said to Mr. Dallas: that, had a separation taken place between different parts of the American Union in an amicable manner, Her Majesty's Government would still have regretted that a Union of States so famous and so conspicuous for its love of liberty and enlightened progress should have been dissolved. That the opposition made by the Government of the United States to the Secession would make us still more averse to take any step to record and recognize that Secession. I explained to Mr. Adams, however, that the despatches of Judge Black and Mr. Seward seemed to ask on our part for a perpetual pledge that we would, under no circumstances, recognize the Seceding States. I had, therefore, thought it necessary to add that Great Britain must hold herself free to act according to the progress of events and as circumstances might require.

I reminded Mr. Adams that the United States had recognized Don Miguel, the usurper of the Throne of Portugal, and had even intended to acknowledge the Hungarian Republic in 1848, when it was obvious that such a Republic could not endure.

I said, that on the other hand, we had taken no step except that of declaring ourselves neutral, and allowing to the Southern States a belligerent character; that the size and population of the Seceding States were so considerable that we could not deny them that character, but that this step implied no recognition nor allowed any other than an intermediate position on the part of the Southern States.

Mr. Adams admitted this, but thought the step we had taken precipitate. He contrasted it with the long period which elapsed between the beginning of the Greek insurrection and our admission of the belligerent character of Greece.

I said that the population of the Seceding States amounting to many millions made them of greater importance than Greece in the early days of her independence, and the critical position of our commerce made it necessary to take some step; that we could not call the Seceding States rebels, nor take part in the war against them.

Mr. Adams declared he had no wish to see us take part in the war, but he did wish us not to give assistance to the South.

I told him we had no thoughts of doing so; that the sympathies of this country were rather with the North than with the South, but we wished to live on amicable terms with both parties.

I pointed out that the blockade recently instituted, and the designation applied to the privateers of the Southern States as pirates, might give rise to difficulties; that, however, the blockade might no doubt be made effective, considering the small number of harbours on the Southern Coast, even though the extent of 3,000 miles of coast were comprehended in terms of that blockade.

Mr. Adams said it was by no means the intention of the United States to institute a paper blockade, a measure against which they had always protested.

With regard to privateers and piracy, I said that although general principles might be proclaimed, the putting them into execution might be accompanied with that forbearance and humanity which might be expected from a nation so cognizant of international relations and so advanced in civilization as the United States.

I touched upon the high protective Tariff recently enacted, and was assured that it was intended rather for revenue than for protection, and that if it failed in bringing revenue it would not be maintained for the sake of monopoly and restriction.

I told Mr. Adams that I did not wish at present to discuss the causes of the Secession or the present state of the conflict; but I assured him that if recognition should ever be in contemplation, I would send to him and allow a full hearing to his exposition of facts and arguments.

I must not omit to state that Mr. Adams, while complaining strongly of our hasty allowance of belligerent rights to the South, expressed throughout a desire on the part of

the Government of the United States to live on the most friendly terms with Great Britain.
I had no hesitation in giving reciprocal assurances of goodwill.

I am, &c.
(Signed)   J. RUSSELL.

No. 42.

Lord Lyons to Lord J. Russell.—(*Received May* 26.)

My Lord,   *Washington, May* 11, 1861.
I HAVE the honour to inform your Lordship that telegraphic intelligence has reached this place that the Southern Congress has declared war against the United States, and authorized the issue of letters of marque. I have not, however, learned that any letters of marque have yet been actually issued.

I do myself the honour to inclose a copy of a despatch on the subject which I have addressed to Rear-Admiral Sir Alexander Milne.

I have, &c.
(Signed)   LYONS.

Inclosure in No. 42.

Lord Lyons to Rear-Admiral Sir A. Milne.

Sir,   *Washington, May* 10, 1861.
WITH reference to my despatch of the 27th ultimo, I have the honour to inform you that telegraphic intelligence has reached this place that the Congress sitting at Montgomery, in Alabama, has declared war against the United States, and has authorized the *de facto* Executive Government of the so-called Confederate States to issue letters of marque. I have not, however, learned that any letters of marque have as yet been actually issued.

Considerable alarm has, you are aware, been expressed to me by some of Her Majesty's Consuls, as well as by merchants and others, lest these privateers should be in fact little better than pirates, and should not confine their depredations to United States' vessels. You are much better able than I am to judge how far it is desirable to take measures at once to protect British merchant-vessels from danger. I do not think it advisable, during the short interval which will now elapse before instructions may be received from Her Majesty's Government, to interfere with these privateers solely on the ground that their letters of marque will proceed from a Government not recognized by Her Majesty. But I presume that it would be perfectly justifiable to take any measures whatever concerning them which were clearly necessary for the security of British trade. The United States' Government has, as you know, declared its intention to treat them as pirates. Almost all the ships of which that Government can dispose will be sent to the coasts of the Southern States for the purpose of blockading the ports and capturing the privateers.

I have, &c.
(Signed)   LYONS.

No. 43.

Lord Lyons to Lord J. Russell.—(*Received May* 26.)

(Extract.)   *Washington, May* 11, 1861.
WITH reference to my despatch of the 22nd ultimo,* I have the honour to transmit to your Lordship copies of a despatch and its inclosures which I have received from Governor-General Sir Edmund Head, relative to an interview which his Excellency had had with Mr. Ashman, the Agent sent by Mr. Seward to Canada.

Your Lordship is aware that Mr. Seward endeavoured in the first place to conceal

* No. 29.

from me that he had sent an Agent to Canada; and secondly, that he refused to give me any information on the subject, even after Mr. Ashman's mission had become so public as to be mentioned in the newspapers.

Inclosure 1 in No. 43.

Sir E. Head to Lord Lyons.

My Lord, *Quebec, May* 3, 1861.

I HAVE the honour to inclose a copy of a letter addressed by me to Mr. Samuel G. Ward, and a copy of his answer on the subject of Mr. Ashman's visit to this Province.

Mr. Ashman has this day visited me, and, in the presence of M. Cartier and M. Vankoughnet, members of my Councils, he informed me that he was requested by the Secretary of State, Mr. Seward, to visit Canada for the purpose of explaining the true position of the United States in the present crisis of their affairs.

I distinctly informed him that I have no authority to recognize him or any other person as the Agent of the United States' Government, or to communicate with him in that capacity; that all official intercourse between the Government of the United States and that of a British Colony must pass through Her Majesty's accredited Representative at Washington.

Mr. Ashman replied that he was not accredited in any way to this Government, or authorized to make any communications to me, but that it was supposed that good might be done by explaining the true position of affairs, as Agents for the Southern States were said to be buying up arms, &c.

I replied that I had no wish to fetter his intercourse with any one, but that I might have a doubt in my own mind whether it was altogether a regular or usual mode of proceeding on the part of any Government to request a person to visit another country on a mission of this kind. Nothing could be more candid or straightforward than Mr. Ashman was. He said he would talk to no one, and return at once if I desired him to do so. I replied, No, I would make no such request. He could talk to whom he pleased; we had nothing to conceal nor any desire to impede his intercourse with anybody.

I have, &c.
(Signed) EDMUND HEAD.

Inclosure 2 in No. 43.

Sir E. Head to Mr. Ward.

Sir, *Quebec, April* 20, 1861.

YOU have probably seen the statement in the "New York Herald" and other papers, to the effect that Mr. Ashman visits Canada as the Agent of the United States' Government. Certainly the impression exists that he comes with some political object—to feel the way, in short, with reference to the disposition of the people here towards the Northern States.

I am perfectly satisfied of the good faith with which you introduced Mr. Ashman to me in the first instance; whether he has since accepted any other mission than that relating to railways I do not know, but the impression to this effect at Washington and elsewhere will make it very difficult for me to communicate with him in any confidential manner.

I understand that he is expected here shortly, and I shall tell him candidly the awkwardness which has been produced by these reports.

Personally, I shall be very glad to see him.

I am, &c.
(Signed) EDMUND HEAD.

Inclosure 3 in No. 43.

Mr. Ward to Sir E. Head.

My dear Sir, *Boston, May* 1, 1861.

MR. ASHMAN apprizes me that he has accepted a mission to Canada on business of the United States' Government. As his previous visits to Canada were noticed by the public press, and as it was rumoured that they were on Government business, it is proper for me to say to you now, that I have had a very frank conversation to-day with Mr. A. on the subject of his present mission, and he authorizes me to say that his prior visits to Canada had reference solely to the business with which he was entrusted by me, relating to the interests of my friends in Grand Trunk Railway, and had no political object whatever; and further, that the object of his present errand is exclusively to explain to the Canadian Government the true position of the United States' Government in this crisis, as he will state to you in person. This done, he returns directly to the United States, not seeking or intending any communications on political subjects in Canada, other than what will come before you.

I am, &c.
(Signed) SAML. G. WARD.

No. 44.

Lord Lyons to Lord J. Russell.—(*Received May* 26.)

(Extract.) *Washington, May* 12, 1861.

LITTLE apparent change in the state of affairs has taken place during the last week. Actual hostilities have not yet begun. Militiamen from the North continue to arrive at Washington, but none have yet attempted to pass into Virginia, or any other of the Seceded States. There are even some people who still hope that a civil war may be avoided. It would be sad to believe that such hopes are altogether unfounded. They rest, however, entirely on the supposition that the existing excitement in the North will wear itself out; that the North, becoming convinced in time of the fruitlessness of a victory, however complete, will acquiesce in the separation which, for a time at least, appears inevitable, and will let the South depart in peace.

No one, I think, the least acquainted with the South assigns a shorter period than a year to the war, if war there must be. Few consider it probable that in a year's time the North will have made any real progress towards subduing the South by force of arms.

It must be admitted, however, that the prognostications on both sides are merely conjectural. Nothing has yet occurred to test either the determination of the North or the endurance of the South. The extent to which it will be possible to establish a blockade by sea and land, which will really straiten the South for provisions, and the amount of suffering which the South will endure rather than submit, have yet to be proved. The troops who must make the first campaign are on both sides almost exclusively composed of regiments of Militiamen, brought together from places widely separated, having little acquaintance with or confidence in each other; more or less well drilled as single regiments, but totally unused to be manœuvred in large bodies. Horses, mules, and other means of transport, necessary for moving troops in masses, are wanting to both the contending parties. The wealth of the North will give it greater facilities for supplying these deficiencies; but, on the other hand, the Southern soldiers, standing on the defensive, and surrounded by a friendly population, can better dispense with them. The courage of both sides may be taken to be equal. The North has numbers and wealth; but the Southern men are more accustomed to the use of arms, and a campaign will much less disturb their ordinary habits or interfere with the demands of business. The North may, perhaps, be more easily induced to sacrifice their pride, and desist from an attempt to crush a rebellion, than the South be forced into a submission which they believe to be incompatible not only with their freedom and their fortunes, but even with their safety in the midst of their slave population.

The Southern cause has gained this week by the secession of Tennessee and Arkansas. To be definitive, however, the secession of these two States must be confirmed by a direct vote of the people. Kentucky and Missouri have not yet declared themselves. The eastern districts of Virginia, in which there are few or no slaves, show symptoms of dissension from the rest of the State. Maryland is in the hands of the Northern troops. The sanguine friends of peace think they see already some signs of relenting in the North; they trust that if peace can be preserved until Congress meets in the beginning of July, a reaction will have taken place, and arrangements be made for an amicable separation: the effect of seven weeks may certainly be very great. Hitherto, however, it must be confessed that the unanimity of the North appears, on the surface, to be unshaken.

To an Englishman sincerely interested in the welfare of this country the present state of things is peculiarly painful. Abhorrence of slavery; respect for law; more complete community of race and language,—enlist his sympathies on the side of the North. On the other hand, he cannot but reflect that any encouragement to the predominant war feeling in the North cannot but be injurious to both sections of the country. The prosecution of the war can lead only to the exhaustion of the North, by an expenditure of life and money on an enterprise in which success and failure would be alike disastrous. It must tend to the utter devastation of the South.

No. 45.

*Lord J. Russell to the Lords Commissioners of the Admiralty.**

My Lords, *Foreign Office, June* 1, 1861.

HER Majesty's Government are, as you are aware, desirous of observing the strictest neutrality in the contest which appears to be imminent between the United States and the so-styled Confederate States of North America; and with the view more effectually to carry out this principle, they propose to interdict the armed ships and also the privateers of both parties from carrying prizes made by them into the ports, harbours, roadsteads, or waters of the United Kingdom, or of any of Her Majesty's Colonies or Possessions abroad.

I have accordingly to acquaint your Lordship that the Queen has been pleased to direct that orders in conformity with the principles above stated should forthwith be addressed to all proper authorities in the United Kingdom, and to Her Majesty's naval and other authorities in all quarters beyond the United Kingdom, for their guidance in the circumstances.

I am, &c.
(Signed) J. RUSSELL.

No. 46.

Lord J. Russell to Lord Lyons.

My Lord, *Foreign Office, June* 1, 1861.

I TRANSMIT herewith, for your Lordship's information, a copy of a letter which I have addressed, by Her Majesty's commands, to the Admiralty, Colonial, War, and India Offices,† desiring that the necessary instructions may be given for interdicting the armed ships and privateers, both of the United States and of the so-called Confederate States, from carrying prizes made by them into the ports, harbours, roadsteads, or waters of the United Kingdom, or of any of Her Majesty's Colonies or Possessions abroad.

I am, &c.
(Signed) J. RUSSELL.

No. 47.

Lord Lyons to Lord J. Russell.—(Received June 4.)

(Extract.) *Washington, May* 21, 1861.

THE only satisfactory intelligence which I am able to give to your Lordship to-day, is that no serious collision has yet taken place between the Northern and Southern forces. The papers, this morning, state that a battery which the Virginians were throwing up in a position inconvenient to the vessels blockading the James river was fired at two days ago by the blockading squadron; that the works were injured or destroyed, and the working parties driven off. This seems to be the only instance in which an actual attack on the South has yet been made.

The State of Maryland, the town of Baltimore included, is now entirely in the hands of the Northern troops. The ordinary communication by railroad through that State between Washington and the North has been re-established.

---

* Similar letters were addressed to the Colonial, War, and India Offices.
† No. 45.

The State of Kentucky appears disposed to maintain a neutral position in the struggle. The Secession tendencies of Missouri have hitherto been checked by the activity of the military officers of the United States. It is hoped by this Government that it will be able so to employ its troops in these two States as to maintain the appearance of a Union party, and to give to such a party the control of the State Executive officers and Legislature.

I cannot myself perceive any signs that the warlike spirit of the North has begun to flag, nor is any symptom apparent that the South is losing courage. The season, however, during which military operations can be safely undertaken in the Southern climate is rapidly passing away, and it is supposed that no attempt will be made by the Northern troops to penetrate into the South farther than Richmond, in Virginia, if, indeed, they should even try to get so far.

No. 48.

Lord Lyons to Lord J. Russell.—(Received June 4.)

(Extract.) *Washington, May 23, 1861.*

THE news from England and France has provoked a violent explosion of wrath from the Press. Your Lordship's declaration in Parliament that Great Britain regards both parties as invested with belligerent rights has been the especial object of attack. Nevertheless, even the immediate effect of the policy declared by England and France has not been disadvantageous.

Upon receiving the intelligence of your Lordship's declaration in Parliament, Mr. Seward drew up a despatch to Mr. Adams to be communicated to your Lordship in terms still stronger than any he had before used. I fear that the President has consented to its being sent, on condition, however, that it is to be left to Mr. Adams' discretion to communicate it or not, as he may think advisable. If sent, it will probably reach London about the same time with this despatch.

No. 49.

Lord Lyons to Lord J. Russell.—(Received June 4.)

My Lord, *Washington, May 23, 1861.*

IT is, I understand, intended by several influential Members of Congress to endeavour to make the special session of that Body, which is summoned for the 4th of July, as short as possible.

Their idea is, that the two Houses should go at once into secret session, in order to avoid speech-making, and pass as rapidly as possible the Acts necessary for the prosecution of the war. These Acts they consider to be three:—

1st. An Army Bill;
2nd. A Navy Bill;
3rd. A Bill increasing and rendering more easy of application the penalties for treason.

To these, I have heard with great regret, that some men of influence think it desirable that a Bill should be added giving the President the right to declare the ports of the Seceded States to be no longer ports of entry, and to confiscate any vessel which shall attempt to resort to them. The apparent object of this measure is to free the Government from the obligation of observing the rules of international law respecting the blockade, and especially to do away with the necessity of keeping at all times a force on the coast sufficient to render it effective.

I have not hesitated to say plainly to those who have consulted me upon this measure, that I consider that it would have a most unfortunate effect on the relations between the United States and the commercial nations of Europe.

When it has been observed to me that no nation can deny to another the right of declaring which of its own ports shall or shall not be ports of entry, I have answered that this was to place the question of recognizing the Southern Confederacy before the Powers of Europe in the light most unfavourable to the views of the United States. I have stated my opinion that in effect, the proposed plan would be simply a paper blockade in a peculiarly objectionable form; and that under whatever form it was attempted to evade the obligations of the laws of nations, the maritime Powers of Europe would recognize no blockade which was not an effective one, carried on in all respects in conformity with those laws.

I have not had any recent conversation concerning this plan, either with Mr. Seward or ony other member of the Executive Government. When I last spoke to Mr. Seward about it he seemed aware that there were serious objections to it.

It has also been proposed to grant to the President power to collect the Customs duties on board ship. I think this plan also very objectionable; but if the ports are to be closed, whether by blockade or otherwise, it cannot, of course, be put into execution, and I do not clearly understand with what object it is brought forward.

I have, &c.
(Signed) LYONS.

No. 50.

Lord Lyons to Lord J. Russell.—(Received June 4.)

My Lord, *Washington, May 23, 1861.*

NO military operations worth recording have taken place since I had the honour of writing to your Lordship the day before yesterday. The war party in the North are impatient for the commencement of hostilities, and urge that an advance should be made to Richmond, or, at all events, that some part of Virginia should be occupied before the beginning of the unhealthy season. It is believed that General Scott is averse to undertaking any considerable movement until his preparations are more complete; but that, nevertheless, some enterprise may, perhaps, be attempted in order to satisfy the popular cry.

The Southern Congress is reported by telegraph to have adjourned at Montgomery the day before yesterday to meet at Richmond on the 20th July next. This announcement will serve to quicken the desire of the North to occupy that city.

It is stated that the Southern Congress, before its adjournment, passed the new Tariff Bill with some important amendments.

Intelligence has also been received by telegraph that North Carolina has passed an Ordinance of Secession unanimously.

The people of Virginia are to vote to-day on the ratification or rejection of the Ordinance of Secession. There seems little or no doubt that the ratification will be carried by a considerable majority; although the Western Division of the State is expected to vote against it, and even to "secede" itself from the rest of the State rather than be carried out of the Union.

I have, &c.
(Signed) LYONS.

No. 51.

Lord Lyons to Lord J. Russell.—(Received June 10.)

My Lord, *Washington, May 25, 1861.*

I HAVE the honour to transmit to your Lordship a copy of a circular addressed to the Customs officers of the United States on the Northern and North-western waters, directing them to detain, with a view to legal proceedings, all vessels attempting to convey munitions of war, provisions, or other supplies to the Seceded States.

I have likewise the honour to inclose extracts from the Washington newspapers "National Intelligencer" and "National Republican," and from the Baltimore "Sun," from which it would appear that a similar circular has since been issued to all the Customs officers of the United States, and that the Administration has declared a long list of articles to come under the head of contraband of war.

Difficulties have been made here about giving copies of the second circular,* but I have directed Mr. Consul Archibald to endeavour to procure one at New York, and to send it to your Lordship by this mail. To inquiries made at the State Department respecting the "Circular" and the "List of Contraband of War," it has been answered that they do

* Not received.

not concern foreign nations, as foreign vessels are already prohibited by the Navigation Laws from carrying any article whatever from one port of the United States to another port of the same States.

I have, &c.
(Signed) LYONS.

Inclosure 1 in No. 51.

Circular addressed to Collectors, Surveyors, and other Officers of the Customs on the Northern and North-Western Waters of the United States.

Treasury Department, May 2, 1861.

ON the 19th day of April, 1861, the President of the United States, by Proclamation, declared the ports of South Carolina, Georgia, Florida, Alabama, Louisiana, Mississippi, and Texas, under blockade; and on the 27th of the same month, by another Proclamation, declared the ports of Virginia and North Carolina also under blockade, since which Proclamation this Department has received reliable information that attempts are frequently made to furnish arms and munitions of war, provisions, and other supplies, to persons and parties in those States in open insurrection against the constitutional authorities of the Union.

It becomes my duty, therefore, to instruct you to cause a careful examination to be made of the manifests of all steam or other vessels departing from your port with cargoes whose ultimate destination you have satisfactory reason to believe is for any port or place under the control of such insurrectionary parties, and to compare the same with the cargo on board; and if any such manifests be found to embrace any articles of the description before mentioned, or any such articles be found to constitute part of the cargo, you will take all necessary and proper means to prevent the departure of the vessel, and to detain the same in your custody until all such articles shall be removed therefrom, and for further proceedings according to law.

You will also make a careful examination of all flat-boats and water-craft without manifests, and of railroad cars and other vehicles arriving at or leaving your port laden with merchandize, the ultimate destination of which you have good reason to believe is for any port or place under insurrectionary control; and if arms, munitions of war, provisions, or other supplies are found, having such destination, you will seize and detain the same to await the proper legal proceedings for confiscation or forfeiture.

In carrying out these instructions you will bear in mind that all persons or parties in armed insurrection against the Union, however such persons or parties may be organized or named, are engaged in levying war against the United States; and that all persons furnishing to such insurgents arms, munitions of war, provisions, or other supplies, are giving them aid and comfort, and so guilty of treason within the terms of the second section of Article III of the Constitution; and you will, therefore, use your utmost vigilance, and endeavour to prevent the prohibited shipments, and to detect and bring to punishment all who are in any way concerned in furnishing to such insurgents any of the articles above described.

You will, however, on the other hand, be careful not to interrupt vexatiously, or beyond necessity, by unwarranted or protracted detentions and examinations, the regular and lawful commerce of your port. You will report forthwith whether any, and if any, what, additional measures may be necessary, in your judgment, to carry into full effect the foregoing resolutions, and you will report to this Department from time to time your action under these instructions.

I am, &c.
(Signed) S. P. CHASE, Secretary to the Treasury.

Inclosure 2 in No. 51.

Newspaper Extracts.

From the " National Intelligencer."

THE Secretary of the Treasury has just issued a circular to all Collectors, Surveyors, and other officers of Customs, precisely similar to that recently addressed to those on the Northern and North-western waters, in relation to commerce with the insurrectionary States, and with the following addition:—

"Among the prohibited supplies are included coals, telegraphic instruments, wire, porous cups, platina, sulphuric acid, zinc, and all other telegraphic material."

From the "National Republican."

The following articles have been officially declared as coming under the head of "contraband of war" by the Administration:—

"Gold and silver coin; cheques or bills of exchange for money; articles of food; clothing and materials for the manufacture of clothing; rifle, pistol, musket, and cannon balls, and shells; gunpowder, and all materials used in its manufacture; ammunition and munitions and implements of war of every description; books of military education; saddles, harness, and trappings for flying artillery, field and staff officers, and cavalry troops; horses; gun-carriages; timber for ship-building; all kinds of naval stores; engines, boilers, and machinery for boats, locomotive engines and cars for railroads; and goods and commodities which might be useful to the enemy in war."

From the "Baltimore Sun."

The Secretary of the Treasury has specially explained what is meant by the words "other supplies" in the enumeration of articles contraband of war, contained in his circular dated May 2nd, addressed to Collectors and other officers of Customs. They mean :—Mercury in all its compounds, chlorate of potash, muriatic acid, chloride of potash, nitrate of soda, chloride of potassium, potash and pearlash, bagging, rope, and nitric acid (the last named could be used for the manufacture of gun-cotton).

No. 52.

Lord J. Russell to Lord Lyons.

(Extract.) *Foreign Office, June* 21, 1861.

I HAVE to state to your Lordship that I have every reason to be satisfied with the language and conduct of Mr. Adams since he has arrived in this country.

The only complaint which he has urged here is, that the Queen's Proclamation announcing her neutrality was hasty and premature.

I said, in the first place, that our position was of necessity one of neutrality; that we could not take part either for the North against the South, or for the South against the North.

To this he willingly assented, and said that the United States expected no assistance from us to enable their Government to finish the war.

I rejoined that if such was the case, as I supposed, it would not have been right either towards our Admirals and Naval Commanders, nor towards our merchants and mercantile marine, to leave them without positive and public orders: that the exercise of belligerent rights of search and capture by a band of adventurers clustered in some small island in the Greek Archipelago or in the Atlantic would subject them to the penalties of piracy: but we could not treat 5,000,000 of men who had declared their independence like a band of marauders or filibusters. If we had done so, we should have done more than the United States themselves. Their troops had taken prisoners many of the adherents of the Confederacy, but I could not perceive from the newspapers that in any case they had brought these prisoners to trial for high treason, or shot them as rebels. Had we hung the captain of an armed vessel of the Southern Confederacy as a pirate we should have done that which a sense of humanity had prohibited on the part of the Government itself whose authority was set at defiance. We surely could not be expected to go beyond the United States' Government themselves in measures of severity.

I had quoted in the House of Commons the case of the Turks and Greeks in order to avail myself of the sound maxim of policy enunciated by Mr. Canning, that the question of belligerent rights is one, not of principle, but of fact; that the size and strength of the party contending against a Government, and not the goodness of their cause, entitle them to the character and treatment of belligerents.

I added that the case quoted by me had been objected to, as if I had compared the United States to Turkey, and the Southern Confederacy to Greeks.

As well might it be said, if any one were to cite the case of Mr. Wilkes in an argument on general warrants, that the case was not applicable because the character of Mr. Wilkes was not entitled to our sympathy or respect.

Mr. Adams maintained that, practically, the so-called Confederate States had no ships of war at sea, and therefore the Royal Proclamation was unnecessary.

The United States' Minister at Paris has made propositions to the Imperial Government founded on the answer of Mr. Marcy to the request formerly made to him to adopt, on the part of his Government, the Declaration of Paris.

The Government of the Emperor entirely concur with Her Majesty's Government in the opinion that these propositions ought to be rejected.*

When I asked Mr. Adams whether he had similar propositions to make to Her Majesty's Government, he informed me that he had no instructions to do so.

No. 53.

Lord Lyons to Lord J. Russell.—(Received June 25.)

My Lord,   *Washington, June 8,* 1861.

WITH reference to my despatch of the 31st ultimo, I have the honour to inclose a copy, cut from a newspaper, of the Act of the Southern Congress prohibiting the export of cotton except through the seaports of the Confederate States.

I have, &c.
(Signed)   LYONS.

Inclosure in No. 53.

Extract from the "Baltimore Sun" of June 5, 1861.

THE "Mobile Register" publishes the Act passed by the Confederate Congress, on the 21st of May, prohibiting the exportation of cotton except through Southern seaports. It reads as follows:—

"Section 1. The Congress of the Confederate States of America do enact that, from and after the 1st day of June next, and during the existence of the blockade of any of the ports of the Confederate States of America by the Government of the United States, it shall not be lawful for any person to export any raw cotton or cotton yarn from the Confederate States of America, except through the seaports of the said Confederate States; and it shall be the duty of all the Marshals and Revenue Officers of the said Confederate States to prevent all violations of this Act.

"Sec. 2. If any person shall violate, or attempt to violate, the provisions of the foregoing section, he shall forfeit all the cotton or cotton yarn thus attempted to be illegally exported, for the use of the Confederate States; and in addition thereto, he shall be guilty of a misdemeanour, and on conviction thereof shall be fined in a sum not exceeding 5,000 dollars, or else imprisoned in some public jail or penitentiary for a period not exceeding six months, at the discretion of the Court, after a conviction upon trial by a Court of competent jurisdiction.

"Sec. 3. Any person informing as to a violation or attempt to violate the provisions of this Act shall be entitled to one-half the proceeds of the article forfeited by reason of his information.

"Sec. 4. Any Justice of the Peace, on information under oath from any person of a violation or attempt to violate this Act, may issue his warrant, and cause the cotton or cotton yarn specified in the affidavit to be seized and retained until an investigation can be had before the Court of the Confederate States.

"Sec. 5. Every steamboat or railroad-car which shall be used, with the consent of the owner or person having the same in charge, for the purpose of violating this Act, shall be forfeited in like manner to the use of the Confederate States. But nothing in this Act shall be so construed as to prohibit the exportation to Mexico, through its coterminous frontier."

---

* See Papers relating to North America, No. 3 ("Correspondence respecting International Maritime Law"), p. 8.

No. 54.

Lord Lyons to Lord J. Russell.—(Received June 25.)

My Lord, Washington, June 8, 1861.

I HAVE the honour to inclose an extract from a despatch from Her Majesty's Consul at New York to me, and copies of a note from me to Mr. Seward, and of Mr. Seward's answer.

These papers relate to a cargo, in part the property of British subjects, which was captured on board the Virginia vessel "Winifred" a short time ago.

The case is not in itself of much importance, and the answer, although unfavourable, does not seem to me to be open to objection. My principal object in sending the papers to your Lordship is to direct attention to the close of Mr. Seward's note, which seems to show that the doctrine of the 3rd Article of the Declaration of Paris is held to be applicable to the existing hostilities between the United States and the South.

I have, &c.
(Signed) LYONS.

Inclosure 1 in No. 54.

Consul Archibald to Lord Lyons.

(Extract.) New York, June 3, 1861.

WILLIAM T. HOLWORTHY, Esq., of the firm of J. L. Phipps and Co., has applied to me for assistance in procuring the release of the cargo of the barque "Winifred," of part of which the said firm are owners, and in the whole of which they are interested.

Mr. Holworthy and the other members of his firm are British subjects. The "Winifred" was bound from Rio Janeiro to Hampton Roads, and the first intimation of a blockade was the vessel's being hailed by the Commander of the United States' vessel "Quaker City," who then took the "Winifred" in charge, and caused her to be sent to this port.

I have the honour to request your Lordship will be pleased to take such steps as you may think necessary for procuring the delivery to Messrs. Phipps and Co. of the cargo of the "Winifred."

Inclosure 2 in No. 54.

Lord Lyons to Mr. Seward.

Sir, Washington, June 5, 1861.

I HAVE the honour to transmit to you herewith a copy of a despatch which I have received to-day from Her Majesty's Consul at New York, and by which I am requested to apply to the Government of the United States for the release of the cargo of the "Winifred," a barque now held as a prize at New York.

The brig is stated to belong to Richmond, in Virginia, to have arrived off Cape Henry from Rio, on the 25th ultimo, in ignorance of the blockade, and to have been captured by the United States' squadron, in consequence of being a Southern vessel.

It appears that the British firm of J. L. Phipps and Co. are owners of part of the cargo and have an interest in the whole of it.

I have the honour to inclose in original affidavits made by the master of the "Winifred," and by Mr. Holworthy, one of the partners of the firm of Phipps and Co., and I beg leave to express my hope that the fact stated may induce the Government of the United States to order the release of the cargo.

I shall be much obliged if you will be so good as to return the original affidavits to me.

I have, &c.
(Signed) LYONS.

Inclosure 3 in No. 54.

Mr. Seward to Lord Lyons.

My Lord,   *Washington, June* 8, 1861.

I HAVE the honour to acknowledge the receipt of your note of the 5th instant, with the accompanying papers, relative to a claim in the case of the cargo of the barque "Winifred," a part of which is represented to belong to British subjects.

In reply, I regret that at this juncture I do not feel at liberty to interfere in the case, as it is understood that the usual proceedings in the Prize Court at New York have been set on foot against the vessel.

If, however, that Court shall be satisfied of the ownership by British subjects of the part of the cargo claimed, it cannot be doubted that restitution will be decreed, as this Government recognizes the right of the property of a friendly nation in the vessels of an insurgent to be exempt from condemnation.

The papers which accompanied your note are herewith returned.

I have, &c.
(Signed)   WILLIAM H. SEWARD.

No. 55.

Lord J. Russell to Lord Lyons.

(Extract.)   *Foreign Office, June* 29, 1861.

MR. ADAMS called upon me yesterday by appointment; the immediate purport of his visit was to inquire what course the Government would pursue in respect to a merchant-vessel called the "Peter Marcy," which had arrived here carrying the flag of the so-called Confederate States, and was now lying in the Victoria Dock in the port of London.

He wished to inquire especially with regard to the clearance outwards of this vessel, as that clearance, if made to a vessel belonging to those whom his Government and he regarded as rebels, might be looked upon as a sort of recognition.

I replied that I knew nothing of this particular case; that however, in contemplation of such a case, we had some time ago called upon the Law Officers of the Crown for an opinion; that they had said that, in point of law, the flag a vessel might bear was immaterial; that in the present case, and in all others, Her Majesty's Government would adhere strictly to the law, and I conceived that course was the one most likely to afford a solution of the difficult questions which might from time to time arise, and perhaps threaten to disturb the friendly relations of the two countries.

In the course of the morning I made the inquiries I had promised, and the result was the letters of which I inclose copies. You will see that our law takes no notice of the authorities ruling, whether *de jure* or *de facto*, in the country from which the vessel proceeds, or to which it may be bound in its outward voyage.

On my side I spoke to Mr. Adams of the Republic of New Granada, which had by Decree closed certain ports, and I said that the legal advice we had received was to the effect that any capture on the high seas made on the ground that certain ports were in the hands of insurgents would be contrary to the law of nations.

That I did not suppose the enactment of a law closing the Southern ports would be proposed by the Government of the United States, but it was possible that in the prevailing heats and animosities such a law might be proposed by some private member of Congress.

Mr. Adams seemed to think that the enactment of such a law would be resisted as contrary to the Constitution of the United States.

I contented myself with repeating that a strict adherence to the law, whether the law of nations or the municipal law, would be the best method of preserving friendly relations.

I was afterwards informed by the New Granadian Minister that no intention was entertained of applying the Decree to which I have here referred, to vessels found on the high seas; it was, he stated, solely applicable to duties of Customs payable in the interior.

Inclosure 1 in No. 55.

Mr. Murray to the Secretary to the Treasury.

(Extract.) *Foreign Office, June* 28, 1861.

I AM directed by Lord John Russell to state to you that his Lordship has been informed by Mr. Adams, the United States' Minister at this Court, that a vessel called the "Peter Marcy" is now lying in the Victoria Docks, and is provided with a register from the so-styled Confederate States; and I am directed by his Lordship to request that you will move the Lords of Her Majesty's Treasury to cause immediate inquiry to be made at the Custom-house respecting this vessel and her papers, and in what manner it is proposed by the Customs to treat her in regard to clearance.

Inclosure 2 in No. 55.

The Commissioners of Customs to the Lords Commissioners of the Treasury.

My Lords, *Custom-House, June* 28, 1861.

YOUR Lordships having referred to us the annexed letter from Mr. Murray, stating that Lord John Russell has been informed by the United States' Minister at this Court that a vessel called the "Peter Marcy" is now lying in the Victoria Docks, and is provided with a register from the so-styled Confederate States, and signifying the request of his Lordship that inquiry may be made at the Custom-house respecting this vessel and her papers, and in what manner it is proposed by the Customs to treat her in regard to clearance, we report—

That by the Customs Consolidation Act, 1853, the masters of vessels are required (Section 50), upon reporting inwards, to state whether the vessel is "British or foreign," if British, "the port of registry, if foreign, the country to which she belongs;" and upon clearing outwards (Section 141), in like manner to state "if British, the port of registry, if foreign, the country:" but neither upon the arrival of a vessel, nor upon her departure, are her papers required to be produced to the officers of Customs.

The entry of a ship, as of America, is quite sufficient to meet the Customs laws; if, however, the master merely stated the town or portion of the country to which she belonged, the Revenue Officers would receive the Report, and enter in the records the name of the State in which the town or district was situated.

We have further to state that the vessel "Peter Marcy" was reported inwards on the 24th instant, as of New Orleans in America, and a similar description would be accepted by our officers on her clearance, and the production of her register would not be required.

We have, &c.
(Signed)   THOS. F. FREMANTLE.
J. GOULBURN.

No. 56.

Lord Lyons to Lord J. Russell.—(Received June 30.)

My Lord, *Washington, June* 17, 1861.

AT the interview which the French Minister and I had the day before yesterday with the Secretary of State of the United States, I announced to the Secretary of State that Her Majesty's Government, with a view to carrying out effectually the principle of neutrality, had interdicted the armed ships, and also the privateers, of both parties in the struggle going on in this country, from carrying prizes made by them into British waters.

Mr. Seward observed that this measure, and that of the same character which had been adopted by France, would probably prove to be a death-blow to Southern privateering.

The newspapers announce that a privateer, the "Savannah," has been captured by the United States' brig "Perry," and sent into New York, the crew being placed in irons on board the "Perry." The question will, therefore, immediately arise whether these prisoners are to be subjected to the penalties of piracy, according to the terms of President Lincoln's Proclamation of the 19th of April. The Southern Government is not without prisoners upon whom to retaliate, should the penalties be enforced.

I have, &c.
(Signed)   LYONS.

No. 57.

Lord Lyons to Lord J. Russell.—(Received June 30.)

My Lord,　　　　　　　　　　　　　　　　　　　*Washington, June* 17, 1861.

IN the course of a conversation which I had with Mr. Seward this morning, he himself introduced the subject of the secret agent whom he sent to Canada in April last. He said that Mr. Ashman, the person sent, was a most respectable man, and that the object of his mission was to ascertain the feeling in Canada with regard to fitting out privateers on the St. Lawrence. Mr. Seward added that as soon as I had spoken to him on the subject, he had recalled Mr. Ashman.

I did not enter into any discussion with Mr. Seward, but, in obedience to the instruction contained in your Lordship's despatch of the 16th ultimo, I said that Her Majesty's Government considered that they had reason to complain that no previous notice had been given to me of the intention to dispatch Mr. Ashman; and that no frank explanation had been given in reply to the inquiry which I had made. I added that I was directed not to conceal from Mr. Seward the unfavourable impression which the transaction had made on Her Majesty's Government.

I have, &c.
(Signed)　　　LYONS.

No. 58.

Earl Cowley to Lord J. Russell.—(Received July 5.)

My Lord,　　　　　　　　　　　　　　　　　　　　*Paris, July* 4, 1861.

M. THOUVENEL has received despatches from Washington, in which M. Mercier alludes to the possibility—he contests the probability—of Congress being called upon to decree the closing of the Southern ports.

M. Thouvenel will write to M. Mercier by the next mail to say that the French Government could not admit the legality of such a Decree, and that they are convinced it will not be proposed to Congress; but in the event of the step being really contemplated, M. Mercier will be instructed to consult with Lord Lyons as to the propriety of drawing the attention of the Northern Government, in a friendly spirit, to the consequences which it may entail.

I have, &c.
(Signed)　　　COWLEY.

No. 59.

Lord J. Russell to Lord Lyons.

(Extract.)　　　　　　　　　　　　　　　　　　*Foreign Office, July* 6, 1861.

HER Majesty's Government entirely concur with the French Government, in the opinion that a Decree closing the Southern ports would be entirely illegal, and would be an evasion of that recognized maxim of the law of nations that the ports of a belligerent can only be closed by an effective blockade.

The Southern ports of the United States are in the hands of persons enemies of the President and Congress of the United States, and whether those enemies be called insurgents, as in one of the letters of Mr. Seward, or the so-styled Confederate States, as they are termed in the Queen's Proclamation, is not material to the question.

But you will not raise the question at all with Mr. Seward, unless, in consultation with M. Mercier, you shall deem it expedient to do so. Her Majesty's Government wish to act in complete accordance with the Government of France.

No. 60.

Lord Lyons to Lord J. Russell.—(Received July 15.)

My Lord,   Washington, July 1, 1861.

IN my despatch of the 25th May last, I had the honour to transmit to your Lordship a copy of a circular addressed by the Secretary of the Treasury to the Collectors of Customs, directing them to take measures to prevent the conveyance of contraband of war to the Seceded States.

I have now the honour to inclose a copy of a circular by which the Secretary of the Treasury instructs Collectors of Customs if they "are satisfied that any merchandise, wherever destined in name, is, in fact, destined for persons or combinations in actual insurrection against the United States, to cause the same to be seized and proceeded against for forfeiture."

By a despatch from Mr. Consul Archibald, I learn that, under this circular, a clearance for Matamoros, a port in Mexico, has been refused to a British vessel at New York. I am also informed that it is intended to introduce a Bill into Congress requiring bonds to be given on the shipment of cargoes in Northern ports, to guard against the transport of merchandise to the Seceded States.

It seems to me to be at the present moment very unadvisable for me to raise any question with the United States' Government which can be avoided. I shall, therefore, if possible, refrain for the present from making any official remonstrance on the subject of these restrictions on commerce, and shall await instructions from your Lordship concerning them.

I have, &c.
(Signed)   LYONS.

Inclosure in No. 60.

Circular addressed to the Collectors of Customs in the United States' Ports.

Sir,   Treasury Department, June 12, 1861.

REFERRING to the circular instructions of the 2nd ultimo, prohibiting the transmission of munitions of war, provisions, or other supplies, to parties in insurrection against the United States, you are now further instructed to exercise the utmost vigilance in arresting and detaining all merchandise, of whatever character, the ultimate destination of which you have satisfactory reason to believe is for insurgents against the United States, or for places under their control.

If you are satisfied, either from the nature of the articles or otherwise, that any merchandise, wherever destined in name, is in fact destined for persons or combinations in actual insurrection against the Government of the United States, you will cause the same to be seized and proceeded against for forfeiture.

If, however, you are satisfied that any merchandise transmitted for States or places under insurrectionary control is not intended for actual insurgents, and has been shipped or forwarded without intent to afford aid and comfort to such insurgents, or otherwise to violate the law, you will simply detain such merchandise, and notify the shippers or forwarders, or their agents, of such detention, and state the cause thereof. If such shipper or forwarder, personally, or by agent, shall satisfy you that the merchandise so arrested will not be sent to any place under insurrectionary control, but will be either returned whence it came, or be disposed of in good faith for consumption within loyal States, you will restore possession of the same, and allow such disposition thereof to be made as the parties in interest may desire.

You will regard all States in which the authority of the United States is temporarily subverted as under insurrectionary control; but any portions of such States in which the laws of the Union and the authority of the Federal Government are acknowledged and respected will be considered as exempt from any interruption of commerce or intercourse, beyond such as may be necessary in order to prevent supplies going to insurgents or to places under their control.

It is the intention of the Department to leave the owners of all property perfectly free to control it in such manner as they see fit, without interference or detention by officers of the Federal Government, except for the purpose of preventing any use or disposal of such property for the aid and comfort of insurgents, or in commerce with States or places controlled by insurgents.

(Signed)   S. P. CHASE, *Secretary of the Treasury.*

No. 61.

Lord J. Russell to Lord Lyons.

My Lord,　　　　　　　　　　　　　　　　　　*Foreign Office, July* 19, 1861.

I HAVE read with great interest the decision of Judge Dunlop pronounced in the District Court of Columbia on the 19th of June, in the case of the "Tropic Wind" schooner.

The general principles laid down in this case are well deserving of attention. The Judge quotes several cases decided in the American Courts, with a view to justify the conclusions at which he ultimately arrives.

In the first place, he cites the case of the "Santissima Trinidad," in the war between Spain and one of her American Provinces. The Court, while refusing to pronounce upon the right of sovereignty in the insurgent Province, observes that the Court, following the Executive Department, have merely declared the notorious fact "that civil war exists between Spain and her American Provinces." The Court adds, " It would be a public and not a civil war if they were Sovereign States. The very object of the contest is to decide whether they shall be sovereign and independent or not. All that the Court has affirmed is, that the existence of this civil war gave to both parties all the rights of war against each other."

The Judge then affirms that the question whether insurrection has culminated in civil war belongs to the political branch of the Government to determine.

Judge Dunlop proceeds to argue that the Proclamation of President Lincoln, declaring that " nine States have resisted," that orders have been given to issue letters of marque in the South; that the President on his side has called out 75,000 men,—show a state of civil war.

" These facts so set forth by the President, with the assertion of the right of blockade, amount to a declaration that civil war exists."

Proceeding in his argument, the Judge says, "I do not find, on examination of the writers on public law, any difference as to belligerent rights in civil or foreign war; and Judge Storey, in 7th Wheaton, as heretofore cited by me, says they are the same. Blockade being one of the rights incident to a state of war, and the President having, in substance, asserted civil war to exist, I am of opinion that the blockade was lawfully proclaimed by the Executive."

It is a question for American Courts to decide whether this power lawfully belongs to the President. But Her Majesty's Government cannot fail to remark the general principles laid down by an American Judge and founded on American authorities bearing on the present state of affairs.

Her Majesty's Government admit that a civil war exists; they admit that whether the Confederate States of the South be sovereign and independent States or not, is the very point to be decided: but Her Majesty's Government affirm, as the United States affirmed in the case of the South American Provinces, that "the existence of this civil war gives to both parties the rights of war against each other."

Arguing from these premises, it is impossible for Her Majesty's Government to admit that the President or Congress of the United States can at one and the same time exercise the belligerent rights of blockade, and the municipal right of closing the ports of the South.

In the present case, Her Majesty's Government do not intend to dispute the right of blockade on the part of the United States with regard to ports in the possession of the Confederate States; but an assumed right to close any ports in the hands of insurgents would imply a right to stop vessels on the high seas without instituting an effective blockade.

This would be a manifest evasion of the necessity of blockade in order to close an enemy's port. Neutral vessels would be excluded when no force exists in the neighbourhood of the port sufficient to carry that exclusion into effect.

Maritime nations would not submit to this excess under pretence of the rights of sovereignty.

Whether, indeed, the United States treat the Southern prisoners in their hands as rebels or as prisoners of war is not a matter in which foreign countries can properly interfere. But Her Majesty's Government cannot allow the Queen's subjects to be deprived of any of the rights of neutrals. They would consider a Decree closing the ports of the South actually in the possession of the insurgent or Confederate States as null and void, and they would not submit to measures taken on the high seas in pursuance of such Decree.

You will concert with M. Mercier as to the best mode of communicating this decision

H

to the President and to the Secretary of State of the United States. You will express strongly to Mr. Seward the wish of Her Majesty's Government to maintain the relations of amity with the United States. But at all events you will take care not to leave him in ignorance of the decision of Her Majesty's Government.

I am, &c.
(Signed) J. RUSSELL.

Judicial Decision on the Blockade of United States' Ports, by Judge Dunlop.

District Court of the United States for the District of Columbia.

Before DUNLOP, J.

United States *et al. v.* Schooner "Tropic Wind" and cargo. June Term, 1861.
In Admiralty.

IN this case, on the 17th instant, Judge Dunlop delivered the following decision:—

A libel has been filed by the United States and the captors in this Court, sitting in Admiralty to condemn as prize the English schooner " Tropic Wind " and cargo, valued at 22,000 dollars, for violating a blockade of the ports of Virginia, proclaimed by the President of the United States on the 27th of April, 1861.

The capture was made in or near the mouth of James river, by the United States' ship "Monticello," Captain ———, on the 21st May, 1861. The blockade of the port of Richmond, Virginia, into which port the "Tropic Wind" had entered before the Proclamation, is alleged to have been made effective on the 30th April, and notice of it brought home to the Captain of the "Tropic Wind," and the British Consul at Richmond, at least as early as the 2nd of May. Fifteen days were allowed by the United States to neutral vessels to leave the blockaded ports of Richmond from the 30th April, the day of the effective blockade.

It appears that the "Tropic Wind" commenced to load her cargo at Richmond, Virginia, on the 13th of May, completed her lading on the 14th May, and sailed from Richmond the same day bound for Halifax, Nova Scotia.

Mr. Carlisle appeared for the vessel and cargo, filed the answer of Captain Layton, and the case has been argued and submitted to me on the libel, answer, evidence taken *in preparatoria*, and official documents.

The authority of the President to institute the blockade is denied by the Respondents, who insist that this power, under the Constitution of the United States, can only be exercised by the National Legislature. And this is the first question to be considered.

It is true no Department of the Federal Government can exercise any power not expressly conferred on it by the Constitution of the United States, or necessary to give effect to granted powers; all others are reserved to the States respectively, or to the people. In Article II, section 2, of the Constitution of the United States, is this provision: " The President shall be Commander-in-chief of the Army and Navy of the United States, and of the Militia of the several States when called into the actual service of the United States."

In the war with Mexico, declared by Congress to exist by the Act of Mexico (see 9th Statute at Large, page 9), the Supreme Court have maintained, in two cases, that the President, without any act of Congress, as Commander-in-chief of the Army and Navy, could exert the belligerent right of levying contributions on the enemy to annoy and weaken him. In the case of Fleming *et al. v.* Page (9th Howard, 615), the present Chief Justice says: " As Commander-in-chief he is authorized to direct the movements of the naval and military forces placed by law at his command, and to employ them in the manner he may deem most effectual to harass and conquer and subdue the enemy." Again, at page 616: " The person who acted in the character of Collector in this instance acted as such under the authority of the Military Commander and in obedience to his orders, and the duties he exacted, and the regulations he adopted, were not those prescribed by law, but by the President in his character of Commander-in-chief. The Custom-house was established in an enemy's country as one of the weapons of war. It was established not for the purpose of giving the people of Tamaulipas the benefit of commerce with the United States or with other countries, but as a measure of hostility and as a part of the military operations in Mexico; it was a mode of exacting contributions from the enemy to support our army, and intended also to cripple the resources of Mexico and make it feel the evils and the burdens of the war. The duties required to be paid were regulated with this view, and were nothing more than contributions levied upon the enemy, which the usages of war justify when an army is operating in the enemy's country."

The other case to which I allude is Cross *et al. v.* Harrison (16th Howard, 189, 190). Judge Wayne, in delivering the opinion of the Supreme Court, says: "Indeed, from the letter of the Secretary of State and from that of the Secretary of the Treasury, we cannot doubt that the action of the Military Governor of California was recognized as allowable and lawful by Mr. Polk and his Cabinet. We think it was a rightful and correct recognition, under all the circumstances; and when we say rightful we mean that it was Constitutional, although Congress had not passed an Act to extend the collection of tonnage and import duties to the ports of California. California, or the port of San Francisco, had been conquered by the arms of the United States as early as 1846. Shortly afterwards, the United States had military possession of all the Upper California. Early in 1847 the President, as Constitutional Commander-in-chief of the Army and Navy, authorized the Military and Naval Commanders of our forces in California to exercise the belligerent rights of a conqueror, and to form a Civil Government for the conquered country, and to impose duties on imports and tonnage as military contributions for the support of the Government and of the army which had the conquest in possession, &c. No one can doubt that these orders of the President, and the action of our Army and Navy Commanders in California in conformity with them, was according to the law of arms," &c. (See also pages 191, 193, 195, 196, 201.)

Blockade is a belligerent right under the law of nations where war exists, and is as clearly defined as the belligerent right to levy contributions in the enemy's country. As the Supreme Court hold the latter power to be constitutionally in the President, without an Act of Congress, as Commander-in-chief of the Army and Navy, it follows necessarily that the power of blockade also resides with him; indeed, it would seem a clearer right, if possible, because, as Chief of the Navy, nobody can doubt the right of its Commander to order a fleet or a ship to capture an enemy's vessel at sea, or to bombard a fortress on shore, and it is only another mode of assault and injury to the same enemy to shut up his harbours and close his trade by the same ship or fleet. The same weapons are used. The Commander only varies the mode of attack.

In Article 1, section 8, clause 11 of the Constitution, under the legislative head, power is granted to Congress "to declare war, grant letters of marque and reprisal, and make rules concerning captures on land and water." These powers are therefore solely confided to and within the control of the Legislature, and cannot be exercised by the President. The President cannot declare war, grant letters of marque, &c., though all other belligerent rights, arising out of a state of war, are vested in him as Commander-in-chief of the Army and Navy. But war declared by Congress is not the only war within the contemplation of the Constitution. In clause 15, Article I, section 8, among the legislative powers is this, "to provide for calling forth the Militia to execute the laws of the Union, suppress insurrections, and repel invasions;" and the Legislature, in execution of this power, passed the Act of 1795 (1st Statutes at Large, 424), vesting in the President, under the terms set forth in the Statute, discretionary power over the Militia in the cases enumerated in this 15th clause of section 8, Article I. The status of foreign nations whose provinces or dependencies are in revolution, foreign invasion of our country, and insurrection at home, are political questions, determinable by the Executive branch of our Government. I refer on this subject to the following cases in the Supreme Court of the United States. The "Santissima Trinidad" (7th Wheaton, 305):—

"This Court has repeatedly decided that it will not undertake to determine who are Sovereign States, but will leave that question to be settled by the other Departments who are charged with the external affairs of the country, and the relations of peace and war. It may, however, be said that both the Judiciary and the Executive have concurred in affirming the sovereignty of the Spanish Colonies now in revolt against the mother-country. But the obvious answer to this objection is, that the Court, following the Executive Department, have merely declared the notorious fact that a civil war exists between Spain and her American provinces; and this, so far from affirming, is a denial of the sovereignty of the latter. It would be a public, and not a civil, war if they were Sovereign States. The very object of the contest is to decide whether they shall be sovereign and independent or not; all that the Court has affirmed is, that the existence of this civil war gave to both parties all the rights of war against each other."

In cases of invasion by a foreign Power, or insurrection at home, in which cases, under the Act of 1795, the President may call out the Militia, the Supreme Court, in 12¼ Wheaton (case of Martin *v.* Mott), pages 29, 30, says it is exclusively with the President to decide whether the exigencies provided for have arisen. These also are political questions, determinable by the Executive alone, and the Courts follow that branch of the Government. In this case, at page 82, the Supreme Court say: "It is no answer that such a power may be abused, for there is no power which is not susceptible of abuse. The remedy for this, as well as for all other official misconduct, if it should occur, is to be found in the Constitution itself."

Whether insurrection has grown to such a head, has become so formidable in power as to have culminated in civil war, it seems to me, must also belong, as to its decision, to to the same political branch of the Government. The President, in his Proclamation relating to the blockade of the ports of the Confederate States, calling out 75,000 Militia to suppress insurrection and the resistance to the Federal laws, alleges, "that nine States have so resisted," and have "threatened to issue letters of marque, to authorize the bearers thereof to commit assaults against the vessels, property, and lives of citizens engaged in commerce on the high seas and in the waters of the United States; that public property of the United States has been seized, the collection of the revenue obstructed, and duly commissioned officers of the United States, while engaged in executing the orders of their superiors, have been arrested and held in custody as prisoners, or have been impeded in the discharge of their official duties, without due legal process, by persons claiming to act under authorities of the States of Virginia and North Carolina, an efficient blockade of the ports of those States will also be established."

These facts, so set forth by the President, with the assertion of the right of blockade, amount to a declaration that civil war exists.

Blockade itself is a belligerent right, and can only legally have place in a state of war; and the notorious fact that immense armies in our immediate view are in hostile array against each other in the Federal and Confederate States, the latter having organized a Government, and elected officers to administer it, attest the executive declaration that civil war exists; a sad war, which, if it must go on, can only be governed by the laws of war, and its evils mitigated by the principles of clemency engrafted upon the war code by the civilization of modern times.

Nor does the assertion of the right in the Proclamation of the 19th April, 1861, to proceed against privateersmen, under the laws of the United States, as pirates, militate against the construction I have above given of the two Proclamations as averring the existence of civil war.

In the case of Rose v. Himely (4th Branch, 272-3), Chief Justice Marshall, in delivering the opinion of the Court says: "It is not intended to say that belligerent rights may not be superadded to those of sovereignty. But admitting a sovereign who is endeavouring to reduce his revolted subjects to obedience, to possess both sovereign and belligerent rights, and to be capable of acting in either character, the manner in which he acts must determine the character of the act. If as a legislator he publishes a law ordaining punishments for certain offences, which law is to be applied by Courts, the nature of the law and the proceedings under it will decide whether it is an exercise of belligerent rights, or exclusively of his sovereign power; and whether the Court, in applying this law to particular cases, acts as a Prize Court, or as a Court enforcing municipal regulations."

In this case I am sitting in Admiralty adjudging a question of prize, under a capture for alleged violation of blockade.

I do not find, on examination of the writers on public law, any difference as to belligerent rights in civil or foreign war, and Judge Story, in 7th Wheaton, as heretofore cited by me, says they are the same. Blockade being one of the rights incident to a state of war, and the President having in substance asserted civil war to exist, I am of opinion that the blockade was lawfully proclaimed by the Executive.

The next inquiry is, when did the blockade become effective, and as such come to the knowledge of the respondents or their Government? Notice, actual or constructive, will do. In the present case, Flag-Officer Pendergrast, commanding the home sqnadron, officially announced the blockade of the ports of Virginia, whose outlet was Hampton Roads, as effective on the 30th April, 1861, and the Secretary of the Navy, in his letter of the 9th May, 1861, states, this notice was sent to the Baltimore and Norfolk papers, and by one or more of them published. In a certificate of the British Consul at Richmond, dated 14th of May, 1861, found on board the "Tropic Wind" at the time of her capture, he states he had received an authoritative communication of the 11th May, which he immediately communicated to the captains of British merchant-vessels and others interested in British trade, that fifteen days would be allowed to leave port after the actual commencement of the blockade, with or without cargoes, "and whether the cargoes were shipped before or after the commencement of the blockade;" and that upon inquiry he found the 2nd of May, 1861, to be the day when the efficient blockade began.

There does not appear in the cause any evidence to show that the United States'

Government agreed to relax the law of blockade, so as to allow British vessels to load cargoes and come out of port after knowledge of effective blockade was brought home to them.

The letter of Mr. Welles to Mr. Seward, dated 9th May, 1861, in answer to inquiries of Lord Lyons, relative to British vessels in Virginian ports, and the operation of the blockade upon them, &c., and which, it must be presumed, was sent to Lord Lyons, does not contain the relaxation of the Law of Blockade referred to in the British Consul's Certificate of the 14th May, 1861 ; by which I mean that it contains no permission to British vessels to come out of port within fifteen days, with cargoes laden on board, after notice of commencement of effective blockade. I give an extract of that letter of the 9th May, 1861 :—

"Fifteen days have been specified as a limit for neutrals to leave the ports after actual blockade has commenced, with or without cargo, and there are yet remaining five or six days for neutrals to leave; with proper diligence on the part of the persons interested, I see no reason for exemption to any."

It also appears in the evidence of the master, Layton, that he heard in Richmond of the blockade as effective before he began to load his cargo, and was informed it commenced on the 2nd of May.

All the testimony concurs in showing that the cargo was laden on board the "Tropic Wind" on the 13th and 14th days of May, 1861. No principle of prize law seems better settled than that such lading violates the blockade, and forfeits both vessel and cargo. In "Weldman on Search, Capture, and Prizes," page 42 :—The act of egress is "as culpable as the act of ingress ; and a blockade is just as much violated by a ship passing outwards as inwards. A blockade is intended to suspend the entire commerce of the place, and a neutral is no more at liberty to assist the traffic of exportation than of importation. The utmost that can be allowed to a neutral vessel is, that, having already taken in a cargo before the blockade begins she may be at liberty to retire with it. If she afterwards takes on board a cargo, it is a fraudulent act, and a violation of the blockade. It is lawful for a ship to withdraw from a blockaded port, in ballast, or with a cargo shipped *bona fide* before notice of the blockade." (See also "Vrouw Judith," Robinson, 150; the "Juno," 2nd Robinson, 119 ; the "Nossa Senhora," 5th Robinson, 52.)

In Weldman's "International Law," vol. ii, page 205, we find this passage :—

"Where the blockade is known at the port of shipment, the master becomes an agent for the cargo ; in such case the owners must at all events answer to the country imposing the blockade for the acts of persons employed by them ; otherwise, by sacrificing the ship, there would be a ready escape for the cargo, for the benefit of which the fund was intended." (See also the "James Cook," Edwards, 261 ; the "Arthur," Edwards, 202 ; the "Exchange," Edwards, 40 ; 1st Kent Commentaries, second edition, 144, 146 ; Olivera *v.* Union Insurance Company, 3rd Wheaton, Supreme Court, Report, 194. See also Wheaton's note to the same case.)

It follows, upon the case as it now stands, there must be condemnation of both vessel and cargo.

June 13, 1861.

(Signed) JAMES DUNLOP.

N.B.—After I had written this opinion on the proofs and papers then before me, but before it was known or copied, I was requested by Mr. Carlisle, by note of the 14th, to ask of the State Department the whole correspondence, a part of which only was in the cause ; and on Saturday evening, the 15th June, the document A was handed to me. I have formed no opinion of the influence this further correspondence has on the legal aspect of the case ; and as the parties concerned on both sides have had no opportunity to see or comment upon it, and may wish further proof as to the relaxation by the United States of the strict law of blockade, I will allow further proof to be taken by either party on this single point, and postpone any decision till the proof is in, and the Counsel on both sides heard. This course is, I believe, consonant with prize practice.

June 17, 1861.

(Signed) JAMES DUNLOP.

No. 62.

Lord Lyons to Lord J. Russell.—(Received July 23.)

(Extract.) *Washington, July* 8, 1861.

I HAVE the honour to inclose four copies of the Message dated the 4th instant, which was sent to Congress on the 5th instant, by President Lincoln.

The President recommends to Congress to place at the disposal of the Government for the suppression of the rebellion, "at least. 400,000 men, and 400,000,000 dollars."

The following is the only passage in the Message which relates to the foreign relations of the country :—

"The forbearance of this Government had been so extraordinary and so long continued as to lead some foreign nations to shape their action as if they supposed the early destruction of our national Union was probable. While this, on discovery, gave the Executive some concern, he is now happy to say that the sovereignty and rights of the United States are now everywhere practically respected by foreign Powers; and a general sympathy with the country is manifested throughout the world."

The Reports of the Secretaries of the Treasury, of War, and of the Navy, are short, and they appear to be sufficiently clear.

The principal change proposed by the Secretary of the Treasury to be made in the Tariff is the imposition of duties on sugar, tea, and coffee. From this source he anticipates deriving a revenue of 20,000,000 dollars.

The other changes recommended are described as follows : "From proposed duties on articles now exempt, or from changed duties on articles now either lightly burdened, or so heavily burdened that the tax amounts to a prohibition, a further increase of revenue to the amount of 7,000,000 dollars may be anticipated."

I trust that these expressions indicate that some move will be made towards a reasonable reform of the Morrill Tariff. The progress, however, in this direction will, I fear, be slow at present.

Your Lordship will perceive that it is proposed to make the interest on a portion of the loan payable in London.

It is not without alarm that I direct your Lordship's attention to the paragraphs towards the end of the Report of the Secretary of the Treasury which refer to the subject of closing the Southern ports by an Act of Congress instead of by a blockade carried on in conformity with the law of nations.

Those who had still dared to hope that union and friendly feeling could be restored between North and South will have seen with pain that the Secretary of the Treasury mentions the forfeiture of the estates of insurgents as a source of future revenue.

In the Report of the Secretary of the Navy the passage relating to the blockades is, I think, worthy of serious consideration. The Secretary calls the attention of Congress, with reference to this subject, to the necessity of some further penal legislation, especially in relation to the law of forfeiture. It is, indeed, as your Lordship is aware, doubted by lawyers of eminence in this country whether, in the present state of the law, any vessel can be condemned for the breach of such a blockade as that now in existence.

The Government had prepared, in concert with the Chairman of the respective Committees of the Senate, before the meeting of Congress, Bills to carry into effect the recommendations made in the Reports of the three Secretaries. The desire of the Cabinet is that these Bills should be passed as rapidly as possible, and that Congress should adjourn without taking up any other business.

In both Houses the great majority of members appear to be inclined towards vigorous, not to say violent measures. In fact, such opposition as has hitherto been manifested to the plan of the Administration comes from the most energetic members. These declare that it is necessary that Congress should continue in Session in order to spur on the Government and General Scott to a more active prosecution of the war.

It is believed that it is in deference to such manifestations of the temper of Congress that a more decided movement forward has been made by the United States' forces in Virginia. It is now very confidently announced that the long-expected battle is positively to be fought this week, and that Manassas Gap is to be the scene of it.

No. 63.

Lord Lyons to Lord J. Russell.—(Received July 26.)

(Extract.) Washington, July 12, 1861.

I HAVE the honour to transmit to your Lordship a copy of a Bill "further to provide for the Collection of Duties on Imports, and for other purposes." This Bill passed the House of Representatives the day before yesterday by a majority of 136 to 10.

The second and third sections of the Bill provide for the collection of duties on shipboard.

The fourth empowers the President to close the ports of entry in districts in which the Customs duties cannot be collected, and subjects to forfeiture ships with their cargoes entering or attempting to enter ports so closed.

The fifth section is intended to put a stop to commercial intercourse between districts in insurrection and the rest of the United States.

It is likely that the Bill will be passed by the Senate also without delay.

It is to be earnestly desired that the Executive Government may see the imprudence of attempting to put the fourth section into execution, without ascertaining the view taken of it by the maritime Powers of Europe.

Inclosure in No. 63.

A Bill "further to provide for the Collection of Duties on Imports, and for other purposes."

BE it enacted by the Senate and House of Representatives of the United States of America in Congress assembled, That whenever it shall, in the judgment of the President, by reason of unlawful combinations of persons in opposition to the laws of the United States, become impracticable to execute the revenue laws and collect the duties on imports by the ordinary means, in the ordinary way, at any port of entry in any collection district, he is authorized to cause such duties to be collected at any port of delivery in said district until such obstruction shall cease; and in such case the Surveyors at said ports of delivery shall be clothed with all the powers and be subject to all the obligations of Collectors at port of entry; and the Secretary of the Treasury, with the approbation of the President, shall appoint such number of weighers, gaugers, measurers, inspectors, appraisers, and clerks as may be necessary, in his judgment, for the faithful execution of the revenue laws at said ports of delivery, and shall fix and establish the limits within which such ports of delivery are constituted ports of entry, as aforesaid; and all the provisions of law regulating the issue of marine papers, the coasting trade, the warehousing of imports, and collection of duties, shall apply to the ports of entry so constituted, in the same manner as they do to ports of entry established by the laws now in force.

Sec. 2. And be it further enacted, That if, from the cause mentioned in the foregoing section, in the judgment of the President, the revenue from duties on imports cannot be effectually collected at any port of entry in any collection district, in the ordinary way and by the ordinary means, or by the course provided in the foregoing section, then and in that case he may direct that the custom-house for the district be established in any secure place within said district, either on land or on board any vessel in said district or at sea near the coast; and in such case the Collector shall reside at such place, or on shipboard, as the case may be, and there detain all vessels and cargoes arriving within or approaching said district, until the duties imposed by law on said vessels and their cargoes are paid in cash: Provided, that if the owner or consignee of the cargo on board any vessel detained as aforesaid, or the master of said vessel, shall desire to enter a port of entry in any other district in the United States where no such obstructions to the execution of the laws exist, the master of such vessel may be permitted so to change the destination of the vessel and cargo in his manifest, whereupon the Collector shall deliver him a written permit to proceed to the port so designated: And provided further, that the Secretary of the Treasury shall, with the approbation of the President, make proper regulations for the enforcement on shipboard of such provisions of the laws regulating the assessment and collection of duties as in his judgment may be necessary and practicable.

Sec. 3. And be it further enacted, that it shall be unlawful to take any vessel or cargo detained as aforesaid from the custody of the proper officers of the Customs, unless by process of some Court of the United States; and in case of any attempt otherwise to take such vessel or cargo by any force, or combination, or assemblage of persons, too great to be overcome by the officers of the Customs, it shall and may be lawful for the President or such person or persons as he shall have empowered for that purpose, to employ such part of the army or navy or militia of the United States, or such force of citizen volunteers as may be deemed necessary for the purpose of preventing the removal of such vessel or cargo, and protecting the officers of the Customs in retaining the custody thereof.

Sec. 4. And be it further enacted, that if, in the judgment of the President, from the cause mentioned in the first section of this Act, the duties upon imports in any collection district cannot be effectually collected by the ordinary means and in the ordinary way, or in the mode and manner provided in the foregoing sections of this Act, then and in that case the President is hereby empowered to close the port or ports of entry in said district, and in such case give notice thereof by Proclamation; and thereupon all right of importation, warehousing, and other privileges incident to ports of entry shall cease and be discontinued at such port so closed, until opened by the order of the President on the cessation of such obstructions: and if, while said ports are so closed, any ship or vessel from beyond the United States, or having on board any articles subject to duties, shall enter or attempt to enter any such port, the same, together with its tackle, apparel, furniture, and cargo, shall be forfeited to the United States.

Sec. 5. And be it further enacted, that whenever the President, in pursuance of the provisions of the second section of the Act entitled "An Act to provide for calling forth the militia to execute the laws of the Union, suppress insurrections, and repel invasions, and to repeal the Act now in force for that purpose," approved February 28, 1795, shall have called forth the militia to suppress combinations against the laws of the United States, and to cause the laws to be duly executed, and the insurgents shall have failed to disperse by the time directed by the President, and when said insurgents claim to act under the authority of any State or States, and such claim is not disclaimed or repudiated by the persons exercising the functions of government in such State or States, or in the part or parts thereof in which said combination exists, nor such insurrection suppressed by said State or States, then and in such case it may and shall be lawful for the President by Proclamation to declare that the inhabitants of such State, or any section or part thereof where such insurrection exists, are in a state of insurrection against the United States; and thereupon all commercial intercourse by and between the same and the citizens thereof and the citizens of the rest of the United States shall cease and be unlawful so long as such condition of hostility shall continue; and all goods and chattels, wares and merchandize, coming from said State or section into the other parts of the United States, and all proceeding to such State or section by land or water, shall, together with the vessel or vehicle conveying the same, or conveying persons to or from such State or section, be forfeited to the United States: Provided, however, that the President may in his discretion license and permit commercial intercourse with any such part of said State or section, the inhabitants of which are so declared in a state of insurrection, in such articles, and for such time, and by such persons, as he in his discretion may think most conducive to the public interest; and such intercourse, so far as by him licensed, shall be conducted and carried on only in pursuance of rules and regulations prescribed by the Secretary of the Treasury. And the Secretary of the Treasury may appoint such officers at places where officers of the Customs are not now authorized by law as may be needed to carry into effect such licenses, rules, and regulations; and officers of the Customs and other officers shall receive for services under this section, and under said rules and regulations, such fees and compensation as are now allowed for similar service under other provisions of law.

Sec. 6. And be it further enacted, that from and after fifteen days after the issuing of the said Proclamation, as provided in the last foregoing section of this Bill, any ship or vessel belonging in whole or in part to any citizen or inhabitant of said State or part of a State whose inhabitants are so declared in a state of insurrection, found at sea, or in any port of the rest of the United States, shall be forfeited to the United States.

Sec. 7. And be it further enacted, that in the execution of the provisions of this Act, and of the other laws of the United States providing for the collection of duties on imports and tonnage, it may and shall be lawful for the President, in addition to the Revenue cutters in service, to employ in aid thereof such other suitable vessels as may in his judgment be required.

Sec. 8. And be it further enacted, that the forfeitures and penalties incurred by virtue of this Act may be mitigated or remitted in pursuance of the authority vested in the Secretary of the Treasury by the Act entitled "An Act providing for mitigating or remitting the forfeitures, penalties, and disabilities accruing in certain cases therein mentioned," approved March third, seventeen hundred and ninety-seven, or in cases where special circumstances may seem to require it, according to regulations to be prescribed by the Secretary of the Treasury.

Sec. 9. And be it further enacted, that proceedings on seizures for forfeiture under this Act may be pursued in the Courts of the United States in any district into which the property so seized may be taken and proceedings instituted; and such Courts shall have and entertain as full jurisdiction over the same as if the seizure was made in that district.

No. 64.

Lord Lyons to Lord J. Russell.—(Received July 26.)

My Lord, *Washington, July* 12, 1861.

I HAVE the honour to inclose a copy of a Joint Resolution, which is now before the Senate, "To approve and confirm certain Acts of the President of the United States for suppressing Insurrection and Rebellion."

Among the acts to be thus confirmed are the Proclamations establishing the blockade.

It is thought that the Resolution will pass both Houses without any material alteration.

I have, &c.
(Signed) LYONS.

Inclosure in No. 64.

Joint Resolution to approve and confirm certain Acts of the President of the United States for Suppressing Insurrection and Rebellion.

WHEREAS, since the adjournment of Congress on the fourth day of March last, a formidable insurrection in certain States of this Union has arrayed itself in armed hostility to the Government of the United States, constitutionally administered; and whereas the President of the United States did, under the extraordinary exigencies thus presented, exercise certain powers and adopt certain measures for the preservation of this government—that is to say: First. He did, on the fifteenth day of April last, issue his proclamation calling upon the several States for seventy-five thousand men to suppress such insurrectionary combinations, and to cause the laws to be faithfully executed. Secondly. He did, on the nineteenth day of April last, issue a Proclamation setting on foot a blockade of the ports within the States of South Carolina, Georgia, Alabama, Florida, Mississippi, Louisiana, and Texas. Thirdly. He did, on the twenty-seventh day of April last, issue a Proclamation establishing a blockade of the ports within the States of Virginia and North Carolina. Fourthly. He did, by an order of the twenty-seventh day of April last, addressed to the Commanding General of the army of the United States, authorize that officer to suspend the writ of *habeas corpus* at any point on or in the vicinity of any military line between the city of Philadelphia and the city of Washington. Fifthly. He did on the third day of May last, issue a Proclamation calling into the service of the United States forty-two thousand and thirty-four volunteers, increasing the regular army by the addition of twenty-two thousand seven hundred and fourteen men, and the navy by an addition of eighteen thousand seamen. Sixthly. He did on the tenth day of May last, issue a Proclamation authorizing the Commander of the forces of the United States on the Coast of Florida to suspend the writ of *habeas corpus*, if necessary. All of which Proclamations and Orders have been submitted to this Congress: Now therefore—

Be it resolved by the Senate and House of Representatives of the United States of America in Congress assembled, That all of the extraordinary acts, proclamations, and orders hereinbefore mentioned, be, and the same are hereby approved and declared to be in all respects legal and valid, to the same intent, and with the same effect, as if they had been issued and done under the previous express authority and direction of the Congress of the United States.

No. 65.

Lord Lyons to Lord J. Russell.—(Received July 27.)

(Extract.) *Washington, July* 15, 1861.

BY my telegram of the 12th instant I had the honour to inform your Lordship that the Act empowering the President to collect duties on shipboard, and to close ports of entry, had passed both Houses of Congress.

I believe that the Act was passed without any other amendment than the verbal one of substituting the word "Act" for "Bill" in the second line of section 6. The copy, therefore, inclosed in my despatch of the 12th instant may be regarded as correct.

Very great efforts were made to awaken members of both Houses to the serious consequences which the Act might have on the relations of the country with the maritime Powers of Europe. The haste with which it was passed, notwithstanding all remonstrance, is an alarming symptom of the temper of the Legislature and of the country at this moment.

No. 66.

Lord Lyons to Lord J. Russell.—(Received July 27.)

(Extract.) *Washington, July* 16, 1861.

CONGRESS has proceeded very rapidly with measures connected with the prosecution of war, to the exclusion of almost all other business. The Bills recommended by the Government have hitherto been passed with little amendment and scarcely any discussion.

The Senate has raised the limit which the volunteers are not to exceed from 400,000 to 500,000 men. The nominal amount of the money to be granted for the support of these troops is, I understand, to be raised from 400,000,000 to 500,000,000 dollars.

Very little allusion to foreign Powers has hitherto been made in Congress. There has, indeed, been scarcely anything like a debate on any subject in either House. Yesterday, however, a motion for the correspondence with foreign Powers relative to the insurrection in the Southern States passed the House of Representatives.

In the very short discussions which have taken place, room has been found for no small degree of violence against the Secessionists. The measures of Congress are intended to intimidate the South. They will certainly go far to do away with any hope that may have remained of a friendly reconstruction of the Union.

The Senate has formally expelled the Senators who represented the Southern States. It has taken a more significant step by admitting two Senators who have been elected by the Legislature which has established itself in the Western counties of Virginia, in opposition to the regularly constituted Legislature, which has gone over with the principal part of the State to the Southern Confederacy. The design of this measure is to encourage any Union men who can obtain the upper hand in detached parts of other Seceded States, to establish a Legislature of their own round which a Union Party may rally.

It seems, however, to be very much doubted whether any beneficial effects can follow sufficiently important to outweigh the disadvantages of this arbitrary and irregular admission of Senators, who can hardly pretend to anything like a legal election, and who certainly do not in any sense represent their State as a whole.

It is thought that Congress may be able to adjourn at the end of this week.

No. 67.

Lord Lyons to Lord J. Russell.—(Received August 4.)

My Lord, *Washington, July* 19, 1861.

WITH reference to my despatch of the 15th instant, and to my previous despatches concerning the Act of Congress empowering the President to collect duties on board ship, and to close ports of entry, I have the honour to inclose a copy of the Act, as passed by both Houses and approved by the President.

* No. 63. † No. 61.

The official title of the Act is, "An Act to provide for the collection of Duties on Imports, and for other purposes."

The copy sent herewith is taken from the "National Republican" newspaper of this morning, to which it has been sent by the Government, according to the usual practice, for publication. No more authentic copy is likely to be printed, until the Statutes at large of the session are published.

It is believed that the Cabinet will to-day deliberate upon the advisableness of issuing the Proclamation which would give effect to the clause providing for the closing of the ports.

I have, &c.
(Signed)   LYONS.

Inclosure in No. 67.

An Act further to Provide for the Collection of Duties on Imports, and for other purposes.

[This is the same as Inclosure 1 in No. 63, the word "Act" being substituted for "Bill" in Section 6.]

No. 68.

Lord Lyons to Lord J. Russell.—(Received August 5.)

My Lord,   *Washington, July* 20, 1861.

I CONSULTED with M. Mercier the day before yesterday on the steps to be taken towards deterring this Government from putting into execution the Act of Congress closing the ports of the Southern States.

We were not very sanguine of success, but we thought it would be advisable to make some effort to turn to account the information respecting the views of our respective Governments which we had received on the previous evening.

M. Mercier showed me a despatch from M. Thouvenel, dated the 4th instant, on this subject; and I, in return, made him acquainted with the substance of your Lordship's despatch of the 6th instant.

M. Mercier proposed that he should go to Mr. Seward, and, without making any formal communication, should tell him, in a friendly and confidential manner, that the French Government could not consider the closing the Southern ports by a Decree as justifiable, and should point out the very serious consequences which an attempt to enforce such a Decree against foreign ships could not but occasion.

I assented to M. Mercier's proposal, and authorized him to mention to Mr. Seward that Her Majesty's Government concurred in the view of the French Government, or to abstain from doing so, as he should think proper at the moment.

M. Mercier went immediately to Mr. Seward. On his return, he told me that Mr. Seward had listened to him with calmness, and without any appearance of dissatisfaction; and had, indeed, appeared to be himself disinclined to issue the Proclamation in virtue of which the Act for closing the ports would be brought into operation. He asked M. Mercier to let him have, for his private use, an extract from the despatch in which the views of the French Government were stated. M. Mercier agreed to send him one. No mention was made either by M. Mercier or Mr. Seward of Her Majesty's Government or of me.

M. Mercier consulted me as to what part of M. Thouvenel's despatch he should give to Mr. Seward, and we agreed upon the extract of which I have the honour to inclose a copy herewith.

Mr. Seward (as, indeed, I expected) sent for me this morning, and after some conversation on the closing of the ports, told me that M. Mercier had given him an extract from a despatch from M. Thouvenel on the subject, and asked whether I had not received any despatch from your Lordship from which I could give him an extract in the same manner.

I was glad to have the opportunity of thus placing myself on exactly the same footing as my French colleague. I accordingly told Mr. Seward that I would read over your Lordship's despatches and see if there was any part of which I could let him have a copy.

I reminded him, however, that I was not charged to make any official communication on the subject to him, and that he must regard anything I might send him as merely a confidential memorandum for his private use.

I have since seen M. Mercier, and with his approval have sent to Mr. Seward the short extract from your Lordship's despatch of the 16th instant of which the inclosed is a copy. I have also given a copy of the extract to M. Mercier.

I have, &c.
(Signed) LYONS.

Inclosure 1 in No. 68.

M. Thouvenel to M. Mercier.

(Extrait.) *Paris, le 4 Juillet,* 1861.

IL me paraît impossible qu'il [le Cabinet de Washington] ne comprenne pas que nous ne pouvions admettre une semblable mesure, que les mêmes considérations qui nous ont amenés à envisager comme deux belligérants les deux fractions de l'Union aujourd'hui en guerre, nous obligeraient à considérer la fermeture par décret des ports du Sud comme la substitution d'un blocus sur le papier au blocus effectif, le seul que les neutres soient tenus de respecter.

Inclosure 2 in No. 68.

Lord J. Russell to Lord Lyons.

(Extract.) *Foreign Office, July* 6, 1861.

HER Majesty's Government entirely concur with the French Government in the opinion that a decree closing the Southern ports would be entirely illegal, and would be an evasion of that recognized maxim of the law of nations that the ports of a belligerent can only be closed by an effective blockade.

No. 69.

Lord Lyons to Lord J. Russell.—(*Received August* 5.)

My Lord, *Washington, July* 22, 1861.

THE main army of the United States, under General McDowell, was defeated yesterday by the Confederate forces under General Beauregard, at a place in Virginia, about five-and-twenty miles from Washington, between a village called Centreville and Manassas Gap.

On the 18th instant the advanced brigade of General McDowell's army, composed of four regiments, encountered the enemy at a place called Bull's Run, and was repulsed. It was near the same spot that the battle took place yesterday.

The United States' army advanced from Centreville to attack General Beauregard's position very early in the morning. By 11 o'clock the two armies were engaged. The fighting appears to have continued without intermission until 4 o'clock in the afternoon. At 3 o'clock the advantage was believed to be on the side of the United States, but about an hour afterwards the United States' troops were seized with a panic, and fled in confusion to Centreville. The rout of the whole army is described by eye-witnesses as complete.

It is supposed here, however, I know not how correctly, that General McDowell's head-quarters are still at Centreville; and that the pursuit was not carried up to that point.

According to the most probable calculation which has been made there were from 50,000 to 60,000 United States' troops engaged, and about the same number on the other side.

It seems to be generally thought that an advance on this place does not enter into General Beauregard's plans. Unless the defeated army rallies on the other side of the Potomac, the Government has little means at this moment of defending the capital. All the troops, with the exception of about 10,000 men, had been sent hence to strengthen General McDowell's army before the battle.

The intelligence of the defeat reached Washington only late last night, and little is certainly known beyond the fact that the rout of the United States' army was complete.

I have, &c.
(Signed)   LYONS.

No. 70.

Earl Russell to Lord Lyons.

My Lord,   *Foreign Office, August* 8, 1861.

I HAVE received your Lordship's despatch of the 12th ultimo.*

The Bill which you have transmitted to me, entitled a "Bill further to provide for the Collection of Duties on Imports, and for other purposes," raises a very serious question.

By the 1st section it is proposed to give to the President the power of closing any ports of the United States "whenever it shall, in the judgment of the President, by reason of unlawful combinations of persons in opposition to the laws of the United States, become impracticable to execute the revenue laws, and collect the duties on imports by the ordinary means in the ordinary way;" and also to give him the power of causing such duties to be collected at any port of delivery.

The 2nd section provides for the establishment of the Custom-house, in such case, in any secure place on land "or on board any vessel in said district, or at sea near the coast," and contains other provisions in aid of this object ; and by the words at the end of the 4th section it is enacted, that "if while said ports of entry are so closed, any ship or vessel from beyond the United States, or having on board any articles subject to duties, shall enter or attempt to enter any such port, the same, together with its tackle, apparel, furniture, and cargo, shall be forfeited to the United States."

It is obvious that this Act gives power to the President to confiscate a foreign vessel, with its cargo, for attempting to enter a port which has not been blockaded and is not in the possession of the Executive, and as to the closing of which none of the parties interested may have received any previous notice.

The Act, it is to be observed, speaks of "unlawful combinations of persons in opposition to the laws of the United States," and seems to contemplate riotous combinations or insurrections of a partial, temporary, or local nature, not constituting a state of war ; combinations of persons simply opposing the laws of the United States. But the joint Resolution of the Senate and Representatives contained in your Lordship's other despatch of the 12th instant† speaks a very different language. In this Resolution we find it affirmed that a formidable insurrection has, since the 4th day of March last, arrayed itself in armed hostility to the Government of the United States ; that the President, on the 15th day of April, issued his Proclamation, calling out 75,000 men to suppress such insurrectionary combinations ; that on the 19th day of April he issued his Proclamation setting on foot a blockade of the ports within seven of the States of the Union ; that on the 27th of April he proclaimed a blockade of two more of the States of the Union ; that on the 3rd day of May he issued a Proclamation increasing the army by 22,714 men, and the navy by 18,000 seamen.

In addition to these acts thus stated by both Houses, we have the information that in his Message to Congress the President has called for 400,000 men and 400,000,000 of dollars.

After the recital of these immense efforts, it seems quite inappropriate to speak of "unlawful combinations." Indeed, it cannot be denied that the state of things which exists, is a state of civil war ; and there is, as regards neutral nations, no difference between civil war and foreign war.

Acting on these principles, Her Majesty's Government has accordingly recognized the state of civil war as existing, and all the rights which belong to a belligerent Her Majesty fully acknowledges to reside in the Government of the United States.

            * No. 63.   † No. 64.

But Her Majesty cannot acknowledge that ports in the complete possession of the (so-called) "Confederate States," and which are not blockaded, shall be interdicted to the commerce of Her Majesty's subjects by decree of the President of the United States, or by a law passed by their Congress. This would be in effect to allow the lawfulness of a paper blockade extending over 3,000 miles of coast. Her Majesty's Government cannot admit a right in any Power not in the possession of the port to erect a so-called "Customhouse" on board a ship "at sea near the coast," and there to exact duties.

The principle is in this case so very clear that it is needless to refer to the case of Spain and Venezuela, or to any other case of a like nature.

Her Majesty's Government decline to discuss the legality or the justice of the conduct of the Confederate States. With the legality or illegality, according to the constitution and laws of the United States, of the acts of the (so-called) Confederate States or their officers and forces, foreign Governments have nothing to do; but they are compelled to recognize this fact, viz., the existence, the extent and continuance of a formidable resistance to the authority of the United States.

The main question is as to the power assumed to be given to the President of instituting a mere paper blockade of ports not in his possession. This power Her Majesty's Government cannot acknowledge as belonging to him by international law, or as consistent with the friendly and commercial relations at present subsisting between the United States and Great Britain, and they would consider its exercise as a violation of the unquestionable rights of neutral nations. Her Majesty's Government trust, however, that the President of the United States will not exercise the power which he is enabled to assume by the Act which I have discussed in this despatch. He has in his own hands the right of blockading the Southern ports in conformity with international law, without raising objections on the part of other maritime Powers.

You will read and give a copy of this despatch to Mr. Seward.*

I am, &c.
(Signed) RUSSELL.

No. 71.

Earl Russell to Lord Lyons.

My Lord,   *Foreign Office, August* 9, 1861.

WITH reference to my despatch of yesterday's date, I have to authorize your Lordship to use your discretion as to communicating that despatch, or not, to Mr. Seward, after consulting M. Mercier, and according to your united judgment on the state of affairs.

I am, &c.
(Signed) RUSSELL.

No. 72.

Lord Lyons to Lord J. Russell.—(Received August 12.)

My Lord,   *Washington, July* 29, 1861.

WITH reference to my despatch of the 16th instant, I have the honour to inform your Lordship that the day before yesterday two Messages from the President, dated the 25th instant, were read in the House of Representatives, transmitting, in answer to Resolutions of the House, Reports from the Secretary of State, declining to produce the correspondence with foreign Powers relative to "maritime rights," and the "existing insurrection."

I have, &c.
(Signed) LYONS.

---

* This despatch was not communicated to Mr. Seward; Lord Lyons having made a similar representation under a previous instruction (see page 72).

No. 73.

Lord Lyons to Lord J. Russell.—(Received August 12.)

(Extract.) *Washington, July* 30, 1861.

VAST loans have been voted by Congress; but great difficulty in raising them is apprehended. Little confidence appears to be felt in the measures taken by the Legislature for increasing the revenue. The duties on tea, coffee, and sugar will, no doubt, be productive; but the probable result of either of the plans now before Congress for altering the Tariff will be a falling-off in the receipts derived from most other articles. The direct taxes have met with great opposition in the House of Representatives. The Bill recommended by the Government and by the Committee of Ways and Means was rejected. A substitute for it, however, passed the House yesterday. But in any form these taxes will be extremely unpopular, and will not produce any appreciable revenue for some months. In the meantime the greatest part of the expenses are provided for by Treasury bonds bearing 6 per cent. interest, which are paid out by the Government at par, but which are already at a discount in the market.

Since the President's Proclamation announcing the determination to coerce the South, the States of Virginia, North Carolina, Arkansas, and Tennessee have gone over to the Confederates. The State of Kentucky, although still in the Union, has declared its intention to hold a neutral position in the struggle. A petty civil war between the Union and Disunion parties is going on in Missouri. The State of Maryland is maintained in obedience only by the presence of a large body of troops, and by the suspension of the writ of *habeas corpus*. The safety of Washington has again depended for several days upon its not entering into the plans of the Confederates to attack it. The confidence of the troops in themselves, and of the people in the troops, has received a severe shock.

But, although the considerations which should make the North willing to listen to proposals for a compromise are so weighty and so numerous, it is nevertheless to be feared that the time for effecting one is still not near. The South will, of course, hear of nothing less than an absolute recognition of the sovereignty and independence of the Confederate States: it will take a great deal to bring the North to consent to this. Present appearances indicate that the war will be persevered in.

The troops in Washington and its neighbourhood have been formed into one division, and placed under the command of General McLlellan.

No. 74.

Messrs. Yancey, Rost, and Mann to Earl Russell.—(Received August 14.)

15, *Half-Moon Street, London, August* 14, 1861.

THE Undersigned, as your Lordship has already on two occasions been verbally and unofficially informed, were appointed on the 16th of March last, a Commission to Her Britannic Majesty's Government by the President of the Confederate States of America.

The Undersigned were instructed to represent to your Lordship that seven of the sovereign States of the late American Union, for just and sufficient reasons, and in full accordance with the great principle of self-government, had thrown off the authority of that Union and formed a Confederacy which they had styled the "Confederate States of America." They were further instructed to ask Her Majesty's Government to recognize the fact of the existence of this new Power in the world, and also to inform it that they were fully empowered to negotiate with it a Treaty of Friendship, Commerce, and Navigation.

At an early day after the arrival of the Undersigned in London, at an informal interview which your Lordship was pleased to accord them, they informed your Lordship of the object of their mission, and endeavoured to impress upon your Lordship that the action of the seven Confederate States had been based upon repeated attempts on the part of the Federal Government, and of many of the more Northern States which composed the late Union during a series of years which extended over near half a century, to rule the people of the Southern section of that Union by means of the unconstitutional exercise of power; and that secession from that Union had been resorted to, as, in the opinion of the Seceding States, the best and surest mode of saving the liberties which their Federal and State Constitutions were designed to secure to them. They also endeavoured to place before your Lordship satisfactory evidence that the justice of this great movement upon the part of the Cotton States was so palpable that it would be indorsed by many, if not by all, of the Southern States which were then adhering to the Union. which would sooner or later become convinced that the security of their rights could only be maintained by pursuing the like process of Secession from the late Federal Union, and accession to the Constitution and Government of the Confederate States of America.

They were especially desirous of convincing your Lordship, and laid before your Lordship reasons for their belief, that the people of the Seceding States had violated no principle of allegiance in their act of Secession, but, on the contrary, had been true to that high duty which all citizens owe to that sovereignty which is the supreme fount of power in a State, no matter what may be the particular form of government under which they live: they were careful to show to your Lordship, however, that the idea of American sovereignty was different from that entertained in Great Britain and Europe; that whereas in the great Eastern hemisphere generally, sovereignty was deemed to exist in the Government, the founders of the North American States had solemnly declared, and upon that declaration had built up American institutions, that " Governments were instituted among men, deriving their just powers from the consent of the governed; that whenever any form of government becomes destructive of these ends (security to life, liberty, and the pursuit of happiness), it is the right of the people to alter or abolish it, and to institute a new Government."

The Undersigned assumed it to be incontrovertible, in order to give practical vitality to this declaration, that the people who were declared to possess this right " to alter or to abolish " such oppressive government, must be the people whose rights such government either assailed, or no longer protected. Whether that government should be administered by one tyrant, or the more heartless and equally effectual despotism of a sectional and tyrannical majority, could make no difference in the application of the principle. When the people who thus act in "abolishing" their form of government are not mere self-constituted assemblages of disaffected individuals, but the sovereign people of great States, each possessing separate Constitutions, and legislative and executive powers, acting in modes prescribed by those Constitutions, and taking votes under form and by virtue of law, the minority yielding cheerfully to the decision of the majority as to the question of redress, it became clear that whatever might be European views as to such action, if developed in Europe, the Seceding States were amply justified by the great America principles of self-government proclaimed by their ancestors in 1776. They submitted that so far from the principle of American allegiance having been violated by the people of the Seceding States, in those States alone is that principle upheld whereby the actions of men claiming to be the representatives of the men of 1776, are to be guided and justified, and that the people and Government of the States upholding Mr. Lincoln, in his war upon the Confederate States, are alone the traitors to that great political truth, and as such must by judged by an impartial world.

In connection with this view, the Undersigned explained to your Lordship the unity, the deliberation, the moderation, and regard for personal and public right; the absence of undue popular commotion during the process of Secession; the daily and ordinary administration of the laws in every department of justice, all of which were distinguishing features of this grand movement. They expatiated upon the great extent of fertile country over which the Confederate States exercised jurisdiction, producing in ample quantity every variety of cereal necessary to the support of their inhabitants; to the great value of the products of cotton and tobacco grown by them; to the number and character of their people; and they submitted to your Lordship that all of these political and material facts demonstrated to the nations of the world that the action of the Confederate States of America was not that of rebels, subject to be dealt with as traitors and pirates by their enemy, but the dignified and solemn conduct of a belligerent Power, struggling, with wisdom and energy, to assume a place among the great States of the civilized world, upon a broad and just principle which commended itself to that world's respect.

The Undersigned have witnessed with pleasure that the views which, in their first interview, they pressed upon your Lordship as to the undoubted right of the Confederate States, under the Law of Nations, to be treated as a belligerent Power, and the monstrous assertion of the Government of Washington of its right to treat their citizens found in arms upon land or sea, as rebels and pirates, have met with the concurrence of Her Britannic Majesty's Government; and that the moral might of this great and Christian people has been thus thrown into the scale to prevent the barbarous and inhuman spectacle of war between citizens so lately claiming a common country, conducted upon principles which would have been a disgrace to the age in which we live.

The Undersigned, however, received, with some surprise and regret, the avowal of Her Britannic Majesty's Government that, in order to the observance of a strict neutrality, the public and private armed vessels of neither of the contending Parties would be permitted to enter Her Majesty's ports with prizes. The Undersigned do not contest the right of the British Government to make such regulations, but have been disposed to think that it has been unusual for Her Majesty's Government to exercise such right, and that in this instance the practical operation of the rule has been to favour the Government at Washington, and to cripple the exercise of an undoubted public right of the Government of the Confederate States. This Government commenced its career entirely without a navy. Owing to the high sense of duty which distinguished the Southern officers who were lately in commission in the United States' navy, the ships which otherwise might have been brought into Southern ports were honourably delivered up to the United States' Government, and the navy, built for the protection of the people of all the States, is now used by the Government at Washington to coerce the people and blockade the ports of one-third of the States of the late Union.

The people of the Confederate States are an agricultural, not a manufacturing or commercial people. They own but few ships. Hence there has been not the least necessity for the Government at Washington to issue letters of marque. The people of the Confederate States have but few ships, and not much commerce upon which such private armed vessels could operate. The commodities produced in the Confederate States are such as the world needs more than any other, and the nations of the earth have heretofore sent their ships to our wharves, and there the merchants buy and receive our cotton and tobacco.

But it is far otherwise with the people of the present United States. They are a manufacturing and commercial people. They do a large part of the carrying-trade of the world. Their ships and commerce afford them the sinews of war, and keep their industry afloat. To cripple this industry and commerce, to destroy their ships or cause them to be dismantled and tied up to their rotting wharves, are legitimate objects and means of warfare.

Having no navy, no commercial marine out of which to improvise public armed vessels to any considerable extent, the Confederate States were compelled to resort to the issuance of letters of marque, a mode of warfare as fully and clearly recognized by the law and usage of nations as any other arm of war, and most assuredly more humane and more civilized in its practice than that which appears to have distinguished the march of the troops of the Government of the United States upon the soil and among the villages of Virginia.

These facts tend to show that the practical working of the rule that forbids the entry of the public and private armed vessels of either party into British ports with prizes operates exclusively to prevent the exercise of this legitimate mode of warfare by the Confederate States, while it is, to a great degree, a practical protection to the commerce and ships of the United States.

In the interview already alluded to, as well as in one of a similar character, held between your Lordship and the Undersigned at a later date, the Undersigned were fully aware of the relations of amity existing between Her Britannic Majesty's Government and that of Washington, and of the peculiar difficulties into which these relations might be thrown if Her Majesty should choose to recognize the nationality of the Confederate States of America, before some decided exhibition of ability upon the part of the Government of those States to maintain itself had been shown. Therefore, they did not deem it advisable to urge Her Majesty's Government to an immediate decision upon so grave a question, but contented themselves with a presentation of the cause of their Government, and have quietly waited upon events to justify all that they had said, with the hope that Her Majesty's Government would soon come to the conclusion that the same sense of justice, the same view of duty under the law of nations, which caused it to recognize the *de facto* Government of Texas while yet a superior Mexican army was contending for supremacy upon its soil, the *de facto* Governments of the South American Republics while Spain still persisted in claiming to be their Sovereign, and the *de facto* Governments of Greece, of Belgium, and Italy, would induce it to recognize the Government of the Confederate Sates of America upon the happening of events exhibiting a deep-seated and abiding confidence that success will attend their efforts. At all events reconstruction of the Union is an impossibility. The brief history of the past confirms them in this belief.

Since the organization of the Government of the Confederate States in February last, and since Mr. Lincoln assumed the reins of government in the United States, and commenced preparing his aggressive policy against the Confederate States, the moral weight of their position and cause, aided by the constitutional action and policy of the new President and his Cabinet, have caused four other great States, viz., Virginia, North

K

Carolina, Tennessee, and Arkansas, containing about 4,500,000 inhabitants, and covering an extent of valuable territory equal to that of France and Spain, to secede from the late Union and join the Confederate States; while the inhabitants of three other powerful States, viz., Maryland, Kentucky, and Missouri, are now agitated by the throes of revolution, and a large part of them are rising in arms to resist the military despotism which, in the name of the Constitution, has been so ruthlessly, and in such utter perversion of the provisions of that instrument, imposed upon them. The Undersigned have also sufficient reasons for the belief that even in the North-Western part of the State of Illinois a part of the people have proclaimed open opposition to Mr. Lincoln's unconstitutional and despotic government, while in several others, public assemblies and their legislatures have condemned the war as subversive of the Constitution. In addition to these striking evidences of the increased strength of the Confederate States, and of great internal weakness and division in Mr. Lincoln's Government, the Undersigned can proudly and confidently point to the unity which exists among the people of the eleven Confederate States, with the solitary and unimportant exception of the extreme north-west corner of Virginia, lying between Ohio and Pennsylvania, and settled almost exclusively by Northern emigrants. Whatever differences of opinion may have been entertained among the people of the United States as to the policy of secession, there was little difference of opinion as to the unconstitutional causes which led to it, and often, by a fair decision at the polls, by the majority in favour of Secession as the means of expressing their liberties, the great mass of the people at once yielded all objections, and are now engaged with their wealth and their persons in the most patriotic exertions to uphold their Government in the course of independence which had been decided upon.

Whatever tribute of admiration may be yielded for the present to the people who submit to Mr. Lincoln's usurping Government, for energy displayed in raising and organizing an immense army for the purpose of imposing the yoke of that Government upon a people who are struggling for the inestimable right of governing themselves, in order to a preservation of their liberties, a just and impartial history will award to the people of the Confederate States an unmixed admiration for an effort which, in the space of six months, has thrown off the authority of the usurper; has organized a new Government, based upon the principles of personal and public liberty; has put that Government into operation; has raised, organized, and armed an army sufficient to meet and defeat in a fair field, and drive in ignominious flight from that field, the myriads of invaders which the reputed first General of the age deemed fit to crush what he termed a rebellion.

The Undersigned call your Lordship's attention to the fact that Mr. Lincoln's Government, though possessed of all the advantages of a more numerous population, of the credit due to a recognized Government of long continuance, of the entire navy of the late Union, has not been able to retake a single fortification of which the Confederate States possessed themselves; but, on the contrary, has been driven out from a mighty fortress upon the Atlantic, and from several forts on the western frontier, by the Confederate arms; that it has not been able to advance more than five miles into the territory of any of the Confederate States where there was any serious attempt to prevent it; and is in danger of losing three great States of the Union by insurrection. Even at sea, upon which the Government of Mr. Lincoln possesses undisputed way, it has not been able to make an effectual blockade of a single port but those which find an outlet through the mouth of Chesapeake Bay; vessels of every class, public and private, armed vessels belonging to the Confederate States, and traders, having found their way in and out of every other port at which the attempt has been made.

In everything that constitutes the material of war, thus far the Confederate States have supplied themselves from their own resources, unaided by that free intercourse with the world which has been open to the United States. Men, arms, munitions of war of every description, have been supplied in ample abundance to defeat all attempts to successfully invade our borders. Money has been obtained in the Confederate States in sufficient quantity. Every loan that has been put upon the market has been taken at and above par, and the Undersigned but state the universal impression and belief of their Government, and their fellow-citizens in the Confederate States, that, no matter what may be the demand for means to defend their country against invasion, sufficient resources of every character, and sufficient patriotism to furnish them, exist within the Confederate States for that purpose.

The Undersigned are aware that an impression has prevailed even in what may be termed well-informed circles in Europe, that the Slave-holding States are poor, and not able to sustain a prolonged conflict with the non-Slave-holding States of the North. In the opinion of the Undersigned, this idea is grossly erroneous; and, considering the importance of a correct understanding of the relative resources of the two contending Powers, in resolving the question of the ability of the South to maintain its position, your Lordship will pardon a reference to the Statistical Tables of 1850, the last authentic exposition of the resources of the United States which has yet been published, and which is appended to this communication. The incontestable truths exhibited in that Table prove that the Confederate States possess the elements of a great and powerful nation, capable not only of clothing, feeding, and defending themselves, but also of clothing all the nations of Europe, under the benign influence of peace and free trade.

The Undersigned are also aware that the anti-slavery sentiment so universally prevalent in England has shrunk from the idea of forming friendly public relations with a Government recognizing the slavery of a part of the human race. The question of the morality of slavery it is not for the Undersigned to discuss with any foreign Power. The authors of the American Declaration of Independence found the African race in the colonies to be slaves, both by Colonial and English law, and by the law of nations. Those great and good men left that fact, and the responsibility for its existence, where they found it; and thus finding that there were two distinct races in the colonies, one free and capable of maintaining their freedom, the other slave and, in their opinion, unfitted to enter upon that contest, and to govern themselves, they made their famous declaration of freedom for the white race alone. They eventually planned and put in operation, in the course of a few years, two plans of government, both resting upon that great and recognized distinction between the white and the black man, and perpetuating that distinction as the fundamental law of the government they framed, which they declared to be framed for the benefit of themselves and their posterity; in their own language, "to secure the blessings of liberty to ourselves and our posterity."

The wisdom of that course is not a matter for discussion with foreign nations. Suffice it to say that thus were the great American institutions framed, and thus have they remained unchanged to this day. It was from no fear that the slaves would be liberated that Secession took place. The very party in power has proposed to guarantee slavery for ever in the States, if the South would but remain in the Union. Mr. Lincoln's Message proposes no freedom to the slave, but announces subjection of his owner to the will of the Union, in other words to the will of the North. Even after the battle of Bull's Run, both branches of the Congress at Washington passed Resolutions that the war is only waged in order to uphold that (pro-slavery) Constitution, and to enforce the laws (many of them pro-slavery), and out of 172 votes in the Lower House they receive all but two, and in the Senate all but one vote. As the army commenced its march the Commanding General issued an order that no slaves should be received into, or allowed to follow, the camp. The great object of the war, therefore, as now officially announced, is not to free the slave, but to keep him in subjection to his owner, and to control his labour through the legislative channels which the Lincoln Government designs to force upon the master. The Undersigned therefore submit with confidence that as far as the anti-slavery sentiment of England is concerned, it can have no sympathy with the North; nay, it will probably become disgusted with a canting hypocrisy which would enlist those sympathies on false pretences. The Undersigned are, however, not insensible to the surmise that the Lincoln Government may, under stress of circumstances, change its policy—a policy based at present more upon a wily view of what is to be its effect in rearing up an element in the Confederate States favourable to the re-construction of the Union than upon any honest desire to uphold a Constitution the main provisions of which it has most shamelessly violated. But they confidently submit to your Lordship's consideration, that success in producing so abrupt and violent a destruction of a system of labour which has reared up so vast a commerce between America and the great States of Europe, which, it is supposed, now gives bread to ten millions of the population of those States, which, it may be safely assumed, is intimately blended with the basis of the great manufacturing and navigating prosperity that distinguishes the age, and that probably not the least of the elements of this prosperity would be visited with results disastrous to the world, as well as to the master and slave.

Resort to servile war has, it is true, as we have heretofore stated, not been proclaimed, but officially abandoned. It has been, however, recommended by persons of influence in the United States, and when all other means shall fail, as the Undersigned assure your Lordship they will, to bring the Confederate States into subjection to the power of Mr. Lincoln's Government, it is by no means improbable that it may be inaugurated. Whenever it shall be done, however, the motive, it is now rendered clear, will not be that high philanthropic consideration which undoubtedly beats in the hearts of many in England, but the base feeling of selfish aggrandisement, not unmixed with a cowardly spirit of revenge.

The Undersigned call your Lordship's attention to what is now so publicly known as a fact—to the great battle of Bull's Run, three miles in front of Manassas Junction, in which a well-appointed army of 55,000 Federal soldiers gave battle to the Confederate States' army of inferior force. After nine hours' hard fighting the Federalists were defeated and driven from the field in open flight, and were pursued by the Confederate States' army to Centreville, the position of the Federal reserve. The enemy lost honour, and nearly all the arms and munitions of war which had been so industriously gathered together for months for an offensive campaign in Virginia; and they did not cease their flight until, under cover of a stormy night, they had regained the shelter of their entrenchments in front of Washington. The Confederate States' forces have commenced offensive movements, and have driven the vaunting hosts of the United States behind entrenchments upon the borders of Virginia, and so far from threatening the integrity of the territory and the existence of the Government of the Confederate States, the Government at Washington seems content at present, and will be rejoiced, if it can maintain a successful defence of its capital, and preserve the remnant of its defeated and disorganized forces.

The Undersigned would also ask your Lordship's attention to the fact, that the cotton-picking season in the cotton-growing States of the Confederacy has commenced. The crop bids fair to be at least an average one, and will be prepared for market and delivered by our planters and merchants as usual, on the wharves of the ports of those States, when there shall be a prospect of the blockade being raised, and not before. As a defensive measure, an embargo has been laid by the Government of the Confederate States upon the passage of cotton by inland conveyance to the United States. To be obtained, it must be sought for in the Atlantic and Gulf ports of those States. They submit to your Lordship the consideration of the fact that the blockade of all the ports of the Confederate States was declared to have commenced by the blockading officer off Charleston, when, in truth, at that time, and for weeks after, there was no pretence of a blockade of the ports in the Gulf. They further submit for consideration, that since the establishment of the blockade there have been repeated instances of vessels breaking it at Wilmington, Charleston, Savannah, Mobile, and New Orleans. It will be for the neutral Powers, whose commerce has been so seriously damaged, to determine how long such a blockade shall be permitted to interfere with their commerce.

In closing this communication the Undersigned desire to urge upon Her Britannic Majesty's Government the just claim which, in their opinion, the Government of the Confederate States has at this time to a recognition as a Government *de facto;* whether its internal peace, or its territory, its population, its great resources for both domestic and foreign commerce, and its power to maintain itself, are considered; or, whether your Lordship shall take into consideration the necessity of commercial relations being established with it, with a view to the preservation of vast interests of the commerce of England. If, however, in the opinion of Her Britannic Majesty's Government, the Confederate States have not yet won a right to a place among the nations of the earth, the Undersigned can only assure your Lordship that while such an announcement will be received with surprise by the Government they represent, and while that Government is to be left to contend for interests which, it thinks, are as important to commercial Europe as to itself, without even a friendly countenance from other nations, its citizens will buckle themselves to the great task before them with a vigour and determination that will justify the Undersigned in having pressed the question upon Her Britannic Majesty's Government; and when peace shall have been made, their Government will at least feel that it will not be justly responsible for the vast quantity of blood which shall have been shed, nor for the great and wide-spread suffering which so prolonged a conflict will have entailed upon millions of the human race, both in the Eastern as well as upon the North American continent.

The Undersigned, &c.

(Signed)   W. L. YANCEY.
P. A. ROST.
A. DUDLEY MANN.

Inclosure in No. 74.

Extract from United States' Census, 1850.

	Non-Slave-holding States.	Slave-holding States.
1. Population	13,330,418	Whites 6,222,418 Blacks 3,204,313
2. Annual value of manufactures, mining, and mechanical arts .. Dollars	845,430,428	167,906,035
3. Cotton .. .. Bales	..	2,445,793*
4. Improved acres of land	58,312,733	54,399,455
5. Average value of farming utensils on each farm .. .. .. Dollars	95	171
6. Horses and mules . .. .. Number	2,290,840	2,570,480
7. Neat cattle . .. . ,,	8,557,786	9,527,915
8. Swine .. .. ,,	9,507,745	20,787,000
9. Wheat, annually .. .. .. Bushels	74,264,580	26,894,000
10. Indian corn .. .. .. ,,	242,718,000	348,992,261
11. Cane sugar .. .. .. Lbs.	..	237,133,000
12. Molasses .. .. Gallons	..	12,700,091
13. Rice .. .. Lbs.	..	215,913,500
14. Tobacco .. .. ,,	14,760,000	185,083,000
15. Salt, annually .. .. .. Bushels	6,029,450	3,754,390

* Crop of 1860, about 4,700,000 bales.

NOTE.—The census of the United States for 1860, now in course of publication, will undoubtedly show an increase of at least 33 per cent. of these resources.

The Report published by the Congress of the United States showing their commerce and navigation for the year ending June 1860, shows that the entire exports for that year were 373,189,274 dollars, of which sum the value of the exports produced exclusively in the South were 247,542,078 dollars, of which 206,779,799 dollars were exported through Southern ports.

No. 75.

Mr. Adams to Earl Russell.—(Received August 15.)

My Lord,   *Legation of the United States, London, August* 15, 1861.

FROM information furnished from sources which appear to me entitled to credit, I feel it my duty to apprize Her Majesty's Government that a violation of the Act prohibiting the fitting out of vessels for warlike purposes is on the point of being committed in one of the ports of Great Britain, whereby an armed steamer is believed to be about to be dispatched with the view of making war against the people of the United States.

It is stated to me that a new screw-steamer called the "Bermuda," ostensibly owned by the commercial house of Fraser, Trenholm, and Levy, of Liverpool, well known to consist in part of Americans in sympathy with the insurgents in the United States, is now lying at West Hartlepool ready for sea. She is stated to carry English colours, but to be commanded by a Frenchman. She is two-masted, brig-rigged, lower part of funnel black, and upper part red; black hull, with a narrow red stripe round the moulding level with the deck; no poop; wheel-house painted white; six white boats slung in iron davits. She has neither figure-head nor bowsprit. Her bottom is painted pink up to the water-line.

This steamer is armed with four guns, and she has been for some time taking in crates, cases, and barrels, believed to contain arms and ammunition of all kinds ordinarily used in carrying on war.

This cargo is nominally entered as destined to Havana, in the Island of Cuba; but her armament and cargo are of such a nature as to render it morally certain that the merchants who claim to be the owners can have no intention of despatching her on any errand of mercy or of peace.

I am informed that this vessel will sail in a day or two. I therefore feel under the highest obligation to submit the information I have obtained, as the ground for an application for a prompt and effective investigation of the truth of the allegations whilst there is time. Not doubting the earnest disposition of Her Majesty's Government faithfully to adhere to the principles of neutrality to which it has pledged itself, I ask, on the part of the United States, for no more than a simple enforcement of the law, in case it shall appear that evil-minded persons are seeking to set it at naught.

I pray, &c.
(Signed)   CHARLES FRANCIS ADAMS.

No. 76.

Earl Russell to Mr. Adams.

Sir, Foreign Office, August 15, 1861.

I HAVE the honour to acknowledge the receipt of your letter of this day calling the attention of Her Majesty's Government to a steam-vessel now fitting out at Hartlepool, which you state it is believed is about to be despatched with a view of making war against the people of the United States; and I have to acquaint you that I have lost no time in communicating with the proper Department of Her Majesty's Government on this subject.

I am, &c.
(Signed) RUSSELL.

No. 77.

Earl Russell to Mr. Adams.

Sir, Foreign Office, August 22, 1861.

I ACQUAINTED you in my letter of the 15th instant that I had lost no time in communicating with the proper Department of Her Majesty's Government respecting the steam-vessel fitting out at Hartlepool, which you believed was about to be despatched with a view of making war against the people of the United States.

I have now the honour to state to you that the result of the inquiries into this case having been submitted to the proper Law Officer of the Crown, Her Majesty's Government have been advised that there is not sufficient evidence to warrant any interference with the clearance or the sailing of the vessel.

The 7th Section of the Foreign Enlistment Act, 59 Geo. III, cap. 69, applies to the equipment of a vessel for the purpose of being employed in the service of a foreign State as a transport or cruizer, but has no reference to the mere nature of the cargo on board, and there is at present no proved intention that the vessel itself is to be employed for a warlike purpose.

The persons engaged in the venture must take the consequences which, according to the law of nations, may happen to ensue during transit, owing to a portion of the cargo loaded by them being contraband of war.

I am, &c.
(Signed) RUSSELL.

No. 78.

Earl Russell to Messrs. Yancey, Rost, and Mann.

Foreign Office, August 24, 1861.

THE Undersigned has had the honour to receive the letter of the 14th instant, addressed to him by Messrs. Yancey, Rost, and Mann, on behalf of the so-styled Confederate States of North America.

The British Government do not pretend in any way to pronounce a judgment upon the questions in debate between the United States and their adversaries in North America; the British Government can only regret that these differences have unfortunately been submitted to the arbitrement of arms. Her Majesty has considered this contest as constituting a civil war, and her Majesty has, by Her Royal Proclamation, declared her intention to preserve a strict neutrality between the contending parties in that war.

Her Majesty will strictly perform the duties which belong to a neutral. Her Majesty cannot undertake to determine by anticipation what may be the issue of the contest, nor can she acknowledge the independence of the nine States which are now combined against the President and Congress of the United States until the fortune of arms or the more peaceful mode of negotiation shall have more clearly determined the respective positions of the two belligerents.

Her Majesty can, in the meantime, only express a hope that some adjustment satisfactory to both parties may be come to, without the calamities which must ensue in the event of an embittered and protracted conflict.

The Undersigned, &c. (Signed) RUSSELL.

No. 79.

Lord Lyons to Lord J. Russell.—(Received August 26.)

My Lord, Washington, *August* 12, 1861.

I HAVE the honour to inclose a copy of an Act of Congress approved on the 5th of August, directing that any vessel or boat built or purchased for piratical purposes shall be seized on the high seas, or in any port of the United States, whether the same shall have actually sailed upon any piratical expedition or not.

Your Lordship is aware that by President Lincoln's Proclamation of the 19th April last, Southern privateers are declared to be amenable to the laws of the United States for the prevention and punishment of piracy.

I have, &c.
(Signed) LYONS.

Inclosure in No. 79.

An Act supplementary to an Act entitled " An Act to Protect the Commerce of the United States, and punish the Crime of Piracy."

BE it enacted by the Senate and House of Representatives of the United States of America in Congress assembled, that any vessel or boat which shall be built, purchased, fitted out, in whole or in part, or held for the purpose of being employed in the commission of any piratical aggression, search, restraint, depredation, or seizure, or in the commission of any other act of piracy, as defined by the law of nations, shall be liable to be captured and brought into any port of the United States if found upon the high seas, or to be seized if found in any port or place within the United States, whether the same shall have actually sailed upon any piratical expedition or not, and whether any act of piracy shall have been committed or attempted upon or from such vessel or boat, or not; and any such vessel or boat may be adjudged and condemned, if captured by a vessel authorized as hereinafter mentioned, to the use of the United States and to that of the captors, and if seized by a Collector, Surveyor, or Marshal, then to the use of the United States, after due process and trial, in like manner as is provided in section 4 of the Act to which this Act is supplementary, which section is hereby made in all respects applicable to cases arising under this Act.

Section 2. And be it further enacted, that the President of the United States be and hereby is authorized to instruct the Commanders of the public armed vessels of the United States, and to authorize the Commanders of any other armed vessels sailing under the authority of any letters of marque and reprisal granted by the Congress of the United States, or the Commanders of any other suitable vessels, to subdue, seize, take, and, if on the high seas, to send into any port of the United States any vessel or boat built, purchased, fitted out, or held, as in the first section of this Act mentioned.

Section 3. And be it further enacted, that the Collectors of the several ports of entry, the Surveyors of the several ports of delivery, and the Marshals of the several judicial districts within the United States be and are hereby authorized and required to seize any and all vessels or boats built, purchased, fitted out, or held as aforesaid, which may be found within their respective ports or districts, and to cause the same to be proceeded against and disposed of as hereinbefore provided.

Approved, August 5, 1861.

No. 80.

Lord Lyons to Lord J. Russell.—(Received August 26.)

My Lord, Washington *August* 12, 1861.

CONGRESS adjourned on the 6th instant without passing the joint Resolution to approve and confirm the acts of the President for suppressing insurrection and rebellion.

I had the honour to transmit a copy of this Resolution to your Lordship in my despatch of the 12th ultimo.* It was introduced into the Senate at the beginning of the Session, and would perhaps have been passed had it been vigorously pushed forward at

* No. 64.

once; but every time it came up for debate, its opponents seemed to increase in number and strength, and at last the Senate separated without coming to a vote upon it.

Men who thought the President justified in taking the measures under the circumstances doubted whether Congress had, under the Constitution, the power to declare them lawful. The few members of the Opposition denounced them as inexcusable violations of the Constitution and the laws, which should bring on the President the penalties of impeachment.

Laws were passed calculated to prevent any practical inconvenience arising at present from the want of a formal confirmation of the President's acts, and it seems to have been deemed prudent not to push the Resolution to a vote.

It was in virtue of this Resolution that the legality of the blockade was to be maintained. It is believed, however, that this is now provided for by a clause, added to an Act on another subject, and providing that all the Proclamations and acts of the President relative to the army and navy be approved and legalized. It is supposed that this may suffice to give legal validity to the Proclamations of the 19th and 27th April, by which the blockades were ordained.

I have, &c.
(Signed)   LYONS.

No. 81.

Lord Lyons to Lord J. Russell.—(Received August 26.)

My Lord,   *Washington, August* 12, 1861.

I CALLED upon Mr. Seward this morning at the State Department, and said to him, in the words of your Lordship's despatch of the 19th ultimo, that Her Majesty's Government "would consider a decree closing the ports of the South actually in possession of the insurgent or Confederate States as null and void, and that they would not submit to measures taken on the high seas in pursuance of such decree."

I proceeded to say that I was instructed to communicate this decision to the Government of the United States, and that M. Mercier, the French Minister, had similar instructions from his Government. I added that having been made aware by confidential conversations with Mr. Seward, that he himself considered that it would not be at this moment expedient for the United States' Government to issue the Proclamation closing the ports, I was willing to leave it to him to decide whether a more formal communication would be desirable or not. I must beg him, however, to regard the statement I had made as a distinct announcement of the determination of Her Majesty's Government. I was willing to stop there, or to make a written declaration, as he thought best.

Mr. Seward thanked me very much for the consideration I had shown; and begged me to confine myself for the present to the verbal announcement I had just made. He said that it would be difficult for me to draw up a written communication which would not have the air of a threat; that just now this might have an unfortunate effect; but that he would ask me hereafter to make a more formal declaration, if it should seem advisable.

I told Mr. Seward that I should always be glad to strengthen his hands in opposing a measure so fraught with danger to the cordial relations between our two Governments, as would be the issuing of the Proclamation declaring the ports to be closed; and I assured him that I was very willing to be guided by his superior knowledge of the feelings of the Government and the country.

Mr. Seward gave me to understand that the question of issuing the Proclamation was dropped for the moment, but he hinted that there were influential persons who were anxious to moot it again.

It was in pursuance of an understanding which I had come to with M. Mercier that I sought this interview with Mr. Seward, and that I spoke to him in the language which I have described. M. Mercier being necessarily in attendance upon Prince Napoleon, was unable himself to hold any long conversation with Mr. Seward before setting out for New York. He had, however, an interview with me on the morning of his departure, at which we agreed on the course to be pursued during his absence.

I have, &c.
(Signed)   LYONS

P.S.—I have caused this despatch to be read to M. de Geoffroy, the First Secretary of the French Legation, in order to enable him to inform M. Mercier accurately of what passed between Mr. Seward and me.

No. 82.

Earl Russell to Lord Lyons.

My Lord,   *Foreign Office, August* 27, 1861.
    HER Majesty's Government approve your proceedings, as reported in your despatch of the 12th instant,* in reference to the announcement which you were instructed to make to the United States' Government, that Her Majesty's Government would not recognize the Decree of Congress closing the Southern ports.
                                                                         I am, &c.
                                                     (Signed)   RUSSELL.

No. 83.

Lord Lyons to Earl Russell.—(Received September 2.)

My Lord,   *Washington, August* 19, 1861.
    I HAVE the honour to inclose a copy, taken from a newspaper, of a Proclamation of the President of the United States, dated the 16th instant, and prohibiting commercial intercourse with the Seceded States. No more authentic copy can at present be procured.
    The Proclamation is issued in virtue of the 5th section of the "Act further to provide for the Collection of Duties on Imports, and for other purposes," of which I had the honour to transmit a copy to your Lordship in my despatch of the 19th ultimo.
    It is the same Act which empowers the President to collect duties on ship-board, and to close ports of entry, but the present Proclamation does not appear to extend to either of those two points.
                                                               I have, &c.
                                                   (Signed)   LYONS.

Inclosure in No. 83.

Proclamation by the President of the United States of America.

    WHEREAS, on the 15th day of April, 1861, the President of the United States, in view of an insurrection against the Laws, Constitution, and Government of the United States, which had broken out within the States of South Carolina, Georgia, Alabama, Florida, Mississippi, Louisiana, and Texas, and in pursuance of the Act entitled "An Act to provide for calling forth the Militia to execute the Laws of the Union, suppress Insurrection, and repel Invasion, and to repeal the Act now in force for that purpose," approved February 28, 1795, did call forth the Militia to suppress said insurrection and to cause the laws of the Union to be duly executed, and the insurgents have failed to disperse by the time directed by the President; and whereas such insurrection has since broken out, and yet exists, within the States of Virginia, North Carolina, Tennessee, and Arkansas; and whereas the insurgents in all the said States claim to act under the authority thereof, and such claim is not disclaimed or repudiated by the person exercising the functions of Government in such State or States, or in the part or parts thereof in which such combinations exist, nor has such insurrection been suppressed by said States:
    Now therefore I, Abraham Lincoln, President of the United States, in pursuance of an Act of Congress approved July 13, 1861, do hereby declare that the inhabitants of the said States of Georgia, South Carolina, Virginia, North Carolina, Tennessee, Alabama, Louisiana, Texas, Arkansas, Mississippi, and Florida (except the inhabitants of that part of the State of Virginia lying west of the Alleghany mountains, and of such other parts of that State and the other States hereinbefore named, as may maintain a loyal adhesion to the Union and the Constitution, or may be, from time to time, occupied and controlled by forces of the United States engaged in the dispersion of said insurgents), are in a state of insurrection against the United States; and that all commercial intercourse between the same, and the inhabitants thereof, with the exceptions aforesaid, and the citizens of other States and other parts of the United States, is unlawful, and will remain unlawful until such insurrection shall cease or has been suppressed; that all goods and chattels, wares and merchandize, coming from any of said States, with the exceptions aforesaid, into

* No. 81.

other parts of the United States, without the special license and permission of the President, through the Secretary of the Treasury, or proceeding to any of said States, with the exceptions aforesaid, by land or water, together with the vessel or vehicle conveying the same, or conveying persons to or from said States, with said exceptions, will be forfeited to the United States; and that from and after fifteen days from the issuing of this Proclamation, all ships and vessels belonging in whole or in part to any citizen or inhabitant of any of said States, with said exceptions, found at sea or in any port of the United States, will be forfeited to the United States; and 1 hereby enjoin upon all District Attorneys, Marshals, and officers of the revenue, and of the military and naval forces of the United States, to be vigilant in the execution of said Act, and in the enforcement of the penalties and forfeitures imposed or declared by it; leaving any party who may think himself aggrieved thereby to his application to the Secretary of the Treasury for the remission of the penalty or forfeiture, which the said Secretary is authorized by law to grant, if, in his judgment, the special circumstances of any case shall require such remission.

In witness whereof I have hereunto set my hand, and caused the seal of the United States to be affixed.

Done at the City of Washington, this 16th day of August, in the year of Our Lord 1861, and of the independence of the United States of America the eighty-sixth.

(Signed) ABRAHAM LINCOLN.

By the President:
(Signed) WM. H. SEWARD, *Secretary of State.*

No. 84.

Lord Lyons to Earl Russell.—(*Received September 2.*)

(Extract.) *Washington, August* 19, 1861.

THE serious alarm caused by the state of the finances has been in some degree dissipated by the result of the negotiation in which the Secretary of the Treasury has been engaged with the banks of New York, Boston, and Philadelphia.

These banks have agreed to take at par, Treasury bonds bonds bearing $7\frac{3}{10}$ per cent. interest, for 50,000,000 dollars (about 10,000,000*l.* sterling). They have reserved to themselves the option of taking 50,000,000 more on the 15th of October next, and 50,000,000 more on the 15th of December next. The Government pledges itself, if the two additional sums of 50,000,000 dollars are taken by the banks, not to issue any other Government stock or Treasury notes until the 2nd February, 1862, excepting Treasury notes payable on demand. The Government is, however, at liberty to raise a loan in Europe.

These and other conditions imposed by the banks are considered to be very onerous for the Government. I have the honour to inclose a copy of the details of the arrangement.

It is not satisfactory that while money can be easily obtained for 4 per cent. on good private security at New York, the Government should have so much difficulty in effecting a loan at $7\frac{3}{10}$ per cent.

Inclosure in No. 84.

Newspaper Extract.

THE GOVERNMENT LOAN.—As the negotiation of the National loan of 150,000,000 dollars, to which we alluded on Saturday last, belongs to the great events which mark the times through which we are passing, we give below the particulars of the terms and conditions on which it was concluded, that the whole subject may be placed clearly before the mind of every reader. We quote the official report of the Bank Convention, held in New York, as made at its final meeting in that city on Thursday last:—

" At a meeting of bank officers held at the American Exchange Bank on Thursday, August 15, 1861, at which thirty-nine banks of New York were represented, the following plan for assisting the United States' Government was unanimously adopted, the votes being taken by a call of names:—

" Section 1. An immediate issue to be made by the United States' Treasury Department of Treasury notes, dated August 15, 1861, bearing interest from that date at 7·30 per cent. to the extent of 50,000,000 dollars.

"Sec. 2. The banks of New York, Boston, and Philadelphia associated to take jointly this 50,000,000 dollars at par, with the privilege of taking at par an additional 50,000,000 dollars October 15th, by giving their decision to the Department October 1st; and also at par 50,000,000 dollars December 15th, by giving their decision December 1st, unless said amount shall have been previously subscribed as a national loan. It being understood and agreed that no other Government stock bonds or Treasury notes (except Treasury notes payable on demand, and the Oregon war loan) shall be negotiated or paid out by the Government until February 1, 1862, should the Associates avail of both privileges, or until December 15, 1861, should they avail of the first only, or until October 15, 1861, if they take but the present 50,000,000 dollars—except that the Government may negotiate in Europe, or through subscriptions to the national loan.

"Sec. 3. An appeal to the people for subscriptions to the national loan to be made by the Government, and as the subscriptions for the notes progress, and the moneys are paid in, the same shall be paid over to the Government, or deposited with banks selected by the Secretary of the Treasury, with the concurrence of a Committee of the Associates; and so much of the proceeds of said loan as shall be required for the purpose, shall be applied in reimbursement of the Associates for subscription, by them paid in, and not otherwise reimbursed. The Treasury notes issued to the Associates, so far as the New York banks are concerned, shall be received by the Loan Committee of New York Banks at 90 per cent., as a basis for using clearing-house certificates to any bank desiring, under the existing arrangement (which must necessarily be continued), and the subscription of the banks shall be in the proportion of capital, except that the interest and proportion of no one institution shall exceed one-tenth of the whole 50,000,000 dollars.

"Sec. 4. On the 1st of October should the Associates for any cause decide not to avail of the privilege of taking the second 50,000,000 dollars, then the balance of notes remaining of the 50,000,000 dollars already taken by them, shall be apportioned and divided among them (*pro rata*), and they shall make payment for their respective proportions.

"Sec. 5. Of the sums subscribed by the Associates, 10 per cent. shall be paid forthwith to the Assistant Treasurer at New York, Boston, or Philadelphia, and the residue shall be placed to the credit of the United States on the books of the banks subscribing. Certificates shall be issued to each subscriber, stating the amount so paid in and deposited, and as the deposits shall be withdrawn or paid into the Treasury (which shall be, as nearly as may be, in proportion of the several subscriptions), Treasury notes bearing 7·30 interest shall be issued in equal amounts to the subscribers respectively. And when the deposits shall be entirely paid to the United States, Treasury notes for the 10 per cent. originally paid shall also be issued, and all notes issued to such subscribers shall bear even date with the certificates, and carry interest from such date.

"Sec. 6. In part payment of deposits for the first 50,000,000 dollars, the Treasury Department will receive from the Associates any past due Treasury notes, or sixty days' Treasury notes. Should the second amount of 50,000,000 dollars be taken by the Associates, the Department will receive on account of deposits any Treasury notes outstanding except 7·30 per cent, notes.

"Sec. 7. The transaction on the part of the Associates may be conducted by a Committee in New York, in which the banks of Boston and Philadelphia should be represented, which Committee should meet daily for the direction of details, and at least weekly for deliberation and consideration of important business.

"Sec. 8. In addition to the banks of New York, Boston, and Philadelphia, it would be desirable that other parties should become associates and trust companies, savings' banks, insurance companies, and private bankers, who, in lieu of *pro rata* of capital should designate, when joining the Association, what amount of interest they decide to take.

"Sec. 9. The capital of the banks of New York, Boston, and Philadelphia, and the respective proportions under a *pro rata* division, would be as follows:—

	Bank capital.	Pro rata proportion of fifty millions.
"New York	$70,000,000	$29,500,000
"Boston	33,000,000	15,500,000
"Philadelphia	12,000,000	5,000,000"

No. 85.

Lord Lyons to Earl Russell.—(Received September 8.)

My Lord,   *Washington, August* 27, 1861.

IN obedience to the instructions contained in your Lordship's despatch of the 9th instant, I purpose to consult M. Mercier before determining whether or not to communicate to Mr. Seward your Lordship's despatch of the 8th instant, stating the views of Her Majesty's Government with regard to the Act of Congress empowering the President to close the Southern ports by proclamation.

M. Mercier is now absent from Washington in attendance upon His Imperial Highness Prince Napoleon; but he is expected to return at the end of the week.

I have, &c.
(Signed)   LYONS.

No. 86.

Earl Russell to Lord Lyons.

My Lord,   *Foreign Office, September* 19, 1861.

I HAVE referred to the Law Advisers of the Crown the Act of Congress inclosed in your despatch of the 12th of August, entitled "An Act supplementary to an Act entitled 'An Act to protect the commerce of the United States, and punish the crime of piracy,'" and I have to acquaint your Lordship that there does not at present seem to be any necessity for the intervention of Her Majesty's Government in relation thereto, provided the Act in its construction and application is limited to "piracy," as defined by the law of nations.

I am, &c.
(Signed)   RUSSELL.

No. 87.

Lord Lyons to Earl Russell.—(Received September 21.)

(Extract.)   *Washington, September* 6, 1861.

LATE on the 30th ultimo I received a telegram from Mr. Consul Archibald, requesting me to obtain an order for his admission to Fort Lafayette, to visit Mr. William Patrick, a British subject who had (it appears) been arrested and sent to that fortress. The order was immediately granted on my causing application for it to be made at the State Department.

I have the honour to inclose copies of correspondence on the subject.

Mr. John Patrick, brother of the Mr. William Patrick who is confined in Fort Lafayette, has come to Washington with very strong applications in behalf of his brother from influential supporters of the Administration at New York. He seems anxious that I should not address any official remonstrance to the United States' Government at this moment, lest my doing so should interfere with the steps which are being taken by his brother's private friends. I have, in consequence, consented to confine myself for the present to the unofficial representation (Inclosure 4) which I have made in order to obtain a diminution of the personal discomfort to which the prisoner has been exposed. As I have little or no hope that he would be released upon an official demand from me, I do not think it fair to him to lessen his chance of obtaining his freedom by private influence.

But I am seriously alarmed and distressed by the system of arbitrary arrest which appears to have been definitively adopted by this Government. British subjects seem to be not less exposed to it than American citizens. I believe it to be entirely illegal; but the case of Quillan, among many others, proves that it is vain to resort to the Courts of law for redress. I think it my duty to recommend the subject to the very serious consideration of Her Majesty's Government.

Inclosure 1 in No. 87.

Consul Archibald to Lord Lyons.

My Lord, New York, August 30, 1861.

I HAVE the honour to report to your Lordship that on Wednesday last, the 28th ultimo, Mr. William Patrick, a resident British merchant of this city, was summarily arrested by the Superintendent of Police without any legal warrant, and imprisoned at Fort Lafayette, where he still continues in the custody of the Commandant of that fort.

Mr. Patrick is a native of Scotland, and has never been naturalized in this country; he is a Director of the Merchants' Bank of New York, and is extensively engaged in business, having numerous correspondents in the Southern States. So far as I can ascertain, the cause of Mr. Patrick's arrest was the detention, at some place in Indiana, of a number of letters addressed to him, or to his care, from parties in the Southern States, in some of which letters it is supposed that expressions favourable to the cause of the insurgents are contained.

It is, however, well known to all who are acquainted with Mr. Patrick, that he is, and ever has been, a strong supporter of the Government of the United States; and I have every reason to believe that he has in no manner committed himself to any act or expression which can furnish evidence of conduct that ought to subject him to suspicion of affording aid or comfort to the insurgents. His friends here feel quite confident that an investigation of the complaint against him, whatever it may be (for as yet they are ignorant of its precise nature), will establish his innocence.

They are desirous that such investigation should take place with as little delay as possible. With the same view, several of the leading bankers and other influential members of the community, by whom Mr. Patrick is justly held in high esteem, propose to forward an application for his early examination to the Government at Washington. Such application will be conveyed by Mr. John Patrick (brother of Mr. William Patrick), who is likewise the bearer of this, and whom I beg leave to introduce to your Lordship, and request that your Lordship will have the goodness to take such steps as you may deem expedient towards procuring the speedy release of Mr. Patrick. Mr. Patrick was hurried off to prison without an opportunity of consulting with his friends, or with me, as to the course which he ought to pursue, and access to him has also been denied to his wife and brother.

It is but just that he should, at least, have an opportunity of communicating with me, and I have the honour to request that your Lordship will be pleased to obtain from the proper Department an order permitting me, as his Consul, to have access to him.

I have, &c.
(Signed) E. M. ARCHIBALD.

Inclosure 2 in No. 87.

Lord Lyons to Consul Archibald.

Sir, Washington, August 31, 1861.

I RECEIVED last night your telegram respecting William Patrick, and, in reply, send you herewith an order which I have procured from the State Department to enable you to visit Patrick at Fort Lafayette.

I am, &c.
(Signed) LYONS.

Inclosure 3 in No. 87.

Consul Archibald to Lord Lyons.

My Lord, New York, September 2, 1861.

I HAVE the honour to acknowledge the receipt of your Lordship's despatch of the 31st ultimo, inclosing an order from General Scott, permitting me to visit Mr. William Patrick, a prisoner at Fort Lafayette.

I visited Mr. Patrick this afternoon, and found that his sleeping-apartment was occupied by nine other prisoners, in common with himself, and in which they are locked up during the night. Mr. Patrick assured me that his health had greatly suffered in consequence, as was evident from his appearance, and begged me to endeavour to obtain an order for his removal to some other place of confinement, where he could have more privacy; and, at all events, be able to sleep at nights, which he finds impossible in the crowded room in which he is now confined.

Ascertaining at the central police-office this evening that any order for this purpose must come from Washington, I have the honour to request that your Lordship will be so good as to submit Mr. Patrick's request for the consideration of the proper Department.

Should his request be complied with, I have further to request that directions may, at the same time, be given for telegraphing the necessary order to New York.

I have, &c.
(Signed)   E. M. ARCHIBALD.

Inclosure 4 in No. 87.

Lord Lyons to Mr. Seward.

(Unofficial.)   *Washington, September* 5, 1861.

LORD LYONS presents his compliments to Mr. Seward, and ventures to ask his immediate attention to a matter of some urgency.

Mr. William Patrick, a British merchant established at New York, has been arrested and sent to Fort Lafayette. Without adverting on the present occasion to any other matter connected with the case, Lord Lyons makes an appeal to Mr. Seward's humanity in behalf of the health of the prisoner, which appears to be seriously endangered.

It seems that Mr. Patrick is locked up at night in a room with nine other prisoners, and that his health has already suffered greatly in consequence. He entreats that he may be removed to some place where he can have more privacy; and, at all events, be able to sleep at nights, which he finds impossible in the crowded room in which he is now confined.

It appears that an order from Washington is necessary for this purpose. Lord Lyons feels sure that Mr. Seward will be desirous to cause the order to be sent without delay; and he takes the liberty of suggesting that if it could be dispatched by telegraph this afternoon, Mr. Patrick might be saved from another sleepless night.

Inclosure 5 in No. 87.

Mr. Seward to Lord Lyons.

Department of State, Washington, September 5, 1861.

THE Secretary of State presents his compliments to Lord Lyons, and, with reference to his unofficial note of this date, has the honour to inform him that directions have been given in the proper quarter to extend to William Patrick any indulgence which his health may require, and which is not incompatible with his safe keeping.

Inclosure 6 in No. 87.

Lord Lyons to Consul Archibald.

Sir,   *Washington, September* 5, 1861.

I RECEIVED, only this morning, your despatch of the 2nd instant concerning the injury to which Mr. William Patrick's health is exposed by his close confinement in Fort Lafayette. I immediately entered into communication with the Secretary of State on the subject. At his suggestion, I wrote to him an unofficial letter concerning it.

I stated in the letter the substance of your despatch, and said that, without adverting, on the present occasion, to any other matter connected with the case, I made an appeal to his humanity in behalf of Mr. Patrick's health. In conclusion, I observed that, if proper orders were sent by telegraph to New York this afternoon, Mr. Patrick might be saved from another sleepless night.

I have just received in answer a letter from Mr. Seward, of which I inclose a copy. It states that directions have been given to extend to Mr. Patrick any indulgence which his health may require, and which is not incompatible with his safe keeping.

I have been in communication with Mr. John Patrick, the brother of Mr. William Patrick, the prisoner. He informs me that he has lost his valise, which contains (I suppose, among other papers) your original report to me of the arrest of Mr. William Patrick. He is confident of recovering the valise; but as I think it very doubtful whether he will do so in time to put me in possession of your despatch to-morrow, I beg you to forward a copy of it yourself to Earl Russell by the steamer which leaves New York on Saturday next, and to send a duplicate to me.

Mr. John Patrick appears to be desirous that I should avoid interfering with the steps which his brother's friends are privately taking to effect his release. I accordingly abstain from any further intervention at present.

I am, &c.
(Signed) LYONS.

No. 88.

Lord Lyons to Earl Russell.—(*Received September* 21.)
My Lord, *Washington, September* 6, 1861.

THE inclosed papers will make your Lordship acquainted with all the information which I possess concerning the arrest of Mr. John Christopher Rahming, another British subject who has been seized and sent to Fort Lafayette.

In compliance with Mr. Archibald's request, I defer taking any further steps in the matter until he has seen the prisoner.

The United States' Government assumes (and, so far as I can discover, without any warrant of law) the right to arrest persons in any part of the country, and to keep them during its pleasure in confinement in charge of the military officers. The Courts of Law are unable to give redress, as the officers of the army decline to make any return to writs of *habeas corpus*. The liability of British subjects to be treated in this arbitrary manner appears to me to be a matter of deep concern.

I have, &c.
(Signed) LYONS.

Inclosure 1 in No. 88.

Consul Archibald to Lord Lyons.

My Lord, *New York, September* 3, 1861.

I REGRET that I am obliged to report to your Lordship the arrest and imprisonment at Fort Lafayette of another British subject, under circumstances, so far as I can learn, of the grossest injustice.

Mr. John Christopher Rahming, a native of the Bahamas, and a member of the Legislative Assembly of that Colony, came to New York about six months since to establish himself as a commission merchant. He was, at 5 o'clock yesterday afternoon, summarily arrested by the police, and taken to the central office in Broome-street, where he could obtain no information whatever, verbal or written, as to the cause of his arrest. At 12 o'clock he was put into a cell, not long enough for him to lie down in, and in which there was merely a bench, and after spending a sleepless night, he was taken out at 9 this morning, and immediately sent off to Fort Lafayette. During the evening he mentioned to those who had him in custody that he was a British subject; and although I was myself at the police office, and saw the Superintendent at about half-past 8 last evening, in reference to Mr. Patrick, the arrest of Mr. Rahming was not reported to me. His friends who have called upon me assure me that Mr. Rahming's conduct and deportment here, both in his business and privately, have been such as could furnish no possible grounds for his arrest for any offence against the Government. The only cause to which he can suppose it to be attributable is the having shipped from Nassau and sent to New York, about six months since, two cannons, part of the wreck of the ship "Arctic," at Nassau, which his agent here, in the ordinary course of business, sold about six weeks since to a dealer in old iron, and which guns are still in this city. I cannot but regard, as I doubt not your Lordship will regard, this mode of seizing and imprisoning a British subject without the ordinary forms of law, and without even making known to him the cause of his imprisonment, as oppressive as it is arbitrary and illegal. I should at once protest, formally, against this proceeding, but that I believe the order for the arrest has been given with the sanction of the United States' Government, and I am enabled thus promptly to report the matter to your Lordship.

I have to request that your Lordship will be so good as to procure an order for my admission to Fort Lafayette, so that Mr. Rahming may have the benefit of my assistance as his Consul. In the meantime, I have instructed his clerk to lock up his books, papers, and effects, and in the event of any application or attempt by the police to obtain possession of them, to refer the applicants to me.

I have, &c.
(Signed) E. M. ARCHIBALD.

Inclosure 2 in No. 88.

Lord Lyons to Consul Archibald.

Sir, *Washington, September* 5, 1861.
AT a quarter before 4 o'clock, P.M., yesterday, I received a telegram from you in the following words:—
"New York, September 4.—Please do nothing respecting my No. 104, except procuring a pass, until you hear further from me."
An hour and a-half later, I received the despatch referred to (No. 104 of 3rd instant). I learned from it that Mr. John Christopher Rahming, a British subject had been arrested and sent to Fort Lafayette, and that you wished me to procure a pass to enable you to visit him there.
The Secretary of State has promised this morning, in compliance with a request from me, to despatch immediately to New York, by telegraph, orders to allow you access to Mr. Rahming.
In compliance with the desire expressed in your telegram, I shall abstain from taking any further steps until I hear again from you on the subject.

I am, &c.
(Signed) LYONS.

Inclosure 3 in No. 88.

Consul Archibald to Lord Lyons.

My Lord, *New York, September* 4, 1861.
I HAD the honour yesterday to report to your Lordship the arrest and imprisonment at Fort Lafayette of Mr. John D. Rahming, a British subject, without the observance of the ordinary forms of law.
The statement of the circumstances I received from his book-keeper and a friend of his, and as yet I have no knowledge that Mr. Rahming has been guilty of any offence deserving such harsh treatment.
I have to-day, however, seen other gentlemen belonging to the Bahamas who are resident here, and I gather from their statements that it is not improbable Mr. Rahming may, through his agents at Nassau, have been interested in some vessel which has violated the blockade.
His arrest, following so closely on the arrival of the mail by the "Karnak" from Nassau, they think it probable the United States' Consul at Nassau may have furnished intelligence which has led to Mr. Rahming's arrest. This is their supposition merely; and although the arbitrary manner in which Mr. Rahming has been imprisoned (no formal complaint being alleged, or at all events made known to him) demands explanation, yet before taking any steps to obtain redress, I think it advisable that I should see him, and hear his own story, taking, if necessary, his affidavit of facts and circumstances.

I have, &c.
(Signed) E. M. ARCHIBALD.

No. 89.

Earl Russell to Lord Lyons.

My Lord,   *Foreign Office, September* 28, 1861.

I AM much concerned to find, by your despatches of the 6th instant, that two more British subjects, Mr. Patrick and Mr. Rahming, have been subjected to arbitrary arrest; and although I learn from your telegraphic despatch that Mr. Patrick has since been released, yet I entirely agree with you that the subject requires the very serious consideration of Her Majesty's Government.

It appears that when British subjects as well as American citizens are arrested, they are immediately transferred to a military prison, and that the military authorities refuse to pay obedience to, or, indeed, to notice, a writ of *habeas corpus.*

This practice is directly opposed to the maxim of the Constitution of the United States, "that no person should be deprived of life, liberty, or property, without due process of law."

Her Majesty's Government are willing, however, to make every allowance for the hard necessities of a time of internal trouble, and they would not have been surprised if the ordinary securities of personal liberty had been temporarily suspended; nor would they have complained if British subjects falling under suspicion had suffered from the consequences of that suspicion.

But it does not appear that the Congress has sanctioned, in this respect, any departure from the due course of law, and it is in these circumstances that the Law Officers of the Crown have pronounced against the legality of the arbitrary arrests of British subjects.

So far as appears, the Secretary of State exercises, upon the reports of spies and informers, the power of depriving British subjects of their liberty, of retaining them in prison, or liberating them, by his sole will and pleasure.

It is obvious that this despotic and arbitrary power is inconsistent with the Constitution of the United States, is at variance with the Treaties of Amity subsisting between the two nations, and must tend to prevent the resort of British subjects to the United States for purposes of trade and industry.

I must instruct you, therefore, to remonstrate against such wanton proceedings, and to say that, in the opinion of Her Majesty's Government, the authority of Congress is necessary in order to justify the arbitrary arrest and imprisonment of British subjects.

                   I am, &c.
               (Signed)   RUSSELL.

No. 90.

Lord Lyons to Earl Russell.—(Received September 30.)

(Extract.)   *Washington, September* 16, 1861.

THE condition of the three Border States, Maryland, Kentucky, and Missouri, is very far from becoming more satisfactory.

It was apprehended that the Maryland Legislature, which was to meet this week, would vote the Secession of the State from the Union, and that upon this Confederate troops would cross the Potomac above or below the defences of Washington, and march to the support of their adherents at Baltimore. The Government has disconcerted one part of the plan by arresting ten of the principal members of the State Legislature, the Mayor of Baltimore, the editors of the three principal Opposition papers, and some other leading men; among these last is Mr. May, a member of the Congress of the United States. Recourse has also been had to petty vexations, such as those which have so often been the reproach of unskilful police authorities under absolute governments in Europe. A war has been made at Baltimore upon particular articles of dress, particular colours, portraits of Southern leaders, and other supposed symbols of disaffection. The violent measures which have been resorted to have gone far to establish the fact that Maryland is retained in the Union only by military force. They have undoubtedly increased the dislike of the people to their Northern rulers.

Alarm is felt lest Kentucky should become the scene of a petty but desolating civil war, like that which is going on in Missouri. The troops, both of the Union and of the Southern Confederation, have entered the State. An end is thus put to the neutrality which the Kentuckians sought to maintain. The hope which remains of saving the State from the fate of Missouri seems to lie in the inhabitants rallying at once to the Union cause.

The proceedings of the Legislature, which has recently assembled, are, if the accounts which reach us be correct, very promising. A series of strongly-worded Resolutions is stated to have passed both Houses, summoning the Confederates to quit the State, and calling upon the Government of the United States to assist in expelling them.

Mr. Magoffin, the Governor, is reported to have returned the Resolutions, with his veto; but the veto is stated to have been cancelled by a majority of two-thirds in each House. The newspapers this morning announce that the Governor has now, in obedience to the Resolutions, issued his Proclamation summoning the Confederate troops to retire. It is very much feared, however, lest the Secessionists in the State should refuse to acquiesce in the Acts of the Legislature, and should oppose them in arms.

I have had the honour to transmit to your Lordship a copy of a Proclamation of General Fremont, placing the State of Missouri under martial law, confiscating property, and bestowing freedom on slaves in certain cases. This Proclamation was displeasing to the President and many members of the Cabinet. It found little favour with moderate men in Missouri; indeed, strong remonstrances against the conduct of General Fremont were made to the Government here by the Union party in that State. They represented that while General Fremont was alienating moderate and constitutional men by his arbitrary proceedings, he was making no military progress. On the contrary, the Secession troops had obtained successes, and were advancing. An immense expenditure was incurred, but no adequate preparations were being made for the great expedition to descend the Mississippi, and restore the mouths of the river to the Union. The declaration concerning the liberation of the slaves was illegal, would give strength to the Disunion party in Kentucky, and shut the door to all hope of reconciliation with any party in the South.

The President appears to have signified privately to General Fremont his disapproval of the clause concerning slaves in the Proclamation. General Fremont seems, however, to have refused to modify it without a public order from the President. This order the President has now given. He has also sent a member of the Cabinet, Mr. Montgomery Blair, the Postmaster-General, to Missouri to arrange matters there.

Arbitrary proceedings, however, are by no means confined to Missouri. The Government at Washington, and, indeed, all the military Commanders, assume and exercise the right all over the coast to arrest any persons, to keep them in confinement without assigning any cause, and to impose such terms as they please as conditions of release. To give one instance, Mr. Berrett, the Mayor of Washington, who was arrested some time ago, has, it is believed, been informed that he will be kept in prison until he resigns the office of Mayor.

The applause with which each successive stretch of power is received by the people is a very alarming symptom to the friends of liberty and law. The case would be much less serious if, in consideration of the emergency, Congress had openly conferred upon the Executive Government certain defined extraordinary powers for a fixed time. The framers of the Constitution were, perhaps, wrong in not conferring upon Congress authority to increase, temporarily, the powers of the Executive. The Constitution does, however, authorize the suspension of the writ of *habeas corpus* in cases of rebellion or invasion; and if the writ had been duly suspended by Act of Congress, the arrests, at least, would have been legal: as it is, the writ is not even formally suspended by Proclamation of the President.

The decision of the banks with regard to taking a second 50,000,000 dollars of the loan is a matter of great moment. It is to be made on the 1st of next month. The ability of the bankers to contribute another 50,000,000 depends very much upon the amount of the original 50,000,000 taken last month, which is covered by the money collected from the people at large by the loan on the French plan, called the People's Loan. It is stated, however, that not more than 10,000,000 dollars (2,000,000*l.*) have yet been raised by it.

No. 91.

Mr. Adams to Earl Russell.—(*Received September* 30.)

Legation of the United States, London, September 30, 1861.

THE Undersigned, Envoy Extraordinary and Minister Plenipotentiary of the United States, regrets to be obliged to inform the Right Honourable Earl Russell, Her Majesty's Principal Secretary of State for Foreign Affairs, that he has been instructed by the President of the United States to prefer a complaint against the authorities of the Island of Trinidad for a violation of Her Majesty's Proclamation of neutrality by giving aid and encouragement to the insurgents of the United States.

It appears by an extract from a letter received at the Department of State from a gentleman believed to be worthy of credit, a resident of Trinidad, Mr. Francis Bernard, a copy of which is submitted herewith, that a steam-vessel known as an armed insurgent privateer, called the "Sumter," was received on the 30th of July last at that port, and was permitted to remain for six days, during which time she was not only furnished with all necessary supplies for the continuance of her cruise under the sanction of the Attorney-General, but that Her Majesty's flag was actually hoisted on the Government flag-staff in acknowledgment of her arrival.

The Undersigned has been directed by his Government to bring this extraordinary proceeding to the attention of Lord Russell, and in case it shall not be satisfactorily explained, to ask for the adoption of such measures as shall insure, on the part of the authorities of the said island, the prevention of all occurrences of the kind during the continuance of the difficulties in America.

The Undersigned deems it proper to add, in explanation of the absence of any official representation from Trinidad to substantiate the present complaint, that there was no Consul of the United States there at the time of the arrival of the vessel. The Undersigned had the honour a few days since, to apprize Lord Russell of the fact that this deficiency had been since supplied by preferring an application for Her Majesty's exequatur for a new Consul, who is already on his way to occupy his post.

The Undersigned, &c. (Signed) CHARLES FRANCIS ADAMS.

Inclosure in No. 91.

Mr. Bernard to Mr. Seward.

(Extract.) *Trinidad, August* 7, 1861.

I BEG to inform you that on the 30th ultimo, a steam-sloop of war (Semmes, Commander), carrying a Secession flag, five guns, some of a large calibre, and a crew of from 120 to 150 men, sailed boldly in our harbour and reported herself to the authorities of this island as being on a cruise. She was last from Puerto Cabello, and since she succeeded in getting out of the Mississippi river she has already captured no less than eleven American vessels. I have ascertained the names of some of them, viz., the "Joseph Maxwell," "Abe Bradford," "Minnie Miller," "Westwind of Westerly," with a cargo of sugar from Havana, and "Golden Rocket," which was burnt by her off the coast of Cuba.

The "Sumter" landed eight of her prisoners here in a destitute condition, but a contribution has been raised here for their benefit, sufficient to supply their immediate wants, and I will take care that they are provided for till an opportunity offers to ship them to the States.

The "Sumter" remained here till the 5th instant, and was allowed to supply herself with coals and other necessary outfits. The British flag was hoisted on the Government flag-staff for her arrival, and the officers of the British war-vessel "Cadmus" appeared to be on amicable terms with those of the "Sumter." The merchant who supplied the "Sumter" with coals did it with the consent and approval of our Attorney-General.

Being a loyal American, I consider it my duty to send you these informations, as there has been no Consul of our nation on this island for many months.

No. 92.

Mr. Adams to Earl Russell.—(*Received October* 2.)

My Lord, *Legation of the United States, London, October* 1, 1861.

IT is with much regret that I find myself receiving at every fresh arrival from the United States, instructions from my Government to make representations to your Lordship concerning alleged violations of Her Majesty's Proclamation of neutrality committed by British subjects, through the channel of the Colonies situated near the United States. I have the honour now to submit to your Lordship's consideration the copy of an intercepted letter from a person named John P. Baldwin, living at Richmond, in Virginia, in the service of the insurgents, addressed to Henry Adderley, Esq., of Nassau, New Providence. It appears by this letter, that Nassau has been made, to some extent, an entrepôt for the transmission of articles contraband of war, from Great Britain to the ports held by the insurgents.

It would be a great source of satisfaction to the Government of the United States to

M 2

learn that Her Majesty's Government felt itself clothed with the necessary power to prevent the exportation of such contraband from the Colonies for the use of the insurgents, and that it would furnish the necessary instructions to the local authorities to attain that end.

I pray, &c.
(Signed) CHARLES FRANCIS ADAMS.

Inclosure in No. 92.

Mr. Baldwin to Mr. Adderley.

My dear Adderley, *Richmond, Virginia, July* 30, 1861.

THE Secretary of the Navy of the Confederate States of America has ordered from England, to be shipped to Nassau, a quantity of arms and powder. I have recommended them to be consigned to you, and I have to ask of you, as a favour to me, to take good care of them.

I will be with you soon, and will expect your aid in transhipping the same.

I must request you to regard this as a confidential communication, and will explain the reasons when we meet. You need not write me on the subject.

Hoping soon to see you, I remain, &c.
(Signed) JNO. P. BALDWIN.

No. 93.

Earl Russell to Lord Lyons.

My Lord, *Foreign Office, October* 3, 1861.

I HAVE had under my consideration, and have referred to the proper Law Adviser of the Crown, your despatch of the 18th of August last, inclosing a Proclamation issued by the President of the United States prohibiting commercial intercourse with the Seceded States; and I have to acquaint you that this Proclamation appears to Her Majesty's Government to be within the competence of the President, and in conformity with the law and usage of nations.

The existence of a war between two Governments implies and involves, in theory, and in the contemplation of international law, the existence of a war between all the individuals voluntarily domiciled within the territory of either Government, which is supposed to represent and act for all such persons; and one of the immediate consequences of war is the entire interdiction of all commercial dealing between the subjects, citizens, or domiciled inhabitants of the belligerents, excepting by the formal and special license or permission of their Government: with this exception, "war" places every individual living within the territory of either Government, as well as the Governments themselves, in a state of hostility, legally and internationally; and trading with the inhabitants of the enemy's territory is "trading with the enemy." These principles have been constantly applied by this country and other foreign Powers, when belligerents.

The fact that the war now existing in North America may, in a certain sense, be viewed as a civil war, and that the President speaks of "the insurrection" of the particular States named in the Proclamation, does not appear to Her Majesty's Government to make any very material or practical difference, more especially as Her Majesty's Government, and all other Governments, have treated both parties as "belligerents engaged against each other in regular war," and consider themselves as "neutrals" internationally. It does not appear to Her Majesty's Government, therefore, that the issuing of this Proclamation requires any international notice on their part.

It remains to be seen how the "forfeiture to the United States" (imposed by the Proclamation) is to be enforced, and carried out in practice, whether by legal proceedings in Court or otherwise, upon which point your Lordship will, doubtless, send further information.

I am, &c.
(Signed) RUSSELL.

No. 94.

Earl Russell to Mr. Adams.

Foreign Office, October 4, 1861.

THE Undersigned has had the honour to receive a complaint from Mr. Adams against the authorities of the Island of Trinidad for a violation of Her Majesty's Proclamation of Neutrality, by giving aid and encouragement to the insurgents of the United States.

It appears from the accounts received at the Colonial Office and at the Admiralty, that a vessel bearing a Secession flag entered the port of Trinidad on the 30th of July last.

Captain Hillyar, of Her Majesty's ship "Cadmus," having sent a boat to ascertain her nationality, the commanding officer showed a commission signed by Mr. Jefferson Davis, calling himself the President of the so-styled Confederate States.

The "Sumter," which was the vessel in question, was allowed to stay six days in Trinidad, and to supply herself with coals and provisions, and the Attorney-General of the Island perceived no illegality in these proceeding.

The Law Officers of the Crown have reported that the conduct of the Governor was in conformity to Her Majesty's Proclamation.

No mention is made by the Governor of his hoisting the British flag on the Government flag-staff, and if he did so, it was apparently in order to show the national character of the island, and not in acknowledgment of the arrival of the "Sumter."

There does not appear, therefore, any reason to believe that Her Majesty's Proclamation of Neutrality has been violated by the Governor of Trinidad or by the commanding officer of Her Majesty's ship "Cadmus."

The Undersigned, &c. (Signed) RUSSELL.

No. 95.

Lord Lyons to Earl Russell.—(Received October 7.)

(Extract.) *Washington, September* 23, 1861.

I HAVE the honour to inclose a copy of a circular letter of the Secretary of State which has been published in the newspapers. It is apparently designed to relieve apprehensions which were entertained that an inquisitorial search was to be made for property belonging to the inhabitants of the Southern States, with a view to confiscating it under Acts of Congress passed last Session. It was even feared that the books of merchants and bankers would be examined, and that balances due to Southern customers, or securities belonging to them, would be confiscated.

Inclosure in No. 95.

Circular addressed by Mr. Seward to the Marshals and District Attorneys of the United States.

Sir, *Department of State, Washington, September* 21, 1861.

IN order to prevent seizures of property belonging to citizens of insurrectionary States, not warranted by the Acts of Congress relating to that subject, it is thought advisable to direct the special attention of Marshals and District Attorneys of the United States to the provisions of these Acts.

The 5th section of the Act of July 13 provides that all goods and chattels, wares, and merchandize, coming from or proceeding to a State or place declared to be in insurrection, together with the vessel or vehicle conveying the same, or conveying persons to or from such State or place, shall be forfeited to the United States.

This section obviously applies to all property in transit, or purchased, or provided with a view to transit, between loyal and disloyal States, and especially to property forming the subject of commercial intercourse. Such property, wherever found, is liable to seizure, and the only redress of parties who think themselves aggrieved, is by appeal to the Secretary of the Treasury, who is invested by and with full power of mitigation and remission.

The 1st section of the Act, approved August 6th, declares, "that if any person or persons, his, her, or their agent, attorney, or employee, shall purchase, or acquire, sell or give any property of whatsoever kind or description, with intent to use or employ the same, or suffer the same to be used or employed in aiding or abetting or promoting such insurrection, . . . or any person or persons engaged therein ; or if any person or persons, being the owners of any such property, shall knowingly use or employ, or suffer the use or employment of the same as aforesaid, all such property is hereby declared to be lawful subject of prize and capture wherever found."

No doubt can be entertained that this section was well considered, and that its operation was intended to be limited to property used in furtherance of the insurrection only.

Seizures under the Act of July 13 should be made by the officers, or under the direction of the officers of the Treasury Department, and all District Attorneys and Marshals of the United States should afford all practicable counsel and aid in the execution of the law.

Seizures under the Act of August 6 should be made by the Marshal of the district in which such property may be found, under the general or particular direction of the District Attorney, or other superior authority. For such seizures there is no power of mitigation or remission in the Secretary of the Treasury, but the District Attorney, or other superior authority, may direct the discontinuance of any proceeding in relation thereto, and the restoration of the property seized.

It will be seen, from an inspection of the Acts of Congress, that no property is confiscated or subjected to forfeiture except such as is in transit, or provided for transit, to and from insurrectionary States, or used for the promotion of the insurrection. Real estate, bonds, promissory notes, moneys on deposit, and the like, are therefore not subject to seizure or confiscation in the absence of evidence of such unlawful use. All officers, while vigilant in the prevention of the conveyance of property to or from the United States, or the use of it for insurrectionary purposes, are expected to be careful in avoiding unnecessary vexation and cost by seizures not warranted by law.

(Signed)   WILLIAM H. SEWARD, *Secretary of State.*

No. 96.

Earl Russell to Mr. Adams.

Sir,   *Foreign Office, October* 8, 1861.

I HAVE had the honour to receive your letter of the 1st instant, inclosing a copy of an intercepted letter from a person named J. P. Baldwin, living in Richmond, Virginia, addressed to Henry Adderley, Esq., of Nassau, New Providence, from which you infer that Nassau has been made, to some extent, an entrepôt for the transmission of contraband of war from Great Britain to the so-called Confederate States; and I have to acquaint you that I have requested the Secretary of State for the Colonies to cause every inquiry to be made into the matter.

I am, &c.
(Signed)   RUSSELL.

No. 97.

Lord Lyons to Earl Russell.—(Received October 14.)

(Extract.)   *Washington, September* 30, 1861.

THE packet which conveys this despatch will, probably, take to Europe the intelligence that the bankers have agreed to take the second 50,000,000 of the loan. Their decision is to be given to-morrow. Little doubt is entertained that it will be favourable; and it is confidently expected that the banks will also take the third 50,000,000 in December. In the meantime the expenditure goes on increasing at a rate which Congress will be called upon to meet by extraordinary measures when the session opens in that month. The regular expenses amount already to, at least, 7,000,000 dollars a-week.

No. 98.

Lord Lyons to Earl Russell.—(Received October 21.)

My Lord,   Washington, October 8, 1861.

A MORE considerable expedition than any yet despatched to act upon the coast of the Southern States is believed to be about to set sail from Chesapeake Bay. The troops embarked will, it is stated, amount to upwards of 10,000. The precise destination of the expedition has not yet become public. The occupation, however, of the port and town of Savannah in Georgia, or of some other port conveniently situated for the exportation of cotton, is very generally supposed to be aimed at.

It is, indeed, well known to have been for some time the purpose of this Government to obtain, if possible, possession of one of the Southern ports before the end of the season for shipping cotton.

It is hoped that if this could be accomplished, a Union Party would immediately show itself in the South, and that this party would be swelled by many whose interest it would be to export cotton through the port seized, which would be the only one open. By this means, too, the manufacturers in the Northern States would obtain their supply of this most important staple, and the danger be escaped that the lack of it will compel the European Powers to interfere in the quarrel.

These calculations rest upon two suppositions, neither of which can be said to be certain, or even very probable.

It is, in the first place, taken for granted that there still exists a Union Party in the Southern States, which only requires encouragement to appear in strength. This may be so; but there have hitherto been no symptoms that any Union Party has survived the rupture and the breaking out of actual hostilities. No such party has yet been seen to greet the appearance of the Union forces in any place in the South which they have hitherto been able to reach.

In the second place it is presumed that the temptation to sell their cotton would be strong enough to overcome the political passions of a large number of the men of influence in the South; that all the rest of the coast being strictly blockaded, they would rather bring their produce down to a port in the hands of the United States than not bring it to market at all; that they would rather receive articles of which they are greatly in need through such a port than do without them altogether.

It seems very doubtful, however, whether this would be the case. The Southern Congress, have, indeed, refused to confirm the prohibition to carry cotton down to the coast at all. But their object appears to have been to afford facilities for running it through the blockade; and with this view they have thrown their whole coast open to trade, without any impediment from Customs' regulations. But even this appears to be more than public opinion sanctions. Mr. Bunch reports that a mercantile house at Charleston is prevented "by the outside pressure" from sending to England a cargo of cotton in a vessel which has arrived after running the blockade. At another port, Wilmington in North Carolina, Mr. Bunch states that several British vessels are hindered from loading by a self-constituted Committee of Safety. Men who ought to know the Southern feeling well, declare that the owners of cotton would rather burn their cotton on their plantations than send it to a port in the occupation of the United States.

I am afraid, therefore, that very little reliance should be placed by European nations upon obtaining a supply of cotton in consequence of the capture by the United States of a Southern port. Still it seems well that this Government should, if possible, put the feelings of the Southern people to the test.

So considerable a success as the seizure and occupation of a port may perhaps not be attained, or if attained may not have the consequences which are hoped. Still these expeditions to various points of the coast appear to be, at all events, judicious military operations. They distract the attention of the enemy's leaders; they cause a wide-spread alarm; they render the individual States less willing to send their fighting men from home to keep up the numbers of the armies on the frontier.

                        I have, &c.
                   (Signed)   LYONS.

No. 99.

Lord Lyons to Earl Russell.—(*Received October* 28.)

My Lord, Washington, *October* 12, 1861.

I HAVE the honour to transmit to your Lordship copies of a despatch and its inclosures which I have received from the Governor-General of Canada, concerning a violation of the British territory, which appears to have been committed by a party of United States' soldiers in pursuit of deserters.

I have also the honour to inclose a copy of a note on the subject which I have addressed to Mr. Seward. I have not yet received any answer from Mr. Seward.

I have, &c.
(Signed) LYONS.

Inclosure 1 in No. 99.

Sir E. Head to Lord Lyons.

My Lord, Quebec, *October* 1, 1861.

I HAVE the honour to forward to your Excellency the annexed paragraph, cut from a provincial newspaper. On reading this notice I caused the telegram of September 30th to be sent to the Sheriff for Essex, to which I have this day received the answer of October 1st.

The newspaper account appears exaggerated, as such things often are ; but if soldiers of the United States' army are to pursue deserters into Canada, it will probably be necessary for me to increase the number of troops in Western Canada very materially.

I have no doubt that the Government at Washington will view with great regret any proceeding of this kind, and will express their disapprobation of the officer's conduct.

I have, &c.
(Signed) EDMUND HEAD.

Inclosure 2 in No. 99.

Mr. Alleyn to Mr. McEwen.

(Telegraphic.) Quebec, *September* 3, 1861.

IS it true that United States' soldiers have lately come over the line into Upper Canada and arrested, or attempted to arrest, persons ? If so, when and where, and what are the particulars ? Answer at once.

Inclosure 3 in No. 99.

Mr. McEwen to Mr. Alleyn.

(Telegraphic.) (*Received at Quebec, October* 1, 1861.)

ABSENT at Ambersthery yesterday ; on hearing that United States' soldiers had come over to arrest deserters, I called at North-ridge, Gisfield, J. P., in this county. Last week Billings, a magistrate, told me that an officer and four men came over from Detroit, and went into the woods off the main road, brought four American deserters in ; that he called on him for his authority ; he said he only had the Colonel's orders to take deserters ; they were not armed, and said he did not intend taking them by force. The magistrate asked the deserters if they wished to go back, they replied " No." He then told them they were free, and the officers and men left for Detroit. I shall send to-day to Billings to get all the particulars and transmit by mail.

Inclosure 4 in No. 99.

Lord Lyons to Mr. Seward.

Sir, *Washington, October* 5, 1861.

I AM requested by the Governor-General of Canada to call the attention of the Government of the United States to a violation of the British territory which appears to have been committed by an officer with a party of United States' soldiers from Detroit, in pursuit of deserters. The inclosed copy of a telegram addressed to the Provincial Secretary by the Sheriff of the county of Essex, in Canada West, will put you in possession of the facts.

The Governor-General entertains no doubt that the Government of the United States will view with great regret a proceeding of this kind, and will express their disapprobation of the conduct of their officer.

I have, &c.
(Signed) LYONS.

No. 100.

Lord Lyons to Earl Russell.—(Received October 28.)

My Lord, *Washington, October* 14, 1861.

I HAVE the honour to transmit to your Lordship herewith, a copy of a note dated to-day, in which, in obedience to the instructions contained in your Lordship's despatch of September 28, I have remonstrated with the United States' Government against the arbitrary arrests of British subjects.

I took an opportunity of mentioning verbally to Mr. Seward the day before yesterday that I had received instructions to make this remonstrance to him.

Mr. Seward said that he should probably reply that this Government had arrested British subjects with the greatest reluctance, and not without strong necessity; and that it had liberated them at the earliest possible moment compatible with the public safety.

I have, &c.
(Signed) LYONS.

Inclosure in No. 100.

Lord Lyons to Mr. Seward.

Sir, *Washington, October* 14, 1861.

HER Majesty's Government were much concerned to find that two British subjects, Mr. Patrick and Mr. Rahming, had been subjected to arbitrary arrest; and although they had learnt from a telegraphic despatch from me that Mr. Patrick had been released, they could not but regard the matter as one requiring their very serious consideration.

Her Majesty's Government perceive that when British subjects, as well as American citizens, are arrested, they are immediately transferred to a military prison, and that the military authorities refuse to pay obedience to a writ of *habeas corpus.*

Her Majesty's Government conceive that this practice is directly opposed to the maxim of the Constitution of the United States "that no person shall be deprived of life, liberty, or property, without due process of law."

Her Majesty's Government are willing, however, to make every allowance for the hard necessities of a time of internal trouble; and they would not have been surprised if the ordinary securities of personal liberty had been temporarily suspended, nor would they have complained if British subjects, falling under suspicion, had suffered from the consequences of that suspension.

But it does not appear that Congress has sanctioned, in this respect, any departure from the due course of law; and it is in these circumstances that the Law Officers of the Crown have advised Her Majesty's Government that the arbitrary arrests of British subjects are illegal.

So far as appears to Her Majesty's Government the Secretary of State of the United States exercises, upon the reports of spies and informers, the power of depriving British subjects of their liberty, of retaining them in prison, or liberating them, by his own will and pleasure.

Her Majesty's Government cannot but regard this despotic and arbitrary power as inconsistent with the Constitution of the United States, as at variance with the Treaties of Amity subsisting between the two nations; and as tending to prevent the resort of British subjects to the United States for purposes of trade and industry.

Her Majesty's Government have, therefore, felt bound to instruct me to remonstrate against such irregular proceedings, and to say that, in their opinion, the authority of Congress is necessary, in order to justify the arbitrary arrest and imprisonment of British subjects.

I have, &c.
(Signed)   LYONS.

No. 101.

Lord Lyons to Earl Russell.—(Received October 31.)

My Lord,   Washington, October 17, 1861.

WITH reference to my despatch of the 12th instant, I have the honour to transmit to you copies of a further despatch, and its inclosures, which I have received from the Governor-General of Canada, relative to the violation of the British territory by a party of United States' soldiers from Detroit in pursuit of deserters. I have also the honour to inclose a copy of a further note on the subject which I have addressed to the Secretary of State of the United States.

I have not yet received any answer, either to this or to my previous note.

I have, &c.
(Signed)   LYONS.

Inclosure 1 in No. 101.

Sir E. Head to Lord Lyons.

My Lord,   Quebec, October 9, 1861.

WITH reference to my despatch of the 1st instant, I now inclose a copy of the Report made by Mr. Billings, the magistrate in the county of Essex in Upper Canada, who discharged the deserters from the United States' army.

I have approved of Mr. Billings' conduct as stated in the inclosed letter, and I now bring the matter formally under your Lordship's notice, in order that the attention of the Government of the United States may be called to the facts.

Your Lordship will see that a portion of the men pursuing the deserters across the frontier were in uniform.

I have, &c.
(Signed)   EDMUND HEAD.

Inclosure 2 in No. 101.

Mr. Billings to Mr. McEwen.

Dear Sir,   North Ridge, October 2, 1861.

AS you wish a statement of the facts concerning the affair of the American soldiers coming down here after deserters, I will give them as nearly as I can.

About 5 o'clock in the afternoon of Saturday the 21st of September, Mr. Wigle, tavern-keeper, came over to my house, and told me that a Captain and five men belonging to the American army had just come to his place hunting after deserters; that they had put their team into his barn, and had gone into the bush after four deserters who were working for farmers living in the bush : he wanted to know if it was lawful for them to take the men. I told him it was not lawful, and that they should not take the men back unless they were willing to go. He said he did not see how I was to hinder them, as he had been told they were all armed with seven-shooters and bowie knives, and that they said they would take them back, dead or alive. Upon hearing this I went down to John Noble, the constable, and told him to go down street and call out a few of the neighbours, and tell them to bring rifles with them, and I would go up street and do the same; and for us all to meet at Wigle's tavern and wait till they came out, which we did. They came out of bush about 8 o'clock in the evening, and the four deserters with them. I asked the Captain by what authority he had arrested those men; he said he had not arrested them, but went to see if they would not go back with him and join the regiment, which they had agreed to, at the same time showing me an order from his Colonel, empowering him to take any deserters from the 8th Michigan Regiment wherever he could find them; he thought that order would justify him even had he arrested the men. I told him we did not acknowledge his Colonel's order this side the river—it might be good enough on the other side; but these men were now under the protection of the British flag, and that he could not take them back unless they were willing to go. I then asked the men if they were willing to go back with their Captain; they each of them said, no. I then asked why they came out of the bush if they did not want to go back—if the Captain or his men had threatened them, or used any force to compel them out; they said he had not, they came out because they thought they had to. I then told the men they were at liberty to go when and where they pleased; they thanked me and left the house. The Captain then asked me if we thought they were wild beasts, as my men were all armed with rifles and so excited. I told him the men brought their rifles with them at my request; that I had been told they were all armed with seven-shooters and bowie knives, and that they had said they would take the deserters back dead or alive; and I said they should not take them back, neither dead nor alive. I thought the rifles might be very useful if they attempted to carry out their threats. The Captain said he had never made any such threat, and he would pledge his word of honour that they had no revolvers about them; that I might search them if I chose. I declined to do so, telling him as he was a military man of rank, and I supposed a gentleman, I would take his word. He said he should complain of me to my Government for discharging the men, and that he would be down next week with fifty men and an order from our Governor to take the deserters back. I told him if he could bring an order from our Governor that the men should be delivered up to him, and make me believe it was a genuine order, he might take them; if not, he could not take them if he fetched the whole regiment.

The Captain and three men were in uniform, two of the men were in plain clothes; two of the men in uniform were non-commissioned officers by the stripes upon their arms, the other men were privates. The deserters were all in uniform.

This being to me an entirely new case, I was perplexed to know what to do. I hope what I have done will meet with your approbation.

I am, &c.
(Signed)   W. H. BILLINGS, J.P.

Inclosure 3 in No. 101.

Mr. Alleyn to Mr. Billings.

Sir,   *Secretary's Office, Quebec, October* 9, 1861.
I HAVE had the honour to submit to his Excellency the Governor-General your letter of the 2nd instant, addressed to the Sheriff of the County of Essex, giving a detailed explanation of the circumstances under which an officer and certain soldiers of the United States' army entered Upper Canada with the view of arresting and conveying to the United States certain alleged deserters from that army; and at the same time stating the steps that you considered it to be your duty, in your capacity as a Justice of the Peace for the county of Essex, to take in reference to the matter.

I am directed by his Excellency to inform you that he approves of your conduct as reported in your letter to the Sheriff, and requests me to express to you such approbation, which I have much pleasure in doing.

I have, &c.
(Signed)   C. ALLEYN, *Secretary.*

Inclosure 4 in No. 101.

Lord Lyons to Mr. Seward.

Sir,   *Washington, October* 15, 1861.
WITH reference to the note which I had the honour to address to you on the 5th instant, I have now the honour to transmit to you a copy of a letter from Mr. Billings, Justice of the Peace in the County of Essex in Canada West, to the Sheriff of the same

county, giving details of the proceedings of the party of United States' soldiers from Detroit who entered the British territory in pursuit of deserters.

This paper has been communicated to me by the Governor-General of Canada, who informs me that he has approved the conduct of Mr. Billings as set forth in it, and who requests me formally to call the attention of the Government of the United States to the matter.

I have, &c.
(Signed) LYONS.

No. 102.

Lord Lyons to Earl Russell.—(Received October 31.)

My Lord, *Washington, October* 17, 1861.

I HAVE the honour to transmit to your Lordship herewith copies of a despatch and its inclosures, which I have received from the Governor-General of Canada, relative to an attempt to enlist men in Canada for the United States' military service.

I have also the honour to transmit to you a copy of a note which I have addressed to the Secretary of State of the United States on the subject. I have not yet received any answer from the Secretary of State.

I have, &c.
(Signed) LYONS.

Inclosure 1 in No. 102.

Sir E. Head to Lord Lyons.

My Lord, *Government House, Quebec, October* 10, 1861

I HAVE the honour to inclose a copy of a letter from Lieutenant-Colonel Booker, the officer of Canadian Militia commanding the Volunteer force at Hamilton in Canada West.

I shall be obliged if your Lordship will call the attention of the United States' Government to the conduct of the person calling himself Lieutenant-Colonel Davies, if indeed he holds the rank in the service of the United States which he professes to do.

It is unnecessary to advert to the principles respecting recruiting on which such stress was laid by the United States' Government in the year 1855. As a matter of course it will be the business of the Law Officers of the Crown here to enforce the observance of the law as interpreted by the Proclamation of Her Majesty.

I ought to add that Lieutenant-Colonel Booker is a gentleman whose assertions may be received with confidence in every respect.

I have, &c.
(Signed) EDMUND HEAD.

Inclosure 2 in No. 102.

Lieutenant-Colonel Booker to the Adjutant-General of Militia, West Quebec.

Sir, *Hamilton, October* 7, 1861.

I HAVE the honour to inclose for your information a circular bill issued in Detroit to further the designs of Colonel Rankin, and circulated broadcast by post and otherwise.

It is said that about 800 copies have been distributed in this city. Several young men have left here and enlisted in Colonel Rankin's Lancers in Detroit. The J. W. Tillman whose name appears at the foot of the printed bills is Lieutenant-Colonel of Rankin's regiment. I refer to this matter in order to add that a man calling himself Lieutenant-Colonel Davies, United States' Army, Grand Rapids, 2nd Regiment Michigan Cavalry, was in this city on Saturday last in United States' regimental uniform: he entered his name in the register of the Royal Hotel, and came here, as I am informed, and by his own confession, in order to offer to Captain Villiers of the Field Battery a Majority in the regiment above-named. He held the authority from his Colonel the Honourable Mr. Kellogg of Michigan, as he said, and was directed to promise to Captain Villiers 200 dollars per month for his services. Davies made no secret of his purpose, but spoke openly in the

Royal Hotel about it. Captain Villiers, as you are aware, is at present in Montreal going through a course of instruction in musketry; he consequently has not seen Davies.

This Lieutenant-Colonel Davies, United States' Army, has, however, left the offer open for Captain Villiers with a person in this city, who is to request Captain Villiers to write to Grand Rapids on his return here. I have every confidence in the discretion of Captain Villiers and that he will act correctly; it is at the same time a source of regret to hear that any officer of the force under my command has been tampered with, or that an attempt to tamper has been made. Several offers of appointments to members of the active force here, with nominally high rate of pay, have been made, and I understand quite openly. Had I been made aware of Lieutenant-Colonel Davies's conversation before he left Hamilton I should have felt called upon to have preferred an information against him at once.

I have, &c.
(Signed) A. BOOKER.

Inclosure 3 in No. 102.

Handbill.

500 men wanted at Detroit, Michigan.

STEADY employment will be given to active young men, of good habits and character, accustomed to farm labour and the care of horses.

I will pay good wages, 13 dollars per month and upwards, with good board and clothing, and will allow to all employed travelling expenses to this place upon the certificate of the Railroad Ticket Agent at the station at which fares are paid will give, which all will be sure to get. Apply at my store, No. 144, Jefferson Avenue, Detroit.

Detroit, September 1861. (Signed) J. W. TILLMAN.

Inclosure 4 in No. 102.

Lord Lyons to Mr. Seward.

Sir, *Washington, October* 15, 1861.

I HAVE the honour to submit to you herewith copies of a despatch and its inclosures which I have received from the Governor-General of Canada, relative to an attempt which appears to have been made to raise recruits in Canada for the United States' army.

In compliance with the request of the Governor-General, I beg to call the particular attention of the Government of the United States to the conduct of the person who announced himself as Lieutenant-Colonel Davies.

I have, &c.
(Signed) LYONS.

No. 103.

Lord Lyons to Earl Russell.—(Received October 31.)

(Extract.) *Washington, October* 18, 1861.

I HAVE the honour to inclose a copy of a note, dated the 14th instant, which I received the day before yesterday from Mr. Seward, in answer to the remonstrance against the arbitrary arrests of British subjects, which I addressed to him by your Lordship's order, and of which a copy was inclosed in my despatch of the 14th instant.

Your Lordship will perceive that Mr. Seward maintains that the President possesses, under the Constitution, the right of suspending, by his own authority, the writ of *habeas corpus* whenever and wheresoever, and in whatsoever extent, the public safety, endangered by treason or invasion in arms, in his judgment requires.

I do not pretend to be myself competent to give an opinion upon this point of American Constitutional law. An opinion pronounced by the Chief Justice of the Supreme Court of the United States is in direct contradiction to the position maintained by Mr. Seward.

It may also be observed that it was not deemed superfluous to endeavour to obtain the sanction of Congress to the suspension of the writ of *habeas corpus.* In a joint Resolution "to approve and confirm certain acts of the President of the United States for suppressing insurrection and rebellion," certain orders of the President for suspending the writ of *habeas corpus* are expressly mentioned among "the extraordinary acts, proclamations, and orders" which it was proposed to declare to be "legal and valid," "to the same extent and to the same effect as if they had been issued and done under the previous authority and direction of the Congress of the United States."

A copy of this proposed Resolution was transmitted to your Lordship with my despatch of the 12th of July last. It was introduced into the Senate at the beginning of the Special Session which opened in July last, and was understood to have been drawn up by Mr. Seward himself. It was at intervals during the session debated in the Senate; but, as I reported to your Lordship in my despatch of the 12th of August last, no vote was taken upon it, and Congress adjourned without passing it.

I had an interview with Mr. Seward at the State Department the day before yesterday, before the note was sent to me. He told me that he had prepared it, and said that he intended to publish it immediately, but would read it first to me to see whether I objected. He accordingly sent for the draft, and read it to me.

When he had finished I asked him what would be his object in publishing it. He answered that he thought it would have a good effect upon public opinion at home and abroad, that the position which the Government of the United States assumed should be made manifest to the world.

I said that, for my part, so far as the question with Great Britain was concerned, I was inclined to think that the publication would tend to produce embarrassment and unnecessary excitement. I must, however, leave all the responsibility with him. I would neither assent nor object to the publication.

I do not perceive that the note has yet been published.

Inclosure in No. 103.

Mr. Seward to Lord Lyons.

My Lord, *Department of State, Washington, October* 14, 1861.

I HAVE the honour to acknowledge your Lordship's note of the present date.

In that paper you inform me that the British Government is much concerned to find that two British subjects, Mr. Patrick and Mr. Rahming, have been brought under arbitrary arrest, and that, although Her Majesty's Ministers have been advised by you of the release of Mr. Patrick, yet they cannot but regard the matter as requiring the very serious consideration of that Government.

You further inform me that Her Majesty's Government perceive that when British subjects as well as American citizens are arrested, they are transferred to a military prison, and that the military authorities refuse to pay obedience to a writ of *habeas corpus.*

You add that Her Majesty's Government conceive that this practice is directly opposed to the maxim of the Constitution of the United States, that no person shall be deprived of life, liberty, or property, without due process of law. You then observe, that Her Majesty's Government are, nevertheless, willing to make every allowance for the hard necessities of a time of internal trouble, and they would not have been surprised if the ordinary securities of personal liberty had been temporarily suspended, nor would they have complained if British subjects falling under suspicion had suffered from the consequences of that suspension. But that it does not appear that Congress has sanctioned in this respect any departure from the due course of law, and it is in these circumstances that the Law Officers of the Crown have advised Her Majesty's Government that the arrests of British subjects are illegal.

You remark further that, so far as appears to Her Majesty's Government, the Secretary of State for the United States exercises, upon the reports of spies, and assumes the power of depriving British subjects of their liberty, or liberating them by his own will and pleasure; and you inform me that Her Majesty's Government cannot but regard this despotic and arbitrary power as inconsistent with the Constitution of the United States, as at variance with the Treaties of Amity subsisting between the two nations, and as tending to prevent the resort of British subjects to the United States for purposes of trade and industry. You conclude with informing me that, upon these grounds, Her Majesty's Government have felt bound to instruct you to remonstrate against such irregular proceedings, and to say that, in their opinion, the authority of Congress is necessary in order to justify the arbitrary arrest and imprisonment of British subjects.

The facts in regard to the two persons named in your note are as follows:—

Communications from the regular police of the country to the Executive at Washington showed that disloyal persons in the State of Alabama were conducting treasonable correspondence with confederates, British subjects and American citizens in Europe, aimed at the overthrow of the Federal Union by armed forces actually in the field and besieging the capital of the United States. A portion of this correspondence which was intercepted was addressed to the firm of Smith and Patrick, brokers, long established, and doing business in the city of New York. It appeared that this firm had a branch at Mobile; that the partner, Smith, is a disloyal citizen of the United States, and that he was in Europe when the treasonable papers were sent from Mobile, addressed through the house of Smith and Patrick, in New York. On receiving this information, William Patrick was arrested and committed into military custody at Fort Lafayette, by an order of the Secretary of War of the United States, addressed to the police of the city of New York. These proceedings took place on the 28th of August last.

Representations were thereupon made to the Secretary of State by friends of Mr. Patrick to the effect that, notwithstanding his associations, he was personally loyal to this Government, and that he was ignorant of the treasonable nature of the correspondence which was being carried on through the mercantile house of which he was a member. Directions were thereupon given by the Secretary of State to a proper agent to inquire into the correctness of the facts thus presented, and this inquiry resulted in the establishment of their truth. Mr. William Patrick was thereupon promptly released from custody by direction of the Secretary of State. This release occurred on the 13th day of September last.

On the second day of September the Superintendent of Police in the city of New York informed the Secretary of State by telegraph, that he had under arrest J. C. Rahming, who had just arrived from Nassau, where he had attempted to induce the owners of the schooner "Arctic" to take cannon to Wilmington, in North Carolina, for the use of the rebels; and inquired what should he do with the prisoner. J. C. Rahming was thereupon committed into military custody at Fort Lafayette, under a mandate from the Secretary of State. This commitment was made on the 2nd day of September. On the 17th day of that month, this prisoner, after due inquiry, was released from custody on his executing a bond in the penalty of 2,500 dollars, with a condition that he should thereafter bear true allegiance to the United States, and do no act hostile or injurious to them while remaining under their protection.

I have to regret that after so long an official intercourse between the Governments of the United States and Great Britain, it should be necessary now to inform Her Majesty's Ministers that all Executive proceedings, whether of the Secretary of War or of the Secretary of State, are, unless disavowed or revoked by the President, proceedings of the President of the United States.

Certainly it is not necessary to announce to the British Government now that an insurrection, attended by civil war, and even social war, was existing in the United States when the proceedings which I have thus related took place. But it does seem necessary to state, for the information of that Government, that Congress is, by the Constitution, invested with no executive power or responsibility whatever; and, on the contrary, that the President of the United States is, by the Constitution and laws, invested with the whole executive power of the Government, and charged with the supreme direction of all Municipal or Ministerial Civil Agents, as well as of the whole land and naval forces of the Union, and that, invested with those ample powers, he is charged by the Constitution and laws with the absolute duty of suppressing insurrection, as well as of preventing and repelling invasion; and that, for these purposes, he constitutionally exercises the right of suspending the writ of *habeas corpus*, whenever and wheresoever, and in whatsoever extent, the public safety, endangered by treason or invasion in arms, in his judgment requires.

The proceedings of which the British Government complain were taken upon information conveyed to the President by legal police authorities of the country, and they were not instituted until after he had suspended the great writ of freedom in just the extent that, in view of the perils of the State, he deemed necessary. For the exercise of that discretion, he, as well as his advisers, among whom are the Secretary of War and the Secretary of State, is responsible by law before the highest judicial tribunal of the Republic, and amenable also to the judgment of his countrymen, and the enlightened opinion of the civilized world.

A candid admission contained in your letter relieves me of any necessity for showing that the two persons named therein were neither known nor supposed to be British subjects when the proceedings occurred; and that in every case subjects of Her Majesty residing in the United States, and under their protection, are treated during the present troubles in the same manner, and with no greater or less rigour, than American citizens.

The military prison which was used for the purpose of detention of the suspected parties is a fort constructed and garrisoned for the public defence. The military officer charged with their custody has declined to pay obedience to the writ of *habeas corpus*, but the refusal was made in obedience to an express direction of the President, in the exercise of his functions as Commander-in-chief of all the land and naval forces of the United States. Although it is not very important, it certainly is not entirely irrelevant to add that, so far as I am informed, no writ of *habeas corpus* was attempted to be served, or was even sued out or applied for in behalf of either of the persons named; although in a case not dissimilar, the writ of *habeas corpus* was issued out in favour of another British subject, and was disobeyed by direction of the President.

The British Government have candidly conceded, in the remonstrance before me, that even in this country, so remarkable for so long an enjoyment by its people of the highest immunities of personal freedom, war, and especially civil war, cannot be conducted exclusively in the forms and with the dilatory remedies provided by municipal laws which are adequate to the preservation of public order in time of peace. Treason always operates, if possible, by surprise, and prudence and humanity therefore equally require that violence, concerted in secret, shall be prevented, if practicable, by unusual and vigorous precaution. I am fully aware of the inconveniences which result from the practice of such precaution, embarrassing communities in social life, and affecting, perhaps, trade and intercourse with foreign nations.

But the American people, after having tried in every way to avert civil war, have accepted it at last as a stern necessity. Their chief interest, while it lasts, is not the enjoyments of society, or the profits of trade, but the saving of the national life. That life saved, all the other blessings which attach to it will speedily return with greater assurance of continuance than ever before. The safety of the whole people has become, in the present emergency, the supreme law ; and, so long as the danger shall exist, all classes of society, equally the denizen and the citizen, cheerfully acquiesce in the measures which that law prescribes.

This Government does not question the learning of the legal advisers of the British Crown, or the justice of the deference which Her Majesty's Government pays to them. Nevertheless, the British Government will hardly expect that the President will accept their explanations of the Constitution of the United States, especially when the Constitution, thus expounded, would leave upon him the sole executive responsibility of suppressing the existing insurrection, while it would transfer to Congress the most material and indispensable power to be employed for that purpose. Moreover, those explanations find no real support in the letter, much less in the spirit, of the Constitution itself. He must be allowed, therefore, to prefer and be governed by the view of an organic national law which, while it will enable him to execute his great trust with complete success, receives the sanction of the highest authorities of our own country, and is sustained by the general consent of the people for whom alone the Constitution was established.

I avail, &c.
(Signed) WILLIAM H. SEWARD.

No. 104.

Earl Russell to Lord Lyons.

My Lord, *Foreign Office, November 5*, 1861.
HER Majesty's Government approve the note of which a copy forms inclosure No. 4 in your despatch of the 12th ultimo, and which you addressed to the United States' Secretary of State, complaining of the violation of Canadian territory by a party of American soldiers in pursuit of deserters.

I am, &c.
(Signed) RUSSELL.

No. 105.

Lord Lyons to Earl Russell.—(Received November 7.)

My Lord, *Washington, October* 24, 1861.
WITH reference to my despatch of the 17th instant, I have the honour to transmit to your Lordship copies of a note from Mr. Seward and its inclosure, relative to the alleged attempt to raise recruits in Canada for the United States' army.

I shall, without delay, transmit copies of these papers to the Governor-General of that Province.

I have, &c.
(Signed) LYONS.

Inclosure 1 in No. 105.

Mr. Seward to Lord Lyons.

My Lord, *Department of State, Washington, October* 24, 1861.
YOUR note of the 15th instant relative to a supposed attempt to raise recruits in Canada for the United States' army was duly received and referred to the Secretary of War. I now have the honour to communicate to you a copy of a letter of this date from him on the subject, the explanation in which, it is hoped, will prove satisfactory to you and to Her Majesty's Government.

I have, &c.
(Signed) WILLIAM H. SEWARD.

Inclosure 2 in No. 105.

Mr. Cameron to Mr. Seward.

Sir, *War Department, Washington, October* 24, 1861.
YOUR communication of the 17th instant, with inclosures from Lord Lyons, was duly received. This Department has not given authority to any officer of the Government or any other person to raise recruits for military service in Canada. The particular case cited is without the slightest foundation in fact. The following has been received from Colonel F. W. Kellogg, of the 2nd Regiment of Michigan Cavalry:—"In reply to your inquiry about Colonel Davies and his visit to Canada I can only say that he asked leave of absence to visit some friends in Hamilton, 320 miles from where he is stationed; that he was neither requested nor authorized to enlist any person for the United States' army; that he was absent four days, and on his return informed me that he believed I could secure the services of a Captain Villiers if I would give him a Major's commission. In reply I told him that the Major of the Regiment had been appointed while he was absent, and I would not offer a commission of any kind to Captain Villiers. This ended the matter, and was all I ever heard of Captain Villiers." All of which is respectfully submitted.
(Signed) SIMON CAMERON.

No. 106.

Lord Lyons to Earl Russell.—(*Received November* 7.)

(Extract.) *Washington, October* 24, 1861.
I DO myself the honour to inclose a report taken from a newspaper. It appears that upon a writ of *habeas corpus* being issued by Judge Merrick in behalf of a minor of the name of Joseph Murphy, the Attorney who served the writ was arrested by the Provost Marshal, and the Judge himself placed under military surveillance. Upon this the Circuit Court issued an order to the Provost Marshal to show cause why an attachment of contempt should not be issued against him. It is announced, however, that the President of the United States has commanded that the rule be returned to the Court with an intimation that he has suspended for the present the writ of *habeas corpus* in cases relating to the army.

Inclosure in No. 106.

Newspaper Extracts.

October 23, 1861.
CIRCUIT COURT.—INTERESTING PROCEEDINGS IN REGARD TO THE ARREST OF JUDGE MERRICK.—Yesterday morning, at the hour of opening the Circuit Court, Judges Dunlop and Morsell appeared in the court-room, but withdrew immediately to the Marshal's office,

where they remained some time in consultation. At noon they returned to the court-room, and after the Court had been formally opened, Judge Dunlop announced that he had received the following communication from Judge Merrick, who is now under the surveillance of the Provost-Marshal, which he read to the bar, there being a large number of them present, as well as a larger number of spectators than is usual:—

Judge Merrick's Letter.

"On Saturday, the 19th of October, 1861, Mr. Foley, a lawyer of this city, called upon me with a petition, supported by affidavit in proper form, praying for a writ of *habeas corpus* to the Provost-Marshal, requiring him to produce before the Undersigned, one John Murphy, who it alleged was a minor under the age of eighteen years, and illegally detained by said Provost-Marshal as an enlisted soldier of the United States. The order was given by me to the clerk, who issued the writ in the usual form. I was informed by Mr. Foley on the afternoon of Saturday, that by reason of the many engagements of the Deputy Marshal of the district of Columbia, he himself took the writ and served it, as by law he rightfully might do, upon the Provost-Marshal, General A. Porter; that when he delivered the writ to the Provost, he was told by him that he would consult the Secretary (I think he said the Secretary of State) whether he should respect the writ or not, and that he (Mr. Foley) must consider himself under arrest, but for the present might go at large as upon his parole. Later in the afternoon Mr. Foley again called at my house with one or two other persons—one, I think, was represented as the elder brother or some near relation of the boy Murphy—and desired to know whether he were now to consider the boy as finally discharged and at liberty to return home to his friends, inasmuch as he had then been dismissed from the guard-house. I declined to make any suggestion to him in the premises, and told him that whatsoever I did in the matter must be done judicially, and after facts had been spread before me upon affidavit, and the appropriate motion, if any, made thereon; and that as the Court would meet on Monday morning, October 21st, in regular term, I should adjourn all proceedings under the writ into Court, for the advice and action of the whole Court.

"He stated that he would reduce all the facts to writing, make affidavit, and file them; for that he expected to be arrested. He then withdrew. On Monday morning, just before the meeting of Court, I went into the Clerk's office and asked Charles McNamee, the Deputy Clerk, if Mr. Foley had filed any affidavits in the case. He examined the papers and reported there was none. I then directed him to indorse upon the papers that they were, by my order, adjourned into the Court for its further action. After the adjournment of the Court I was informed by a member of the bar, that about 11 o'clock that morning Mr. Foley had been arrested and placed in the guard-house, by order of the Provost-Marshal, and he announced his purpose to apply for his release. I told him that whatever application he had to make must be in writing, upon proper affidavit, and that as the whole Court was in regular session, he must make it to the Court in full sitting; and he withdrew to confer with some of his brother lawyers upon his course. After dinner I visited my brother Judges in Georgetown, and returning home between half-past seven and eight o'clock, found an armed sentinel stationed at my door, by order of the Provost-Marshal. I learned this guard had been placed at my door as early as 5 o'clock; armed sentries from that time continuously, until now, have been stationed in front of my house. Thus, it appears that a military officer against whom a writ in the appointed form of law has issued, first threatened with, and afterwards arrested and imprisoned, the attorney who rightfully served the writ upon him. He continued, and still continues, in contempt and disregard of the mandate of the law, and has ignominiously placed an armed guard to insult and intimidate by its presence the judge who ordered the writ to issue, and still keeps up this armed array at his door in defiance and contempt of the justice of the land. Under these circumstances, I respectfully request the Chief Justice of the Circuit Court to cause this memorandum to be read in open Court, to show the reasons for my absence from my place upon the bench; and that he will cause this paper to be entered at length on the minutes of the Court, alongside the record of my absence, to show through all time, the reason why I do not, this 22nd of October, 1861, appear in my accustomed place.

(Signed) "WM. M. MERRICK,
"*Assistant Judge of the Circuit Court of the District of Columbia.*"

Judge Dunlop then announced that Judge Morsell and himself, the two remaining Judges, had, upon consultation, thought best to order the letter to be entered on the minutes, agreeably to the request of their fellow-Judge. They also thought that, as the writ alluded to in the letter had been regularly issued, it was proper to state the matter was now before this Court to be tried.

The statement of their fellow-Judge presents a case where the progress of the law is obstructed, and the remedy it is the duty of the Court to afford, and, if the facts were as stated, to cause the law to be respected. As the Provost-Marshal had obstructed a process regularly issued by the Court, it would order a rule to be served on General Andrew Porter to appear before the Court, and show cause why an attachment for contempt of Court should not be issued against him.

Judge Morsell said that this proceeding was a palpable gross obstruction to the administration of justice to prevent a Judge of this Court from taking his seat, because he issued just such a writ as the law requires. The placing of a sentinel before Judge Merrick's house was evidently for the purpose of embarrassing him in this particular subject, and to prevent his appearance in Court. He would make the rule broader, so as to have Mr. Provost satisfy the Court in both matters. The Court has its duty to perform, as Judges are sworn to do, and that duty is the administration of justice according to law. What is the real state of things? If martial law is to be our guide, we look to the President of the United States to say so. He (Judge Morsell) did not pretend to controvert the right of the President to proclaim martial law, but let him issue his proclamation. The Judges have their duty to do under the law, and they are liable to be punished if they do not do it.

The Judge proceeded to speak of the rule which would be served, and concluded by saying, "I intend to do my duty, and vindicate the character of this Court as long as I sit here. I am an old man, and have but a few years to live."

The following writ was then issued on General Porter:—

"District of Columbia to wit.

"*The United States of America,*

"To Andrew Porter, Provost-Marshal of the District of Columbia, greeting:

"It is, this 22nd day of October, 1861, ordered by the Circuit Court of the district of Columbia, that you show cause why an attachment of contempt should not be issued against you, for obstructing the process and course of justice, and administration of it in the Circuit Court in the particular case set forth in the letter of the Honourable Judge Merrick, hereto annexed, on Saturday the 26th day of October instant, at 10 o'clock A.M. of that day, in said Circuit Court, in the City Hall of the city of Washington.

"Hereof fail not, as you will answer the contrary, at your peril.

"Witness: the Honourable James Dunlop, Chief Judge of the Circuit Court of the district of Columbia.

"Issued this 22nd day of October, 1861.
(Signed) "JNO. A. SMITH, *Clerk.*"

The larger part of the spectators then left the Court-room, and the balance of the day was occupied in calling the docket.

October 24, 1861.

We learn that the President yesterday instructed the United States' Marshal for this district, in respect to the rule placed in his hands by the Circuit Court to be served upon the Provost-Marshal (General Porter) for his appearance before that Court, not to serve the rule, but to return it to the Court with the information that he (the President) had for the present suspended the privilege of the writ of *habeas corpus* in cases relating to the military.

No. 107.

Earl Russell to Lord Lyons.

(Extract.) *Foreign Office, November* 9, 1861.

WHATEVER instructions I might otherwise have been prepared to give your Lordship respecting Mr. Rahming's application to be indemnified for his recent imprisonment, the answer returned by Mr. Seward, as inclosed in your despatch of the 18th of October, to your representation against the arbitrary imprisonment of British subjects, and specifically of Mr. Rahming, induces me to defer, at all events for the present, any directions to renew the discussion on the subject.

The President of the United States maintains that he has the right to arrest, without cause or reason assigned, any British subject residing in the United States; and it would serve no purpose to ask the President to give indemnity in a case in which he maintains that he has acted lawfully.

Nor would it be of any use to appeal to an American Court of Justice, as it does not appear that attention is paid to the decisions of those Courts if unpalatable to the Executive. Where a writ of *habeas corpus* has been granted, it has not been obeyed.

No. 108.

Lord Lyons to Earl Russell.—(Received November 19.)

My Lord, Washington, November 4, 1861.

WITH reference to my despatches of the 12th and of the 17th ultimo, I have the honour to transmit to your Lordship copies of a note from Mr. Seward, and of two letters annexed to it, relative to the violation of the Canadian territory by a party of United States' soldiers from Detroit in pursuit of deserters.

I have sent copies of these three papers to the Governor-General of Canada.

I have, &c.
(Signed) LYONS.

Inclosure 1 in No. 108.

Mr. Seward to Lord Lyons.

My Lord, Department of State, Washington, November 2, 1861.

I HAVE had the honour to receive your two communications dated respectively the 5th and the 15th ultimo, relative to the pursuit of deserters from the United States in Canada.

Having referred the matter to the Secretary of War, I now have the honour to inclose you a copy of that officer's reply, which it is hoped will prove satisfactory to his Excellency the Governor-General of Canada, especially as it appears that the persons who went in quest of the deserters were unarmed, and had no intention to employ force for their apprehension, but merely to persuade them to return to their duty.

I avail, &c.
(Signed) WILLIAM H. SEWARD.

Inclosure 2 in No. 108.

Mr. Cameron to Mr. Seward.

Sir, War Department, November 1, 1861.

YOUR communications of the 7th and 15th ultimo, inclosing copies of notes from the British Minister relative to the pursuit of deserters from the United States in Canadian territory, have been received by this Department and referred to the General-in-chief.

The General-in-chief has transmitted to this Department the Report of Lieutenant-Colonel Buckers (who is stationed at Detroit) upon the case, together with the accompanying papers showing the facts and the circumstances.

I have the honour to transmit herewith the Report and its inclosures.
(Signed) SIMON CAMERON.

Inclosure 3 in No. 108.

Lieutenant-Colonel Buckers to Colonel Townsend, U.S.A.

Colonel, Detroit, Michigan, October 21, 1861.

YOUR letter of the 11th of October, in reference to the apprehension of deserters from the United States' army in Canada, was received on the 15th instant, but, owing to my indisposition, and the absence of Sheriff McEven, my answer has been delayed until the present date.

It appears, from all the evidence I have been able to collect, that, on the 21st of September ultimo, Captain Church, of the Michigan 8th Infantry Volunteers, was ordered by his Colonel, Fenton, to proceed from Fort Wayne, near Detroit, to Canada, with a party of four or five unarmed soldiers, and, if possible, to induce four deserters to return to the regiment. He was directed to use no force, but to persuade the men to return, on a promise that no proceedings should be had against them.

Captain Church proceeded to Canada with his unarmed party, found the men he sought, and was proceeding homeward with them when he was interrupted by a magistrate named W. H. Billings, with a posse of about thirty men, armed with rifles, and somewhat excited. A conversation occurred between the magistrate and Captain Church, which resulted in the release of the four deserters, as they informed the magistrate that they did not wish to return to the United States.

Captain Church and his party were not armed, but inasmuch as he was accused of being armed with seven-shooters and bowie-knives, he proposed that the magistrate should examine him and his party, which Mr. Billings declined to do.

Captain Church returned, without the deserters, to Fort Wayne.

Colonel Fenton is probably near Washington, or Annapolis, Indiana, with his regiment, and may throw more light on the subject than I can.

No violence or force was used towards the deserters, and neither Mr. Billings, J. P., nor Sheriff McEven seem to entertain the idea that Captain Church designed to use force in executing the duty assigned him.

I inclose herewith copies of the following papers, furnished me through the politeness of Sheriff McEven:—

1. A telegram from C. Alleyn, Provisional Secretary, to Sheriff McEven, of September 30, 1861.
2. A letter from C. Alleyn, Secretary, to W. H. Billings, dated Quebec, October 9, 1861.
3. A letter from W. H. Billings, J.P., dated North Ridge, October 2, 1861, to John McEven, Esq., Sheriff of Essex County.

In the absence of Colonel Fenton and his regiment, my means of obtaining precise information are limited, but I believe the above statement embraces all the principal points at issue, and is as definite as my information will enable me to make it.

I have, &c.
(Signed) E. BUCKERS.

No. 109.

Lord Lyons to Earl Russell.—(Received November 19.)

My Lord, Washington, November 4, 1861.

MR. SEWARD spoke to me, the day before yesterday, respecting the admission of the Confederate vessel "Sumter" into British and Dutch ports.

With regard to the Dutch Government, Mr. Seward said that he had been obliged to cause very serious remonstrances to be addressed to them, but that he had now been informed that they had given orders that the Southern privateers should not be allowed to remain more than twenty-four hours in a Dutch port. It was true, he said, that it had been declared that these orders had not been issued in deference to the representations of the United States' Government: but this was immaterial; so long as the privateers were excluded in practice, he did not care to inquire on what ground that was done.

Mr. Seward then mentioned the reception of the "Sumter" at Trinidad, and alluded to your Lordship's note to Mr. Adams of the 4th of October, on the subject. He said he had been obliged to send immediately instructions to Mr. Adams with regard to that note. He did not tell me the nature of those instructions, but he spoke to me of the affair in a tone of complaint, and dwelt especially on the length of time during which the "Sumter" had been allowed to remain at Trinidad, and on the supplies which she had obtained there. He said that France, and, he thought, all the other Powers of Europe, refused to allow privateers to remain for more than twenty-four hours in their ports. He could hardly conceive that England wished to stand alone as the only Power which admitted the enemies of the United States, without restriction, into its harbours. He supposed that the matter could hardly have been presented in this light to Her Majesty's Government.

I observed to Mr. Seward, that I supposed that in this matter each Power had looked back to precedents, and taken the course which had been usual with it on similar occasions in former times. In one point the English rule was, I said, more stringent than that of France and many other Powers, for armed vessels were not allowed to carry their prizes into British ports for any time, however short.

Mr. Seward did not pursue the conversation. He merely said that he had wished to mention the matter to me in the hope that I might do something towards getting it satisfactorily settled.

I have, &c.
(Signed) LYONS.

No. 110.

Lord Lyons to Earl Russell.—(Received November 19.)

(Extract.)   *Washington, November* 4, 1861.

IN my immediately preceding despatch of this date, I have reported to your Lordship the substance of observations which Mr. Seward made to me the day before yesterday, with regard to the reception of "Confederate vessels" in British ports. Mr. Seward concluded by saying that he earnestly wished this matter could be satisfactorily settled, because it now constituted the only "difficulty" between the United States and Great Britain. Perceiving that I did not immediately assent to this, Mr Seward added, "It is, at all events, the only question we have against you; you may, perhaps, have something against us."

I thought it well to take advantage of the opening thus given to me, and to make some remarks to Mr. Seward on certain matters in which it appears to me that the course taken by the United States' Government is likely to have an unfortunate effect on the relations between the two countries.

I said to Mr. Seward that I could not but think that the extreme punctiliousness which he displayed with regard to communications between the British and French Governments and the *de facto* Government in the South was neither politic nor reasonable: the effect of it must be to keep open a constant source of irritation. It was impossible that such communications should not take place. Under present circumstances there was no authority in the Southern States which could afford protection to the persons and property of the large number of British and French subjects established in those States, except the so-called Confederate Government. It was impossible, therefore, that we should "ignore" the existence of that Government. The necessary intercourse with it had been hitherto carried on in the most unofficial manner, and with the most delicate regard to the susceptibility of the Government and people of the United States. Was it a reasonable ground of complaint, or of strong—or, at least, discourteous—proceedings on the part of the Cabinet of Washington? To put an extreme case—which, however, might not impossibly have happened in old times in Italy—suppose a band of brigands obtained possession of a town in which there were foreign Consuls, foreign residents, and foreign property: could the Government of the country be justly offended if the Consuls made the best terms they could for their countrymen with the Chief of the Brigands, so long as their lives and fortunes were in his hands? I proceeded to give some instances of matters in which communication with the Southern *de facto* authorities was necessary. I mentioned, among other cases, that of British property on board a vessel captured by a Southern privateer. Was it an offence to the United States if the British Consul should take steps to obtain the restitution of this property? Was it wise to push England and France to the wall? What could be the advantage of rendering it difficult to conduct this necessary intercourse in the quiet and unobtrusive manner which had been adopted?

Mr. Seward said that probably he should not think it necessary to take notice of an application from the restitution of captured property.

I went on to say that there was another matter which caused me still more serious alarm. The numerous military arrests of British subjects, and, I was pained to add, the ill-treatment to which in some instances British subjects had been exposed, constituted in my eyes a grave danger to the cordial relations between the two countries. I mentioned the case of the nine seamen so unjustifiably treated in Fort Lafayette, and said that there were, I was afraid, instances in which the crews of British vessels captured for alleged breach of blockade had been placed in irons or subjected to other indignities. These things had, I knew, made a very painful impression upon Her Majesty's Government. They would have a great effect upon public opinion in England; the English people did not enter far into abstract questions of national dignity, but they felt very strongly on the subject of the treatment of their fellow-countrymen abroad; nothing inspired them with so strong or so lasting a resentment as injuries and indignities inflicted by foreign Governments on Her Majesty's subjects.

Mr. Seward replied that he had already sent me a written answer respecting the nine seamen, and that as to the recent arrests they had almost all been made in view of the Maryland elections; that those elections would be over in about a week's time, and that he hoped then to be able to set at liberty all the British subjects now under military arrest.

No. 111.

Lord Lyons to Earl Russell.—(Received November 19.)

(Extract.) *Washington, November* 4, 1861.

MR. SEWARD asked me whether any special communication concerning American affairs had recently taken place between the British and French Governments. I replied that the two Governments were constantly in confidential communication on the present state of this country, but that I did not know of anything of a special character which had lately passed between them on the subject. Mr. Seward then said that I must have seen the reports in the newspapers about the proceedings of the French Chambers of Commerce with regard to the cotton supply. Had anything passed lately on that subject between the British and French Governments? I replied, Not to my knowledge.

No. 112.

Earl Russell to Lord Lyons.

My Lord, *Foreign Office, November* 22, 1861.

I HAVE received your despatch of the 4th instant, reporting the substance of a conversation you had had with Mr. Seward relative to the reception of the privateers and vessels of the so-styled Confederate States in foreign ports, and I have to state to you that it appears from that despatch that Mr. Seward never chooses to understand the position of Her Majesty's Government. Her Majesty has declared entire neutrality in the unhappy contest now carried on in the United States. Her Majesty admits the ships of war and privateers of the United States to British ports, there to remain to victual and take in coals. If Her Majesty were to refuse similar facilities to the vessels of war and privateers of the so-styled Confederate States, Her Majesty would be at once declaring herself a party to the war.

If Mr. Seward is desirous that the ships of war of the Confederate States should not be allowed to stay more than twenty-four hours in a British port, he should declare it in plain terms. In any case Her Majesty's Government are determined to treat the ships of war and privateers of the so-styled Confederate States in the same manner as the ships of war and privateers of the United States.

I am, &c.
(Signed)   RUSSELL.

No. 113.

Earl Russell to Lord Lyons.

My Lord, *Foreign Office, November* 22, 1861.

SOME misapprehension appears to have prevailed in respect to the note which your Lordship addressed to Mr. Seward regarding the two British subjects, Messrs. Patrick and Rahming.

Your Lordship very properly, according to the instructions I had given, stated to Mr. Seward that in the opinion of the Law Officers the arrest of British subjects, and the refusal of the writ of *habeas corpus,* was illegal.

It seems to have been inferred, and Mr. Seward himself countenances this mistake, that the British Government pretended to set up their reading of the American Constitution as of greater authority than the authority of the President of the United States.

Such was obviously not your Lordship's meaning nor mine. It is necessary in every case where a British subject complains, to consult the law of the country in which the complaint arises.

Thus when a British subject complained last year of detention in a Prussian prison, Her Majesty's Government took pains to ascertain the provisions of the Prussian law on the subject. Thus a few days ago I directed Her Majesty's Minister at Madrid to complain of the treatment of a British vessel and her commander on the ground that the Spanish law had been violated by that treatment.

It is obvious that, so long as the British or any other Government complains of the violation of right, it is necessary to ascertain the nature of the laws of which the violation is alleged. Otherwise the complaint can only be directed against harshness of administration and excess of rigour.

That Her Majesty's Government were not singular in believing that the writ of *habeas corpus* can only be suspended by authority of Congress has, since the date of your note, been abundantly shown. A Judge issues a writ of *habeas corpus* to bring up the body of a minor enlisted and detained in the ranks of the United States' army; not only is the writ disobeyed, but a sentinel is placed at the door of the Judge. The Circuit Court of which he is a member, having the matter before them, decide that they do not doubt their power to regard the return made by the Deputy-Marshal as insufficient in law, and to proceed against the officer who had made it, and that if they do not proceed further, it is because they have no physical power. If this view required confirmation, it may be said that very able lawyers have written in support of this doctrine.

To recur, however, to the remonstrance which I directed your Lordship to address to Mr. Seward, I have to observe that Her Majesty's Government never had it in contemplation to controvert an authoritative declaration of the law of the United States in respect to the liberty of persons residing therein.

What Her Majesty's Government doubted was, the authority of the President to set aside the law and privilege of *habeas corpus* by his sole will and pleasure. That doubt has been shared by the Circuit Court of Washington, and by many of the most eminent lawyers of a country fertile in men of legal attainments and judicial fame.

In the particular case of Mr. Patrick, it appears that that gentleman was a partner in a firm with another gentleman who has taken part with the South, and that the correspondence of enemies to the Government was supposed to be conveyed by means of their firm.

When it is considered that a year ago two members of a firm who belonged one to the Northern and the other to the Southern States were considered equally loyal citizens; that a commercial firm cannot be dissolved in a day; that letters sent through a firm are not usually submitted to the principal partners of that firm; that no pains were taken to ascertain the character and political sentiments of Mr. Patrick before he was subjected to the indignity and pain of an arrest, this case unavoidably suggests the reflection that the possession of arbitrary power, in whatever hands it may be placed, is sure to lead to abuse.

Among the necessities of civil war this wanton and capricious arrest of Mr. Patrick cannot be reckoned, and the remonstrance of Her Majesty's Government must remain on record.

You may give a copy of this despatch to Mr. Seward.

I am, &c.
(Signed) RUSSELL.

No. 114.

Lord Lyons to Earl Russell.—(Received November 25.)

My Lord, *Washington, November 9, 1861.*
WITH reference to my despatch of the 4th instant, I have the honour to inform your Lordship that this morning Mr. Seward spoke to me again on the subject of the admission of Confederate vessels into British ports. He used very nearly the same language on this as on the former occasion. He seemed, however, to wish now to be understood as requesting me positively to suggest to Her Majesty's Government to adopt the rule in this respect which had, he said, been adopted by all the other Powers of Europe. He seemed to desire to make this suggestion through me, rather than in a more formal manner through the United States' Minister in London.

I said to Mr. Seward that Great Britain had, I thought, been the first Power to place any restriction upon the admission into her ports of the armed vessels of the belligerents in the present war; and that she had no doubt followed the precedents afforded by her own previous conduct in similar cases. I did not make any difficulty about conveying Mr. Seward's suggestion to your Lordship, but I did not express any opinion as to the reception it would meet with.

I have, &c.
(Signed) LYONS.

No. 115.

Messrs. Yancey, Rost, and Mann to Earl Russell.—(*Received November* 30.)

London, November 30, 1861.

THE Undersigned have been instructed by the President of the Confederate States to communicate to Her Britannic Majesty's Government copies of the list of vessels which have arrived at and departed from the various ports of the Confederate States since the proclamation of a blockade of those ports, up to the 20th of August last, by which it will be seen that up to that time more than 400 vessels had arrived and departed unmolested.

Since the date of these Reports, other and most important violations of the blockade are known to have occurred. The Undersigned will instance a few of the most prominent and well-known:—

The British steamer "Bermuda" went into the port of Savannah from Falmouth, England, on the 28th of September, and left that port for Havre on the 1st instant.

The Confederate States' steamer "Theodora" left Charleston on or about the 1st of October, put to sea, and returned on the same day.

The same steamer left Charleston on the 11th of October for Havana, proceeded to that port, took in cargo, and entered the port of Savannah about the 20th of the same month.

The Confederate ship "Helen" left the port of Charleston on the 2nd of November, and arrived at Liverpool on the 25th instant.

Three ships, with cargoes, arrived from Havana in the Confederate port of Savannah about the 24th of October.

On the 26th of October the Confederate States' steamer "Nashville" left the port of Charleston, and arrived at Southampton on the 21st instant.

It was declared by the five Great European Powers, at the Conference of Paris, that "blockades, to be binding, must be effective—that is, maintained by a force sufficient really to prevent access to the enemy's coast;" a principle long before sanctioned by leading publicists, and now acknowledged by all civilized nations. When these Resolutions were communicated to the Government of the United States, though that relating to privateers was rejected (without a required modification), the principle there applied to blockades was unequivocally affirmed. On the 13th of August last the Government of the Confederate States acknowledged the same principle, in its full extent, by a Declaration of its Congress.

The Undersigned confidently submit that the annexed list of vessels that have arrived at and cleared from the ports of the Confederate States since the blockade was proclaimed by the Government of the United States, is conclusive evidence that this blockade has not been effective, and is therefore not binding.

May not the Government of the Confederate States, then, fairly suggest that the five Great Powers owe it to their own consistency, to the rule of conduct so formally laid down for their guidance, and to the commercial world (so deeply interested), to make good their Declaration, so solemnly and publicly made? Propositions of such gravity, and emanating from sources so high, may fairly be considered as affecting the general business relations of human society, and as controlling, in a great degree, the calculations and arrangements of nations, so far as they are concerned in the rules thus laid down. Men have a right to presume that a law thus proclaimed will be universally maintained by those who have the power to do so, and who have taken it upon themselves to watch over its execution; nor will any suppose that particular States or cases would be exempted from its operation under the influence of partiality or favour. If, therefore, we can prove the blockade to have been ineffectual, we perhaps have a right to expect that the nations assenting to this Declaration of the Conference at Paris will not consider it to be binding. We are fortified in this expectation, not only by their own declarations, but by the nature of the interests affected by the blockade. So far, at least, it has been proved that the only certain and sufficient source of cotton supply has been found in the Confederate States. It is probable that there are more people without than within the Confederate States who derive their means of living from the various uses which are made of this important staple. A war, therefore, which shuts up this great source of supply from the general uses of mankind is directed as much against those who transport and manufacture cotton as against those who produce the raw material. Innocent parties who are thus affected may well insist that a right whose exercise operates so unfavourably on them shall only be used within the strictest limits of public law. Would it not be a movement more in consonance with the spirit of the age to insist that, among the many efficient means of waging war, this one should be excepted in deference to the general interests of mankind, so many of whom

P

depend for their means of living upon a ready and easy access to the greatest and cheapest cotton-market of the world? If, for the general benefit of commerce, some of its great routes have been neutralized, so as to be unaffected by the chances of war, might not another interest, of a greater and more world-wide importance, claim at least so much consideration as to demand the benefit of every presumption in favour of its protection against all the chances of war save those which arise under the strictest rules of public war?

This is a question of almost as much interest to the world at large as it is to the Confederate States. No belligerent can claim the right thus to injure innocent parties by such a blockade, except to the extent that it can be shown to furnish the legitimate, or, perhaps we might go still further and say, the necessary means to prosecute the war successfully. If it has become obvious, as would now seem to be the case, that no blockade which they can maintain will enable the United to subdue the Confederate States of America, upon what plea can its further continuance be justified to third parties who are so deeply interested in a ready and easy access to the cheapest and most abundant sources of cotton supply? Perhaps we had the right to expect, inasmuch as by the Proclamation of Her Britannic Majesty neutrality had been declared as between the belligerents, that one of the parties would not have been allowed to close the ports of the other by a mere proclamation of blockade without an adequate force to sustain it.

The Undersigned submit to Her Majesty's Government that a real neutrality calls for a rigid observance of international and municipal law in their application to both belligerents, and that a relaxation of the principles of public law in favour of one of the parties violating them can be nothing more nor less than an injury done to that extent to the other side. Any considerations of sympathy for the embarrassed condition of the United States, if allowed to relax the application of those laws, must be justly considered as so much aid and comfort given to them at the expense of the Confederate States, and the Undersigned cannot for a moment believe that such a policy can influence Her Majesty's Government.

The Undersigned have forborne to press these great questions upon the attention of Her Majesty's Government with that assiduity which, perhaps, the interests of the Confederate States would have justified, knowing the great interests of Her Majesty's Government in the preservation of friendly relations with both the belligerent Powers. They cannot but think that the facts connected with this nominal blockade, and the great interests of the neutral commerce of the world, imperatively demand that Her Majesty's Government should take decisive action in declaring the blockade ineffective.

These views are affirmed as much in the general interests of mankind as in that of the Confederate States, who do not ask for assistance to enable them to maintain their independence against any Power which has yet assailed them.

The Undersigned have been further instructed by their Government to communicate to that of Her Britannic Majesty a copy of Resolutions adopted by the Congress of the Confederate States, August 13, 1861. It is annexed as Inclosure No. 2.

The Undersigned, &c. (Signed) W. L. YANCEY.
P. H. ROST.
A. DUDLEY MANN.

Inclosure 1 in No. 115.

List of Vessels which have broken the Southern Blockade.

Inclosure 2 in No. 115.

Resolution touching certain Points of Maritime Law, and defining the Position of the Confederate States in respect thereto.

WHEREAS the Plenipotentiaries of Great Britain, Austria, France, Prussia, Russia, Sardinia, and Turkey, in a Conference held at Paris on the 16th of April, 1856, made certain declarations concerning maritime law, to serve as uniform rules for their guidance in all cases arising out of the principles thus proclaimed;

And whereas, it being desirable not only to attain certainty and uniformity, as far as may be practicable, in maritime law, but also to maintain whatever is just and proper in the established usages of nations, the Confederate States of America deem it important to declare the principles by which they will be governed in their intercourse with the rest of mankind: Now, therefore, be it

Resolved by the Congress of the Confederate States of America ;—

1st. That we maintain the right of privateering, as it has been long established by the practice and recognized by the Law of Nations.

2nd. That the neutral flag covers enemy's goods, with the exception of contraband of war.

3rd. That neutral goods, with the exception of contraband of war, are not liable to capture under enemy's flag.

4th. That blockades, in order to be binding, must be effectual; that is to say, maintained by a force sufficient really to prevent access to the coast of the enemy.

Signed by the President of Congress, on the 13th August, and approved same day by the President of the Confederate States of America.

No. 116.

Lord Lyons to Earl Russell.—(*Received November* 24.)

(Extract.)   *Washington, November* 15, 1861.

IF the great naval expedition has not realized the sanguine expectations of those who supposed it would immediately reduce New Orleans, or some other large city, it has, nevertheless, rendered an important service. It has obtained for the United States the possession of Port Royal, a harbour situated about midway between Charleston and Savannah. The command of this harbour will very much facilitate the operations of the blockading squadron. If, as does not seem improbable, the troops are able to hold the position which they have taken up at the small town of Beaufort at the head of the harbour, their presence will be a constant source of disquietude both to Savannah and Charleston, and will afford this Government the means of landing at leisure as large a force as they think fit at this important strategic point.

This success in South Carolina was closely followed by what appears to be a serious defeat of the Confederate troops in Kentucky. If the published accounts can be trusted, General Nelson, commanding the United States' troops in that State, completely defeated the Confederates at Pikeville, taking a considerable number of prisoners, and among them the officer in command, Colonel John S. Williams.

Scarcely less importance is attached to the destruction of the railroad bridges which is reported to have been effected by the Union party in Eastern Tennessee. It is even hoped that the result of this interruption of communication may be nothing less than the restoration of Eastern Tennessee to the Union.

All these events taken together have not, perhaps, as yet made any very great change in the relative strength of the North and the South; but they are sufficiently discouraging to the South to afford a test of the spirit and feeling which really prevail there. If there be in truth a considerable Union party, it can hardly fail to give some signs of its existence. If a considerable part of the people be willing to accept a return to the Union as a less evil than the sufferings, hardships, and dangers which Secession has brought upon them, they have an opportunity to make their voices heard. If the slaves be ready to rise on their masters, or to desert them, the presence of a Federal army at Beaufort, in the midst of a large slave population, will give many of them an opportunity to do so with impunity. If, on the other hand, the present reverses are not followed by dissension in the South, and cause no abatement of the resolution of the Southern people, the presumption will still be that the war must end either in the reduction of the South to the condition of a conquered country, or in its complete independence.

No. 117.

Lord Lyons to Earl Russell.—(*Received December* 2.)

My Lord,   *Washington, November* 18, 1861.

I HAVE the honour to inclose a copy of a despatch from the Governor-General of Canada, stating that he accepts as satisfactory the explanation of the violation of the Canadian territory contained in the note from Mr. Seward of which I transmitted a copy to your Lordship in my despatch of the 4th instant.

                                                                        I have, &c.
                                                           (Signed)   LYONS.

Inclosure in No. 117.

Viscount Monck to Lord Lyons.

My Lord, Quebec, November 11, 1861.
 I HAVE the honour to acknowledge the receipt of your despatch of the 4th instant, inclosing copies of a note and papers accompanying it, received from the United States' Secretary of State, in reply to the representations made by your Excellency, of the violation of British territory, by a party of soldiers from Detroit, in pursuit of deserters.
 Though it would appear that a certain amount of force must have been used in bringing back the deserters, as on Mr. Billings' offering them their choice they refused to accompany the United States' party any further, yet, as Mr. Seward admits the justice of the remonstrance, and does not defend the act of aggression, I accept his explanation of the transaction as satisfactory. I have, &c.
            (Signed) MONCK.

No. 118.

Lord Lyons to Earl Russell.—(Received December 2.)

My Lord, Washington, November 18, 1861.
 I HAVE the honour to transmit to your Lordship herewith a copy of a despatch from Mr. Cridland, Acting Consul at Richmond, reporting proceedings taken under the Sequestration Act of the so-called Confederate States, for the seizure of 2,500 hogsheads of tobacco, the property of Messrs. Auguste Belmont and Co., of New York.
 I do not know that any English interests are directly involved in this particular seizure. I have, &c.
            (Signed) LYONS.

Inclosure in No. 118.

Acting Consul Cridland to Lord Lyons.

My Lord, Richmond, October 19, 1861.
 I HAVE the honour to report, for the information of your Lordship, the following proceedings now going on in the District Court of the Confederate States of America for the Eastern District of Virginia, in regard to a case in which perhaps British interests may be involved.
 In the aforesaid Court, now sitting in this city, I learn that the Receiver, acting under the requisitions of the Sequestration Act of the Confederate Congress, has filed a petition against 2,500 hogsheads of tobacco in the hands of Mr. John Jones, probably a warehouseman of this city, and purporting to belong to Auguste Belmont and Co., of New York.
 The value is estimated at $250,000. The alleged owners have apparently no counsel here, and it is supposed that the firm may consist of Mr. Belmont, in New York, and the Messrs. Rothschild, of London.
 Under the General Consular Instructions I have taken no proceedings in the case, for want of any proof of the said tobacco being British property, but I concluded that it would be proper to respectfully represent the case to your Lordship and await instructions.
            I have, &c.
            (Signed) FRED. J. CRIDLAND.

No. 119.

Earl Russell to Acting Consul Cridland.

Sir, Foreign Office, December 6, 1861.
 LORD LYONS has transmitted to me a copy of your despatch of the 19th of October respecting certain proceedings which have been instituted in the District Court of the Confederate States of America for the Eastern District of Virginia, for putting into operation the Sequestration Act of the Confederate Congress in regard to certain

merchandize supposed to be owned by a foreign house at New York, and in which Messrs. Rothschilds of London are also considered to be interested.

The Congress of the Confederate States appears to have enacted by an Act of the 21st of August last, that property of whatever nature, except public stocks and securities, held by an alien enemy since the 21st of May, 1861, shall be sequestrated and appropriated in the manner pointed out in the Act; and the Attorney-General of the Confederate States has distinctly laid down in an instruction dated September 12, that all persons who have a domicil within the States with which the Government of the Confederate States is at war, no matter whether they be citizens or not of such Government, are subject to the provisions of the Act.

Her Majesty's Government have received urgent representations from parties in this country connected in business with, and having establishments in, the Northern States of America, of the hardship and injustice which this Act of the Confederate States, if applied to British subjects domiciled in the United States, cannot fail to inflict upon them.

Now, whatever may have been the abstract rule of the law of nations on this point in former times, the instances of its application in the manner contemplated by the Act of the Confederate Congress, in modern and more civilized times, are so rare and have been so generally condemned that it may almost be said to have become obsolete. The conclusion expressed by Wheaton on the subject ("Elements," 6th edition, page 369) is as follows :—

"It appears, then, to be the modern rule of international usage, that property of the enemy found within the territory of the belligerent State, or debts due to his subjects by the Government or individuals at the commencement of hostilities, are not liable to be seized and confiscated as prize of war. This rule is frequently enforced by Treaty stipulations, but unless it be thus enforced it cannot be considered as an inflexible, though an established, rule. The rule, as it has been beautifully observed, like other precepts of morality, of humanity, and even of wisdom, is addressed to the judgment of the Sovereign : it is a guide which he follows or abandons at his will, and although it cannot be disregarded by him without obloquy, yet it may be disregarded. It is not an immutable rule of law, but depends on political considerations which many continually vary."

The observations of Wheaton which I have cited apply to the existence of an ordinary state of war between two independent and foreign nations. But in the present case they apply with still more force against the exercise of the right in question ; for the present is a case of civil war between the different parts of one Confederation, during whose union the subjects of foreign States were invited and induced to settle indiscriminately in its various States, without any ground for contemplating such a disruption as has now occurred. No notice has been given to them, nor time allowed, which would enable them to prepare for such an emergency, or to separate their affairs from those of the citizens of either belligerent ; and though technically they are liable to be considered enemies by one or other of the belligerents, as the case may be, it is impossible to treat them as such without gross injustice and a breach of that faith to which every State of the American Union was originally a party.

Under these circumstances I have to instruct you to remonstrate strongly with the Secretary of State of the so-called Confederate States on the hardship and injustice of confiscating the property of neutrals under the Sequestration Act of the Confederate Congress.

I am, &c.
(Signed) RUSSELL.

No. 120.

Earl Russell to Her Majesty's Consuls in the Confederate States.

Sir, *Foreign Office, December* 6, 1861.

I TRANSMIT to you herewith, for your information and guidance, a copy of an instruction which I have addressed to Her Majesty's Acting Consul at Richmond, in Virginia,* respecting the Sequestration Act of the Confederate Congress of the 21st of August last; and I have to instruct you, if the necessity for doing so should arise, to protest, on the grounds stated in that instruction, against the confiscation of British property in your district under the Act in question.

I am, &c.
(Signed) RUSSELL.

---

* No. 119.

No. 121.

Mr. Hammond to the Secretary to the Admiralty.

(Extract.) *Foreign Office, December 6, 1861.*

I AM directed by Earl Russell to transmit to you herewith certain packets addressed to Her Majesty's Consuls in the so-styled Confederate States of North America, together with copies of the despatches which they contain,* for the information of the Lords Commissioners of the Admiralty.

I am to request that these packets may be forwarded to Vice-Admiral Sir Alexander Milne, with instructions to send them on under cover to one of Her Majesty's Consuls in the Southern or Confederate States as may be most convenient, directing such Consul to forward them, by post or otherwise, to their respective addresses, as he may judge best to ensure their safe arrival.

No. 122.

Earl Russell to Lord Lyons.

My Lord, *Foreign Office, December 6, 1861.*

I INCLOSE, for your Lordship's information, and with reference to your despatch of the 18th ultimo, a copy of an instruction which I have addressed to Her Majesty's Acting Consul at Richmond, Virginia,† respecting the appplication of the Sequestration Act of the so-styled Confederate States to the property of British subjects.

I also inclose a copy of an instruction which I have given to Her Majesty's other Consuls in the Confederate States, and a copy of a letter to the Admiralty,‡ conveying instructions for Vice-Admiral Sir A. Milne as to the manner of forwarding these despatches to their destination.

It will not be necessary for your Lordship to make any communication to the Government at Washington with reference to these despatches.

I am, &c.
(Signed) RUSSELL.

No. 123.

Lord Lyons to Earl Russell.—(Received December 7.)

(Extract.) *Washington, November 22, 1861.*

WITH reference to my despatch of the 23rd of September last I have the honour to inclose four copies of a Circular issued on the 12th instant by the Secretary of the Treasury with regard to the seizure of ships under the 6th Section of the Act of Congress of the 13th July last.

I have also the honour to inclose a copy of an unofficial note which I have received from the Secretary of the Treasury, to whom I applied privately for authentic copies of the circular. The Secretary states that he trusts I shall find the circular to be conceived in a liberal spirit towards all not actually involved in rebellion.

Inclosure 1 in No. 123.

Circular to Collectors and other Officers of the United States' Customs.

Treasury Department, November 12, 1861.

THE following Regulations will be observed in regard to seizures of vessels made in pursuance of the 6th section of the Act of July 13, 1861 :—

First. All such seizures must be made by the Collector of Customs, or other proper revenue officer, except in case of his absence or disability, or where immediate action is necessary, and no such officer is at hand to make the seizure.

Second. In all cases of seizure the Collector, or other officer acting in his stead, shall notify the proper District Attorney, who will at once institute proceedings for the condemnation of the vessel. After the commencement of such proceedings, if it shall appear to

---

* Nos. 119 and 120.   † No. 119.   ‡ Nos. 120 and 121.

the satisfaction of the District Attorney instituting them that the vessel is owned in part by persons not citizens of any State or part of a State in insurrection against the United States, and not residing therein, and that she will not be employed in aiding the existing rebellion, or in violating any law of the United States, such vessel may be discharged on bail being given, according to the course of Admiralty proceedings, for the share or shares owned by any person or persons residing in any such insurgent State or part of State; in which case the proceedings so instituted will be prosecuted, without delay, to condemnation and sale of such insurgent interest, and as to the remainder of the vessel, the forfeiture thereof will be remitted.

Third. Should there be any unusual delay in the commencement of such proceedings, or should there be any other circumstances rendering it proper, in the judgment of the Collector, or other officer acting in his stead, that the vessel should be released from custody before the commencement of proceedings, the same may be done; provided the Collector or other officer acting in his stead shall be satisfied that no such improper use as before mentioned, is to be made of said vessel; and one or more of the owners residing in loyal States shall give a bond, with sufficient sureties, to the United States, in double the value of the share or shares thereof owned in any such insurgent State or part of a State, with the condition that the vessel shall be safely, and in good order, returned to the Collector or other officer in whose custody she may be, within such time as he shall direct, and without any change in the ownership of said share or shares; and with the further condition that the vessel shall at all times be subject to any order or decree of the Court in which any proceedings for her condemnation may be instituted, or of any appellate Court to which the same may be removed; and with the further condition that any costs or other moneys which shall be awarded by either of said Courts in said proceedings shall be paid; together with such other conditions as the Collector or other officer shall deem just and expedient, in order to secure the objects contemplated by the Act aforesaid. The execution of such bond and the discharge of the vessel shall not delay the institution or prosecution of proceedings for the condemnation of the insurgent interest, but the same shall be commenced and prosecuted, in all respects, so far as practicable, in the same manner as if the vessel still remained in the custody of the officer.

The District Attorney will notify the Collector, or other officer making the seizure in his stead, of the commencement of proceedings for the condemnation of the vessel, of the time of trial of the suit, of the result of the trial, and of the time of sale (if a sale be ordered), and the result thereof.

(Signed) S. P. CHASE, *Secretary of the Treasury.*

Inclosure 2 in No. 123.

Mr. Chase to Lord Lyons.

My Lord, *Treasury Department, November* 21, 1861.

IT gives me very great pleasure to comply with your request for copies of the recent circular of this Department, relating to the seizure and confiscation of vessels owned in whole or in part by citizens of States in insurrection.

I trust you will find them to be conceived in a liberal spirit towards all not actually involved in rebellion.

Twelve copies are transmitted.

I have, &c.
(Signed) S. P. CHASE.

No. 124.

Earl Russell to Messrs. Yancey, Rost, and Mann.

Foreign Office, December 7, 1861.

LORD RUSSELL presents his compliments to Mr. Yancey, Mr. Rost, and Mr. Mann. He has had the honour to receive their letters and inclosures of the 27th and 30th of November; but, in the present state of affairs, he must decline to enter into any official communication with them.

No. 125.

Lord Lyons to Earl Russell.—(*Received December 9.*)

My Lord, Washington, November 25, 1861.

MORE recent and more accurate accounts have, in some degree, diminished the splendour of the achievements of the United States' sea and land forces at Port Royal. Nevertheless, the expedition appears to have attained, in great part, the objects for which it was sent. It has given the United States the command of a harbour, which will be of great use to their blockading squadron. It has enabled them to establish a body of troops in a position threatening the important towns of Savannah and Charleston. On the other hand, however, it would seem to have completely failed in producing any demonstration of Union feeling in the South. The country in the neighbourhood of the United States' troops appears to have been entirely abandoned by the white population. No voice in favour of a return to the Union has yet made itself heard in any part of the Southern States.

The success of this expedition has, however, been sufficiently great to induce the Government to prepare another of the same kind. The destination has, of course, not yet become public. The plan, too, of obstructing the inlets and harbours on the Southern coast by sinking vessels laden with stones in them has been resumed. The inclosed extracts from newspapers give details of the preparations which are being made for this purpose.

Rumours of an advance of the grand army of the Potomac under General McClellan are again rife, but the weather has become very unfavourable for military operations.

The details of the accounts from Missouri which appear in the newspapers cannot be relied upon. There is, however, a general impression that the Secessionists are again making head in that State.

I have, &c.
(Signed) LYONS

Inclosure in No. 125.

Newspaper Extract.

FLEET OF STONE VESSELS.—The fleet of stone-laden vessels for sinking in the harbours of the Southern Coast, which has been for some time preparing, sailed on the 20th instant, and we give below a list of the vessels composing it, with their tonnage. They are all old, but substantial, whaling-vessels, double decked to give them greater firmness; they were stripped of their copper and other fittings which were not necessary for so short a voyage as they will make, and loaded with picked stone as deeply as was safe.

In the bottom of each ship a hole was bored, into which was fitted a lead-pipe five inches in diameter, with a valve so fixed that though perfectly safe even for a long voyage, it can be quickly removed. It is calculated that the ship will be filled and sunk to the bottom in twenty minutes after the removal of this valve.

The crew consists of six men each. These will be returned by the men-of-war who will assist in the work of sinking. Each ship will be anchored in the place chosen for her, and will then be sprung round broadside to the channel, thus effecting as great a stoppage as is possible. When this is done, and she is in position, the valve will be withdrawn, and when the vessel is nearly level with the water's edge the men will leave in a small boat. It is reported that an enterprising rigger has gone down with the fleet with the intention to take off what pieces of spars and rigging may remain above the water's edge after the ships are sunk.

Each Captain received on the day he sailed sealed orders not to be opened till after the pilot left his vessel. The following is a copy in blank of these orders. If the blanks were filled the enemy might know too soon where the fleet is bound:—

Secret Orders.

"To Captain ———, Sir: The ———, now under your command, having been purchased by the Navy Department for service on the Southern Coast of the United States, the following are your orders for your proposed voyage:

"You will proceed from this port on ——— the ——— instant, or with the first fair wind, and when clear of the land make a direct passage to the port of ———, and there deliver your ship to the Commanding officer of the blockading fleet off said port, taking his receipt for her to return to me. After the delivery of your vessel, yourself and crew will be provided with passages to the port of New York by the Navy Department, and on arrival there you will call on ———, who will furnish you funds to return to this port.

"On the voyage down it would be well, as far as practicable, to keep in company of your consorts, to exhibit lights by night and sound horns or bells in case of fog near the coast.

"You will also examine daily the pipe in the quarter of your ship under water, to see that it remains safe.

"The only service required of you is the safe delivery of your vessel; and as she is old and heavily laden, you will use special care that she sustains no damage from unskilful seamanship or want of prudence and care.

"On a close approach to your port of destination begin to put between-decks cargo into lower hold, and before anchoring permanently, have your second anchor and chain (if you have one) secured on deck. On leaving your vessel, unless otherwise ordered, you will bring away papers, chronometer, charts, compasses, spy-glass, and any other portable articles not required by the Commander of the blockading fleet there, and return them safely to me.

"In case of disaster, to preclude going on, you can call at Fortress Monroe, Hampton Roads, to repair damages, reporting to the flag-officer there.

"Wishing you a safe and speedy passage, I am, &c.

" ——————."

THE FLEET.

The following is the List of Vessels to be sunk.

Ships.	Tons.	Port.	Barques.	Tons.	Port.
Corea	356	New London.	Tenedos	245	New London.
Lewis	308	Ditto.	Fortune	292	Ditto.
Robin Hood	395	Mystic.	Cossack	254	New Bedford.
Archer	322	New Bedford.	Amazon	318	Fair Haven.
Timor	289	Sag Harbour.	Henrietta	407	New Bedford.
Meteor	324	Mystic.	Garland	243	Ditto.
Rebecca Sims	400	Fair Haven.	Harvest	314	Fair Haven.
L. C. Richmond	341	New Bedford.	America	329	Edgartown.
Courier	381	Ditto.	Peter Demil	300	New York.
Maria Theresa	330	Ditto.	Leonidas	231	New Bedford.
Kensington	357	Ditto.	South America	606	Ditto.
Herald	274	Ditto.			
Potomac	356	Nantucket.	Total	8,375	
Phenix	404	New London.			

25 Vessels, average 335 tons.

No. 126.

Lord Lyons to Earl Russell.—(Received December 12.)

My Lord, *Washington, November 29, 1861.*

IN my despatch of the 25th instant, I inclosed extracts from newspapers giving details of the preparations made by order of the Government of the United States to obstruct the inlets and harbours on the coast of the Southern States by sinking vessels laden with stones. Several vessels are stated to have been already despatched for this purpose, and Charleston and Savannah are announced by the press (I know not on what authority) as the ports against which they are directed.

This mode of closing the ports has given rise to a great deal of discussion. By some it is characterized as an odious and barbarous measure, not sanctioned by the usages of civilized warfare. Others maintain that it is perfectly fair and proper. The question seems to depend on the extent to which the harbours will be permanently injured. If the obstructions cannot be completely removed on the cessation of hostilities, the measure is certainly open to grave objection.

I have, &c.
(Signed) LYONS.

No. 127.

Earl Russell to Lord Lyons.

My Lord,   *Foreign Office, December* 20, 1861.

I OBSERVE it is stated, apparently on good authority, that it is the intention of the President of the United States to send vessels laden with stones to be sunk at the mouths of the Southern harbours, with a view to choke up the passage to those harbours.

It is stated that this is to be done, not with a view to assist military operations, and as a temporary measure of war, but with the declared object of destroying these harbours for ever, and reducing to misery the numerous inhabitants of the cities connected with them.

I must remark, in the first place, that this cruel plan would seem to imply utter despair of the restoration of the Union, the professed object of the war; for it never could be the wish of the United States to destroy cities from which their own country was to derive a portion of its riches and prosperity: such a plan could only be adopted as a measure of revenge and irremediable injury against an enemy.

But even in this view, as a scheme of embittered and sanguinary war, such a measure is not justifiable. It is a plot against the commerce of nations, and the free intercourse of the Southern States of America with the civilized world. It is a project worthy only of times of barbarism.

I wish you to speak in this sense to Mr. Seward, who will, I hope, disavow the alleged project.

                                                           I am, &c.
                                                (Signed)   RUSSELL.

No. 128.

Earl Russell to Lord Lyons.

My Lord,   *Foreign Office, December* 20, 1861.

YOU may speak to Mr. Seward on the subject of letters of marque.

Should Great Britain and the United States ever unhappily be at war against each other, Her Majesty will be ready to relinquish her prerogative, and abolish privateering as between the two nations, provided the President would be ready to make a similar engagement on the part of the United States.

                                              I am, &c.
                                    (Signed)   RUSSELL.

No. 129.

Earl Russell to Lord Lyons.

My Lord,   *Foreign Office, December* 20, 1861.

I HAVE received your Lordship's despatch of the 22nd of November, inclosing a copy of a circular issued by the Treasury Department of the United States, with regard to the seizure of ships, under the 6th section of the Act of Congress of July 18, 1861; and I have to state to you in reply that as the instructions contained in the circular do not in themselves appear to be illegal or unreasonable, and as you do not suggest that any particular difficulties or objections are likely to arise in the working of the Act, or from the effect of the circular, or that any special injury to British interests is to be apprehended, Her Majesty's Government see no reason for interfering in this matter.

                                                I am, &c.
                                    (Signed)   RUSSELL.

No. 130.

Lord Lyons to Earl Russell.—(*Received December 25.*)

(Extract.) Washington, December 6, 1861.

I HAVE the honour to transmit to your Lordship a copy of the Papers relating to Foreign Affairs which were laid before Congress with the President's Message.* As the earliest copies did not come from the press until yesterday afternoon, I have not had time to do more than read somewhat hastily that part of the correspondence which relates to England and France.

A great deal of the space devoted to both countries is occupied by the negotiations concerning the adherence of the United States to the Declaration of Paris. Mr. Adams writes frequently and at great length concerning his misapprehension of your Lordship's intentions as to transferring the negotiation to Washington. The simple explanation of this misapprehension is, that Mr. Seward refused to see the despatch in which your Lordship's proposals were made. Your Lordship will recollect that Mr. Seward, having been permitted by M. Mercier and me to read and consider in private that despatch, and a despatch of a similar tenor from the Government of France, refused to receive the formal copies we were instructed to place in his hands, or to take any official notice of their contents. The English despatch was, however, subsequently communicated officially by your Lordship to Mr. Adams, and appears at page 110 of the printed papers inclosed herewith.

From several of the papers now published, it appears that it was only an act of common prudence, on the part of the Governments of Great Britain and France, not to accept the accession of this country to the Declaration of Paris, without stating distinctly what obligations they intended by doing so to assume with regard to the Seceded States. Little doubt can remain, after reading the papers, that the accession was offered solely with a view to the effect it would have on the privateering operations of the Southern States; and that a refusal on the part of England and France, after having accepted the accession, to treat the Southern privateers as pirates, would have been made a serious grievance, if not a ground of quarrel.

The papers on this subject which have struck me as most worthy of notice will be found at pages 76, 77, 79, 186, 187, 194, 198, 202, 207. In the letter from Mr. Seward to Mr. Dayton of the 22nd June, which appears at page 186, the following passage occurs:—

"We shall continue to regard France as respecting our Government until she practically acts in violation of her friendly obligations to us, as we understand them. When she does that, it will be time enough to inquire whether if we accede to the Treaty of Paris she could, after that, allow pirates upon our commerce shelter in her ports, and what our remedy should then be. We have no fear on this head."

Your Lordship will find at page 51 extracts from the menacing despatch from Mr. Seward to Mr. Adams, which was mentioned in my despatch to your Lordship of the 23rd May last. Your Lordship is aware that it is supposed that Mr. Seward's despatch was originally drawn up in still stronger terms.

At page 126 appears a despatch to Mr. Adams identical with, or very closely resembling, that announcing the revocation of Mr. Consul Bunch's exequatur, which was read to me by Mr. Seward on the 26th of October last. I communicated as much of it as I could recollect to your Lordship in my despatch of the 28th of that month. I observe that in one part of his despatch, Mr. Seward states that the Government "must revoke" the exequatur; and in another he desires Mr. Adams to inform your Lordship that the exequatur has been withdrawn. I have no reason to suppose that the formal act revoking the exequatur has yet been signed. When the exequaturs of three British Consuls were revoked in 1856, the form adopted was that of Letters-Patent published in the newspapers, in the same way in which exequaturs are published. This is, I believe, the usual practice. I have not observed in the newspapers any such Letters-Patent with regard to Mr. Bunch's exequatur. I have not received any notice of such letters having been signed. Indeed, I have no official knowledge of there having been any intention to revoke Mr. Bunch's exequatur.

In a despatch from Mr. Seward to Mr. Adams of the 1st July last, which appears at page 75, there is an allusion to the affair of the "Peerless," and to the mission of Mr. Ashman to Canada. Mr. Seward says cursorily, "I asked Lord Lyons to request the Governor-General of Canada to look into the facts and prevent the departure of the vessel, if he should find the report to be true. Lord Lyons answered that he had no authority to do so." I presume that the "he" in this last sentence refers to the Governor-General of Canada; for, of course, I could never have said that I had no authority to make a request to the Governor-General. What I did say was (as I reported to your Lordship at the time), that "if the ship's papers were in order, and there was no direct proof of her being actually engaged in any unlawful enterprise, the Governor-General might not have legal power to interfere with her." This question of the "Peerless" ended in a strange manner. It turned out that the ship had all the time been purchased by the United States' Government itself. This purchase appears to have been the cause of the proceedings of the vessel which were looked upon as suspicious.

Of Mr. Ashman it is said that he was sent to Canada to watch and prevent just such transactions as the sale or fitting out of the "Peerless" for a pirate would have been. Mr. Seward adds that it was not supposed that his visit would be thought objectionable by the British Government. If so it is difficult to understand why the intention to send him was concealed from me, or why, when I asked for information to be communicated to your Lordship on the objects of the mission, Mr. Seward refused to give it. Mr. Ashman was not recalled until the character of his reception by the Governor-General had made his position untenable.

Copies of Mr. Seward's note to me of the 8th June, 1861, appear to have been sent both to Mr. Adams and Mr. Dayton, in order to dispel any doubt which the British or French Governments might entertain that the principle laid down by the third Article of the Declaration of Paris on Maritime Law would be observed by the United States in the present civil war. (Pages 63 and 187.)

I have not time to make sure of the fact before the departure of my messenger, but I am nearly certain that eventually the exequatur of the Russian Consul mentioned in the second paragraph of page 53 was not revoked.

I have thought it right to send to your Lordship at once the observations which have occurred to me during the hasty perusal of the papers which is all I have had time for. A more complete examination of them would perhaps suggest more important reflections.

Inclosure in No. 130.

Papers relating to Foreign Affairs, laid before Congress with the President's Message of December, 1861.

[See Papers relating to North America, No. 2, presented to Parliament same time.]

No. 131.

Lord Lyons to Earl Russell.—(*Received December* 26.)

(Extract.) *Washington, December* 13, 1861.

THE expenditure for the year ending June 30, 1862, is estimated at 543,406,422 dollars 6 cents (about 111,000,000*l.* sterling).

The revenue, exclusive of loans and of the balance in the Treasury at the beginning of the year, 54,552,665 dollars 44 cents (about 11,200,000*l.* sterling), or little more than one-tenth of the expenses.

In the estimate of the revenue, 20,000,000 dollars are set down for the produce of the direct taxes. No portion of the direct taxes is yet due, and as the attempt to collect any direct taxes at all for the Federal Government is an entirely new experiment, the result can only be a matter of conjecture.

It is calculated by the Secretary that the Public Debt, which amounted to 90,867,828 dollars 68 cents (about 19,000,000*l.* sterling) on the 1st day of July, 1861, will be on the 1st day of July, 1862, 517,732,802 dollars 93 cents (about 106,000,000*l.* sterling).

The calculations for the year ending June 30, 1863, are less unfavourable, principally because the Secretary hopes to add about 8,000,000 dollars to the receipts from Customs, and 30,000,000 dollars to the receipts from direct taxes, internal duties, &c. It is for that year, 1862-63, that Congress is called upon to provide during the present session, and to which, consequently, the recommendations of the Secretary principally apply.

He proposes an addition to the duties on tea, coffee, and sugar; but recommends that no other alterations should be made during the present session in the Tariff of import duties. He appears to think that it is undesirable to encourage trade with nations who are neutral in the present struggle.

"While other nations," he says, "look with indifferent or unfriendly eyes upon this work (the re-establishment of the Union), sound policy would seem to suggest, not the extension of foreign trade, but a more absolute reliance, under God, upon American labour, American skill, and American soil. Freedom of commerce is, indeed, a wise and noble policy; but to be wise and noble, it must be the policy of concordant and fraternal nations."

He proceeds to recommend an increase of the income tax, and of other internal duties; and then enters at great length upon plans for substituting United States' Treasury notes payable at sight, for the notes now circulated by private banks.

He renews the suggestion that confiscation of the property of insurgents should be looked to as a source of revenue.

He gives a statement of the views of the Government with regard to granting licenses to trade with the Southern States, and to the re-establishing commercial intercourse, as its forces advance into Southern territory.

The Board which regulates the lighthouses and beacons on the coast of the United States being subordinate to the Treasury Department, the Secretary mentions that as districts on the Southern coasts have been occupied by the United States' forces, the lights which had been extinguished by the Southern people have been rekindled. "Already," he says, "from the coasts of the Chesapeake, the banks of Hatteras, from the Islands of Port Royal entrance, and from Chandeleur Island in the Gulf, they shine once more as the safeguards and symbols of fraternal commerce and peaceful civilization. May we not," he adds, " hope that the time is not far off when every extinguished light shall be in like manner restored, amid the rejoicings of a reunited people?"

In the last paragraph but one the Secretary recommends the adoption of a uniform system of weights and measures by all commercial nations.

No. 132.

Earl Russell to Mr. Adams.

Sir, *Foreign Office, January* 8, 1862.

WITH reference to my letter of the 8th of October last relative to the alleged consignments to Mr. Henry Adderley, of Nassau, New Providence, of warlike stores for the use of the forces of the so-styled Confederate States, I have now the honour to inform you that the Secretary of State for the Colonies has communicated to me a copy of a despatch from the Lieutenant-Governor of the Bahamas, inclosing a copy of a letter which his Excellency has received from Mr. Adderley, denying the allegations brought against him, together with a Report from the Receiver-General of the port of Nassau stating that no warlike stores have been received at that port, either from Great Britain or elsewhere, and that no munitions of war have been shipped from thence to the Confederate States.

I am, &c.
(Signed) RUSSELL.

Inclosure 1 in No. 132.

Lieutenant-Governor Nesbitt to the Duke of Newcastle.

My Lord Duke, *Government House, Nassau, Bahamas, November* 20, 1861.

IN compliance with the instructions contained in your Grace's despatch of the 15th ultimo, with the inclosures, copy of a letter from the Foreign Office, with one from the United States' Minister in London, covering the copy of an intercepted letter which had been addressed by a Mr. Baldwin, living at Richmond, Virginia, to Mr. Henry Adderley, of Nassau, New Providence, consigning to his care certain warlike stores then shipping from Great Britain, I have made inquiry into the circumstances, and have the honour to inclose, for your Grace's information,—

1st. A letter from Mr. Henry Adderley.

2nd. A letter from the Receiver-General of this port, by which your Grace will perceive that no warlike stores have been consigned to Mr. Adderley from Great Britain for transport to the Confederate States, or to any other place, and that no warlike stores have been received at this port, either from the United Kingdom or elsewhere, nor have any munitions of war been shipped from Nassau to the Confederate States.

I have, &c.
(Signed) C. R. NESBITT.

Inclosure 2 in No. 132.

Mr. Adderley to Lieutenant-Governor Nesbitt.

Sir, *Nassau, November* 19, 1861.

I HAVE the honour to acknowledge the receipt of your letter of 16th instant with the inclosures, one of which I notice is a copy of an intercepted letter said to be from Mr. Baldwin, living in Richmond, Virginia, and addressed to me.

I am rather surprised that the American Government should have countenanced the intercepting of letters passing through their Post Office.

For your information I beg leave to state that no warlike stores have been consigned to me from Great Britain for transport to the Confederate States, or to any other place.

I have, &c.
(Signed) HENRY ADDERLEY.

Inclosure 3 in No. 132.

Mr. Whitty to Lieutenant-Governor Nesbitt.

Sir, *Receiver-General's Office, Nassau, November* 20, 1861.

IN reply to your Excellency's memorandum respecting the importation into this Colony of any warlike stores from the United Kingdom for the use of the Confederate States, I beg leave to state that no such stores have been received at this port, either from the United Kingdom or elsewhere; neither have any munitions of war been shipped from Nassau to the Confederate States.

I have, &c.
(Signed) F. WHITTY, *Receiver-General.*

No. 133.

Mr. Adams to Earl Russell.—(Received January 13.)

My Lord, *Legation of the United States, London, January* 10, 1862.

I HAVE the honour to acknowledge the reception of a note from your Lordship of the 8th instant, in reply to mine of the 1st of October last, soliciting the attention of Her Majesty's Government to certain passages of an intercepted letter of one Baldwin, of Richmond, in Virginia, tending to throw suspicion upon Mr. Henry Adderley, of Nassau, New Providence, as privy to the transmission of warlike stores from Great Britain through that point to the insurgents in the United States.

It gives me, as I doubt not it will give the Government which I have the honour to represent, the highest satisfaction to learn that the letter of Mr. Baldwin was an impudent assumption on his part, and that there is not a shadow of reason for the suspicion naturally thrown upon the authorities of Nassau by that unwarrantable act.

I have, &c.
(Signed) CHARLES FRANCIS ADAMS.

No. 134.

Lord Lyons to Earl Russell.—(Received January 15, 1862.)

My Lord, *Washington, December* 31, 1861.

THE Secretary of State of the United States has informed me, that having learned that Messrs. J. W. Zacharie and T. J. Rogers, American citizens, were taken from a vessel called the "Eugenia Smith," under the British flag, and under circumstances similar to those involved in the case of Messrs. Mason and Slidell, and that they are now confined in Fort Lafayette, he has caused orders to be given for their discharge, and permission for them to return to Norfolk, in Virginia, by way of Fortress Monroe.

I have, &c.
(Signed) LYONS.

No. 135.

Lord Lyons to Earl Russell.—(*Received January* 15, 1862.)

My Lord,   *Washington, December* 31, 1861.

THE principal banks at New York and Boston, and, I believe, in other towns, have suspended specie payments. The Treasury of the United States yesterday followed the example.

The banks have apparently found it impossible to furnish to the Government the large loans which they have engaged to make to it. They have not found that support from the public on which they reckoned when they entered into the contracts for the loans. On the contrary, the call on the banks for specie by their private customers has been extraordinarily large. The amount of specie in the New York banks has sunk from about 42,000,000 dollars to about 26,000,000 dollars during the three weeks ending on the 28th instant (three days ago); nearly 10,000.000 dollars were withdrawn by private customers during the last of those weeks.

Under these circumstances, it became impossible for the banks to continue specie payments; and as the Treasury may be said at the present moment to have no other resources than the produce of the loans from the banks, it is as unable as they are to make payments otherwise than in paper.

The remedy suggested is the immediate imposition of high taxes. A reduction of the tariff of import duties would afford a means of increasing the revenue to a large extent, but this has not yet been proposed.

                                                     I have, &c.
                                            (Signed)   LYONS.

No. 136.

Lord Lyons to Earl Russell.—(*Received January* 15, 1862.)

My Lord,   *Washington, December* 31, 1861.

I HAVE the honour to inclose herewith to your Lordship, a copy of a note from Mr. Seward to the Secretary of the Navy, which has been communicated to me to-day by Mr. Seward. It refers to the circumstance of a promise having been exacted, as a condition of release, by the Commander of the United States' steamer from three British seamen captured for breach of blockade, to the effect that they should undertake not to be employed in similar proceedings for the future. Your Lordship will see that Mr. Seward strongly condemns this act, and releases the seamen from the obligation taken by them.

The inclosed correspondence between Her Majesty's Vice-Consul at Key West and Commander Woodhall of the "Connecticut," which has been forwarded to me by Her Majesty's Consul-General at Havana, will put your Lordship in possession of all the facts of the case, such as they have been represented to me.

                                                       I have, &c.
                                            (Signed)   LYONS.

Inclosure 1 in No. 136.

Mr. Seward to Mr. Welles.

Sir,   *Department of State, Washington, December* 31, 1861.

THIS Department has been informally apprized that Commander Woodhall, of the United States' steamer "Connecticut," recently exacted as a condition of the release of members of the crew of the British schooner "Adeline," captured for a breach of the blockade, that they should enter into an engagement not to be employed in a similar proceeding in future.

It occurs to this Department that as the requirement referred to is not warranted by public law, the Commanders of blockading vessels should be instructed not to exact any similar condition for the release of persons found on board vessels charged with a breach of the blockade. It may be lawful to detain such persons as witnesses, when their testimony may be indispensable to the administration of justice, but when captured in a neutral ship they cannot be considered, and ought not to be treated, as prisoners of war. Angus Smith, John Mooney, and John H. McSlaney, the alleged British subjects above referred to, are consequently to be considered as absolved from the obligation represented to have been required of them by Commander Woodhall.

I have, &c.
(Signed) WILLIAM H. SEWARD.

Inclosure 2 in No. 136.

Vice-Consul Welch to Captain Woodhall, U.S.N.

Sir, *Key West, December* 9, 1861.

AFTER my very pleasant visit on board your ship on Saturday last, I went down to Fort Taylor, and had an interview with Captain Angus Smith, John Mooney, and John H. Mc Slaney, a part of the crew of the British schooner "Adeline," of Nassau, which vessel was captured by the United States' war-steamer "Connecticut," under your command, on or about the 17th day of November last past, and brought here, and have since been confined in Fort Taylor.

The above-named persons assure me most positively that they are British subjects, and, in fact, persons residing in this city knew the pilot, John H. Mc Slaney, and I believe the mate, John Mooney, to have been in the Bahamas.

As you signified your intention of taking them to New York in your ship as prisoners of war, I hope you will, upon due reflection, alter your mind, and order them to be set at liberty, inasmuch as Great Britain and the United States are not at war.

I believe it is not the practice of nations to treat neutrals violating blockades as enemies, and hold them as prisoners of war, after the confiscation of the property found in their charge. I therefore beg leave to call your attention to this point, and I hope, after due consideration, you will conclude to set them at liberty; but if you conclude not to do so, but keep them as prisoners of war, I shall feel obliged, as the British Vice-Consul, to protest against their further imprisonment.

Hoping that we may come to a satisfactory understanding, and that the men may be set at liberty, I have, &c.

(Signed) R. M. WELCH.

Inclosure 3 in No. 136.

Captain Woodhall, U.S.N., to Vice-Consul Welch.

Sir, *Key West, December* 9, 1861.

YOURS of this day's date has been received, asking the release of Captain Angus Smith, John H. Mc Slaney, and John Mooney, persons belonging to the prize-schooner "Adeline," captured by me on or about the 17th day of November last, stating your reason for this request, that they are British subjects.

I had determined to take these persons to the North, and deliver them to the custody of the United States' Marshal subject to the further orders of the United States' Government, believing sincerely that the said persons were perfectly aware of the purpose and object of the voyage, and had a full knowledge of the consequences likely to ensue in case of capture, their transactions being clearly in violation of the express command of Her Majesty's Government.

However, as you have requested, I have so far considered and do modify (upon advisement) my intentions (yesterday expressed to you), as to agree to permit the liberation of these persons above-mentioned, upon the condition that they will give me their written promises not to again embark on a like enterprise, or interfere with the legitimate object of the United States' Government in suppressing the wicked rebellion now unhappily existing in our once happy and prosperous country.

If your views coincide with mine, and you will take this in charge, and furnish me the said document, I will, on its receipt, release the parties you have interested yourself so earnestly for.

I have, &c.
(Signed) N. WOODHALL.

Inclosure 4 in No. 136.

Promise exacted from part of the Crew of the British Steamer " Adeline."

WE the Undersigned, Angus Smith (master), John Mooney (mate), and John H. McSlinney (pilot), a part of the crew of the British schooner "Adeline," of Nassau, which was captured by the United States' steamer "Connecticut," about the 17th day of November, 1861, and brought to the port of Key West, and now in confinement in Fort Taylor, do each for ourselves, in consideration of our release from confinement, promise not to again embark in a like enterprise, or interfere with the legitimate object of the United States' Government in suppressing the wicked and causeless rebellion now unhappily existing in this once happy and prosperous country.

(Signed) ANGUS SMITH.
JOHN H. MOONEY.
JOHN H. McSLINNEY.

Witness:
(Signed) R. M. WELCH, *British Vice-Consul.*
British Vice-Consulate, West Key, December 9, 1861.

I hereby certify that the above-named persons signed the above in my presence, of their own free will.

(Signed) R. M. WELCH, *British Vice-Consul.*
West Key, December 9, 1861.

No. 137.

Lord Lyons to Earl Russell.—(Received January 15, 1862.)

My Lord, *Washington, December* 31, 1861.

I HAVE the honour to inclose herewith to your Lordship a copy of a note from Mr. Seward to the Secretary of the Navy, which has been communicated to me to-day by Mr. Seward, referring to the fact of a British schooner, the "James Campbell," captured for breach of blockade, having been brought into New York with the British flag flying under that of the United States.

Mr. Seward condemns this act in the strongest terms; and your Lordship will see, from the inclosed copies of correspondence between Flag Officer Paulding and Her Majesty's Consul at New York, and between the same officer and Commander Lyons, of Her Majesty's ship "Racer," that the act was disavowed with equal promptitude by the naval authorities of the United States, under whose notice it was brought.

I have, &c.
(Signed) LYONS.

Inclosure 1 in No. 137.

Mr. Seward to Mr. Welles.

Sir, *Department of State, Washington, December* 31, 1861.

THIS Department has received unofficial information that the schooner "James Campbell," captured by the blockading squadron, was carried into New York, with the British flag flying under that of the United States. This unseemly act must have been occasioned by a misapprehension of his duty by the officer who ordered or allowed it. I will consequently thank you to give such orders as may tend to prevent a repetition of the same.

I have, &c.
(Signed) WILLIAM H. SEWARD.

Inclosure 2 in No. 137.

Consul Archibald to Lord Lyons.

My Lord,   New York, December 28, 1861.

I HAVE the honour to transmit to your Lordship, herewith inclosed, a copy of a letter this day received by me from Captain Paulding, United States' Navy, commanding at the Naval Yard, Brooklyn, in reference to an act of discourtesy to our flag by the prize-master of a British schooner called the "James Campbell," recently captured by the Atlantic blockading squadron, and sent to this port.

Your Lordship will learn, I am sure, with satisfaction the prompt proceedings of Captain Paulding in disapproving of the conduct of the prize-master, and in reporting the transaction to the Secretary of the Navy.

                I have, &c.
          (Signed) E. M. ARCHIBALD.

Inclosure 3 in No. 137.

Flag Officer Paulding to Consul Archibald.

Sir,   Navy Yard, New York, December 27, 1861.

IT has been reported to me that the schooner "James Campbell," a prize to the North Atlantic blockading squadron, came into port with the English flag flying under the American, and that it was kept so, until ordered to be hauled down by the officers of this yard.

I beg leave to assure you that I very much regret the circumstance, which I can only attribute to ignorance on the part of the mate having charge of the schooner, whom I have reported to the Honourable Secretary of the Navy for his action in the premises.

                I am, &c.
          (Signed) H. PAULDING.

Inclosure 4 in No. 137.

Commander Lyons to Lord Lyons.

My Lord,   "Racer," Staten Island, New York, December 29, 1861.

I HAVE the honour to inclose herewith, for your Lordship's information, copies of a correspondence which has taken place between Flag Officer Paulding and myself, relative to a schooner passing close to two of Her Majesty's ships, with the United States' flag flying over the English ensign.

                I have, &c.
          (Signed) ALGERNON LYONS.

Inclosure 5 in No. 137.

Commander Lyons to Flag Officer Paulding.

Sir,   "Racer," Staten Island, December 27, 1861.

I BEG most respectfully to bring before your notice the following circumstances.

Between the hours of 2 and 3 P.M. yesterday, the 26th instant, an United States' steamer, having in tow a schooner with the flag of the United States flying over the English ensign, passed close to two ships of Her Britannic Majesty, lying off Staten Island, and passed in the direction of New York.

I feel assured, Sir, from your well-known courtesy, of which you were so good as to give me a proof but a very few days since, and which called forth my best thanks, that a proceeding so unusual, and to the British flag so offensive, will not be approved by you.

                I have, &c.
          (Signed) ALGERNON LYONS.

Inclosure 6 in No. 137.

Flag Officer Paulding to Commander Lyons.

Sir, Navy Yard, New York, December 28, 1861.
I HAVE the honour to acknowledge the receipt of your communication of yesterday's date.

In reply, I take leave to assure you, that so soon as the circumstance referred to in your note was made known to me, I immediately expressed my regret at the occurrence to Her Britannic Majesty's Consul, E. M. Archibald, Esq., and reported the officer who caused it to the Honourable Secretary of the Navy.

The officer, recently from civil life, who had charge of the schooner, a prize to the United States' blockading squadron, committed the offence through ignorance, and I promptly disavow, in behalf of the Government of the United States, any intention of disrespect to Her Britannic Majesty's flag or officers, by the act of one of its officers.

I have, &c.
(Signed) W. PAULDING.

Inclosure 7 in No. 137.

Commander Lyons to Flag Officer Paulding.

Sir, "*Racer,*" Staten Island, December 28, 1861.
I HAVE had the high gratification of receiving your communication of this day's date, in reply to my letter of yesterday, and I hasten, Sir, to assure you that the explanation you have been so good as to give me relative to the circumstances referred to is most perfectly satisfactory.

I have, &c.
(Signed) ALGERNON LYONS.

No. 138.

Lord Lyons to Earl Russell.—(Received January 16.)

(Extract.) Washington, January 2, 1862.
I VERY much regret to have to inform your Lordship that the question of closing the ports of the Southern States by an Act of Congress, instead of by a blockade under the law of nations, has been again mooted in the House of Representatives. Mr. Stevens, who, as Chairman of the Committee of Ways and Means, is regarded as the leader of the House, introduced, on the 30th ultimo, a Bill to repeal all laws creating ports of entry in the States which now are, or hereafter may be, in rebellion against this Government.

I have the honour to inclose copies of the Bill, and of the speech with which it was brought forward by Mr. Stevens. It appears to be a far more objectionable measure than the Act empowering the Executive Government to close the ports by proclamation, which was passed by Congress last Session, and approved on the 13th July by President Lincoln. It does not leave any option to the Government in the matter, but abolishes the ports of entry at once by an Act of Congress. Authority is, indeed, given to the President to declare any harbour a port of entry, when in his judgment it shall be expedient to do so. But this is evidently done with a view to those harbours only in the Southern States which the United States now hold, or of which they may hereafter obtain possession. If the Bill were to pass both Houses, and be sanctioned by the President, he could hardly proceed to make it of no effect, by restoring forthwith by Proclamation, the ports of entry which it would abolish.

The provisions which the Bill contains for enforcing the prohibition to enter or come out of the ports to which it applies, are certainly not deficient in stringency. Vessels with their cargoes and everything pertaining to them are to be seized and forfeited; every person is authorized to make the seizure; it may be made at any place at sea or in any port; the goods may be taken wherever found, either on land or water; the ship, cargo, and officers may be tried in any Court of the United States into the jurisdiction of which they may be taken.

Mr. Stevens has postponed the further consideration of the Bill until the second Tuesday in next month. It is to be hoped that in the interval the Executive Government may use their influence to defeat it, and that reflection may convince the majority of the House, if not the mover himself, of the imprudence of any attempt to close the ports otherwise than by a blockade in comformity with the Law of Nations.

Inclosure in No. 138.

Extract from the "National Intelligencer" of December 31, 1861.

MR STEVENS' BILL ABOLISHING CERTAIN PORTS OF ENTRY.—THE following is the Bill introduced in the House to-day by Mr. Stevens on leave:—

1st. That all laws, or parts of laws, creating and establishing ports of entry or delivery in any State now in rebellion be, and the same are hereby repealed.

2nd. Hereafter no vessel, either foreign or domestic, except such as belong to or are employed by the Government of the United States, shall enter or leave any of said ports, unless driven there by stress of weather.

3rd. If any vessel shall violate, or attempt to violate, the provisions of this Act, the said vessel, cargo, and everything appertaining thereto, shall be forfeited, the one-half to go to the captors, and the other half to the United States; and every person is hereby authorized to make such seizure, and the captain or commander of said vessel shall be fined not exceeding 500 dollars.

4th. The said vessel and cargo may be seized at any place at sea, or in any port, and the goods may be taken wherever found, either on land or water.

5th. The proceeds shall be divided among the captors according to the law now regulating prizes.

6th. The ship and cargo may be tried, as well as the officers, in any Court of the United States into whose jurisdiction the same may be taken.

7th. The States now in rebellion are Virginia, North Carolina, South Carolina, Georgia, Alabama, Florida, Texas, Louisiana, Mississippi, Tennessee, and Arkansas. If any other States should hereafter become rebellious, the President shall proclaim the fact, and the provisions of this Act shall then apply to such State or States.

8th. The President shall have power to declare any harbour or harbours ports of entry, when in his judgment it shall be expedient.

HOUSE OF REPRESENTATIVES, MONDAY, DECEMBER 30, 1861.

PORTS OF ENTRY.—*Mr. Stevens.* I should be glad to introduce a Bill of which I gave notice some time ago, with a view of having it placed upon file and printed. I will afterwards move that its consideration be postponed until some future day. The Bill is to repeal certain Acts creating ports of entry.

There being no objection, the Bill was received and read a first and second time.

Mr. Stevens. As the House is rather thin to-day, I propose to make some observations upon this subject. I think a Bill providing for the repeal of all laws creating ports of entry in the rebellious States ought to have been passed at the last Congress. I reported such a Bill, but there were too many Peace Conventions, and Border State Conferences, and too much amiable timidity in this House to allow it to pass—it might offend the rebels. I again reported it at the extra session; it was referred to the Committee on Commerce, and smothered. I now intend to ask a vote of the House on it. The Government has suffered serious disadvantage for the want of it. They have been compelled to put themselves in a false position by attempting to close the ports, and calling it a blockade. Nations do not, correctly speaking, blockade their own ports; that term applies only to operations against foreign nations. When a blockade is declared, it is a quasi admission of the independent existence of the people blockaded. Foreign Powers have then a right to raise the question of the efficiency of the blockade. Evading it when imperfectly maintained is legitimate trade. Nations may lay embargo on their own ports at pleasure. Every nation has a right to say how many of their harbours shall be ports of entry. Foreign nations can enter none other. Collectors and Custom-houses are maintained in none but ports of entry. No duties can be collected in any other, and any trade with them is smuggling. With this right foreign nations cannot interfere. The right to create and indicate ports of entry and delivery is one of the acknowledged prerogatives of sovereignty. Harbours not declared ports of entry need no blockade to exclude commerce: the law blockades them. Respect for that law is safer than fleets. If not respected, its violation creates no international trouble. The offending party is not protected by its Government. We might confine our whole trade to New York, Boston, and Charleston if we chose, and foreign nations could not complain or dictate. How much easier would it be to stop trade with the rebel States if they had no ports of entry than now. The hopes of the forfeiture would induce swarms of private vessels to watch the smugglers.

Mr. Olin.—I wish to ask the gentleman from Pennsylvania whether the provisions of his Bill are consistent with that clause of the Constitution which gives to all ports of entry the same privileges.

Mr. Stevens.—The Constitution, it is true, provides that all ports of entry shall be treated alike, but it does not provide that you shall create certain ports of entry.

Mr. Olin.—But you have created them.

Mr. Stevens.—You have created them ports of entry, and you can repeal the laws so creating them. There is no doubt at all upon this point. No gentleman will deny that. You must put all ports of entry upon the same footing; but when you have passed laws making certain places ports of entry, you can repeal those laws. This bill places all ports of entry now existing in the rebel States upon the same footing. We are not compelled to create ports of entry anywhere, unless we choose. That is for Congress alone to determine

It may be said that commercial nations would respect the ports of entry created by the rebel States. That would be a violation of the law of nations, unless they first acknowledged their independence, and put them on an equality with other nations. It would be just cause of war. In China a widely extended rebellion has existed for years. It has established a regular government, and has several important sea-ports in possession. They lately held Shanghae. Yet Europe ignores their existence, and treats with the legitimate Government for those very ports.

The insurrection in India embraced many more people than ours, many of them well trained to arms ; yet what nation ever thought of recognizing their *de facto* existence, or of treating them as a Power ? When Ireland was in arms against the Government, what would England have said had we negociated with them for ports of entry and recognized their letters of marque ? She would instantly and justly have declared war. I have no fear that any foreign Power will recognize the rebel States. I know very well what deep interest England feels in this question, for, while sealing the Southern ports would ruin the South, it would undoubtedly seriously injure British interests. The second city in her empire is greatly dependent for her prosperity on her cotton manufactories. A half million of people there, as well as many others scattered over the kingdom, earn their living in her factories. It is said five million of people are dependent on them. The products swell the capital of the cotton lords, and contribute largely to commerce. Eighty-five per cent. of the raw material to supply these mills comes from America, and about fifteen per cent. from all other countries (India nine, others six per cent.) Hence it is obvious that England would suffer more by the suppression of Southern commerce than any other nation. It would greatly injure the factories in the loyal States. It would bankrupt the rebel States.

Hence we see the reason why certain leading journals in England sympathize with the South, and suggest means to evade our blockade, and kindly advise us peaceably to settle with the rebels. Why did not England succumb to the Sepoy rebellion ? While the English people hate slavery, the Manchester School would prefer that 4,000,000 slaves should continue in perpetual bondage than that her 5,000,000 dependents should suffer some inconvenience. I doubt not she will use every means in her power to keep open Southern ports. England made war upon the most innocent people in the world to compel them to take her opium. The wise legislation of China had excluded that poisonous drug from the empire. England violated every law of nations and every principle of morality by compelling the people, at the mouth of the cannon, to swallow 80,000,000 dollars worth of it per year.

Nor have we the countervailing advantage of the anti-slavery feeling of England. That feeling among the masses is more intense than the greed for cotton. Were it believed that we were engaged in a war that would abolish slavery, the Government of England would not dare aid our enemies. The whole civilized world now abhors slavery. But in this contest we have the sympathy of none of them. Thus far our war has virtually been made to rivet still stronger the chains of human bondage. Christian nations —civilized nations, whether Christian, Mohammedan, or Pagan, do not sympathise with slave-mongers.

But even now, with the moral sense of the world against us, I do not believe that there is any danger of war with England. The late difficulty, which was so threatening, has been happily settled without any loss of dignity on our part. Nations do not now, and ought not to, go to war on mere questions of regularity, where no vital principle is involved. Much may be waived or yielded on such points unless it impairs the honour of glory of the nation ; then not a tittle can be surrendered, for the honour and glory of a nation are as much a part of her real strength as her fleets and armies. The most unpleasant thing which I have observed in this affair is the impertinent interference of France. Why should she intervene uninvited unless for the purpose of intimidation? The letter of M. Thouvenel is harsh and dictatorial. When we have settled our domestic affairs it may be well to look into this holy alliance of these Powers, and see how far their dictation is to control the conduct of nations.

The statesmen of England feel kindly towards the South for another reason. As Slave States can never become a manufacturing or navigating people, they sympathize with her free-trade folly. We as a nation are bound to maintain our principles and our independence, no matter what difficulties surround us. I have no fear that any foreign Power will recognize the rebel States. But if Manchester should drive England to give aid to the traitors, the free people of America will not quail before it. We have survived two wars with her: one when our population was but 3,000,000; the other when it was 8,000,000, including slaves. Now, when the free States alone have 20,000,000, what have we to fear? A nation great in intellectual as well as material power shows to best advantage in her worst distress. When Rome was deserted by most of her Italian allies, and the Carthaginians were under her walls, she found the King of Macedon tampering with her enemy, and instantly declared war against her, instead of tamely negotiating. A nation is always great according to the energy and courage of the Government. The people are everywhere brave; but timid, faltering, hesitating rulers may soon make them cowards. A nation of 20,000,000 of brave men will always be great, if the Government have energy and power with which to inspire them. Alexander infused his indomitable courage into 20,000 confiding soldiers, and overthrew the countless armies of a timid prince. Let this nation determine to be invincible, and the world in arms, distant as we are from them, cannot conquer her. Let them handle war with silken gloves, and the softest satraps of Asia would defeat them.

War is always a mighty evil. With England it would be especially deplorable. But war with all nations is better than national dishonour and disgrace. We should be better able to meet England in arms with the rebel States in alliance with her than if they were still loyal. They have a vastly extended defenceless frontier easily accessible by a maritime enemy. Most of the army and navy of the nation during the last war were required for its defence. If we were relieved from protecting them, we could use all our forces in other quarters. We should then do what we ought long since to have done—organize their domestic enemies against them, who would find themselves and their allies sufficient employment at home without invading the North. If such a deplorable war should be forced upon us we should do what we ought to have done in the last war—rectify our Eastern and Northern boundaries; and our banner would wave over freemen, and none but republican freemen, from the Gulf of Mexico to the Arctic Ocean, and from the Bay of St. Lawrence to Puget Sound.

Now, Mr. Speaker, unless some gentleman wishes to discuss the bill further at this time, I will move that it be postponed until the second Tuesday in February next, and that it be printed.

The motion was agreed to.

No. 139.

Lord Lyons to Earl Russell.—(Received January 16.)

My Lord, *Washington, January 2, 1862.*

IN my despatches of the 25th and 29th of November last, I had the honour to convey information to your Lordship concerning the preparations which were being made by this Government to obstruct the entrance to ports in the Southern States, by sinking vessels laden with stones in the channels.

Mr. Consul Molyneux, in a despatch dated the 7th of last month,* reported to your Lordship that the measure was, when he wrote, in course of execution at Savannah.

The inclosed extracts from the "National Intelligencer" newspaper of the day before yesterday seem to show that the entrance to Charleston harbour has been effectually obstructed.

I have, &c.
(Signed) LYONS.

---

* Extract from Consul Molyneux' despatch:—"I beg to acquaint your Lordship with the fact that the Federal Government has adopted an unusual mode of blockading the Savannah river; namely, by sinking across the channel vessels heavily laden with stone. A few days ago a large fleet of such vessels, accompanied by seven vessels of war, arrived off Tybee, some of which are now being sunk in such a manner as to prevent the passage of any vessel. It is reported to be the intention of the Federal Government to block up all the Southern harbours in the same manner."

Inclosure in No. 139.

Extract from the "National Intelligencer" of December 31, 1861.

THE STONE FLEET AT CHARLESTON.—THE official Report of Commodore Dupont in relation to the sinking of the stone fleet has been received at the Navy Department. The substantial part of the document consists in the Report of Captain Charles Henry Davis, who had command of the fleet. In this Report Captain Davis says:—

"On the night of my arrival off Charleston the lighthouse was blown up, by which the purpose of my visit was essentially promoted. After the bar had been sounded out two ships were sunk—one on the eastern, and one on the western limits of the channel—which served to limit the field of operations. After all the ships which were to be sunk, sixteen in number, had been brought here and placed in a position to be easily moored, they were towed in by the smaller steamers and placed upon and inside the bar, in a checkered or indented form, lying as much as possible across the direction of the channel in several lines, some distance apart; and they are made so nearly to overlie each other that it would be difficult to draw a line through them in the direction of the channel which would not be intercepted by one of the vessels."

Commander Davis states that he was guided by several principles in choosing the place and manner for sinking the vessels, viz.:—

First. The bar was selected because it is the principal and culminating point of the natural deposit on this line. By adding the material contained in the hulks to those already placed there by Nature, it may be expected that the natural forces which aggregate the latter will tend to keep the former in their assigned positions.

Secondly. By putting down the vessels in an indented line to create a material obstruction to the channel, without seriously impeding the flow of water. If it were possible to build a wall across the channel, the river, which must flow to the sea, would undoubtedly take another and similar path. But if, on the contrary, the blocking up of the natural channel is only partial, the water may retain a part of its old course, and require the addition of only a new channel of small capacity.

Thirdly. The mode of sinking the vessels is intended to establish a combination of artificial interruptions and irregularities resembling, on a small scale, those of Hell Gate or Holmes Hole, and producing, like them, eddies, whirlpools, and counter-currents, such as render the navigation of an otherwise difficult channel hazardous and uncertain.

No. 140.

Lord Lyons to Earl Russell.—(Received January 16.)

My Lord, *Washington, January* 3, 1862.

IT is announced that great efforts are about to be made to give a serious blow to the Southern cause.

A naval and military expedition, as formidable as that which obtained possession of Port Royal, is believed to be on the point of assembling at Fortress Monroe, at the mouth of Chesapeake Bay. The number of soldiers embarked is stated to be about 14,000. It is to be commanded by General Burnside.

Another naval and military expedition, on nearly the same scale, is said to be almost ready.

Numerous gun-boats have been prepared on the Upper Mississippi, in order to descend that river. It is understood that some of the United States' officers do not despair of carrying troops as far as New Orleans by this means, and obtaining possession of that important town.

It is stated, but with less confidence, that the Grand Army of the Potomac is about to make a forward movement.

The destination of General Burnside's expedition has not become public. The general opinion is that it will attempt to approach Richmond by one or more of the three rivers (the Rappahannock, the York river, and the James river) which fall into Chesapeake Bay below the mouth of the Potomac. General Burnside might in this way make a diversion which would very much facilitate an attack by the Grand Army on the Confederate forces in front of Manassas Gap.

By many, however, it is thought that the expedition under General Burnside is intended either to seize another port on the Southern Coast, in the same way as Port Royal was taken possession of by General Sherman, or to reinforce the troops on Ship Island, with a view to an attack from that point on New Orleans.

However this may be, the magnificent promises which have on so many previous occasions been followed by very small performance render people incredulous, and dispose them to expect small rather than great results from these expeditions, so loudly vaunted beforehand.

I have, &c.
(Signed)   LYONS.

No. 141.

The Chairman of the Liverpool Shipowners' Association to Earl Russell.—(Received January 14.)

My Lord,   *Shipowners' Association, Liverpool, January* 13, 1862.

IT has come to the knowledge of the Liverpool Shipowners' Association through the public prints, that the Federal Government of the United States have sunk a stone squadron in the main channel of Charleston harbour.

This proceeding cannot fail seriously and permanently to injure the entrance to that harbour.

The Association fears that unless strong representations and remonstrances are promptly made, a similar course may be immediately followed in the case of the other harbours of the Confederate States.

The Association does not think it necessary to dwell at length on the importance of this question as affecting the general interests of commerce, but feels called upon, as representing an important interest, to address your Lordship on the subject.

I am therefore instructed by the Association respectfully to press this matter on your Lordship's earnest consideration.

I have, &c.
(Signed)   FRANCIS A. CLINT, *Chairman.*

No. 142.

Mr. Hammond to the Chairman of the Liverpool Shipowners' Association.

Sir,   *Foreign Office, January* 15, 1862.

I AM directed by Earl Russell to acknowledge the receipt of the letter which, on behalf of the Liverpool Shipowners' Association, you addressed to him on the 13th instant, calling his attention to the course which the Federal Government of the United States have adopted for closing the main channel of Charleston harbour, by sinking there vessels laden with stone; and expressing the fear of the Association that, unless strong representations and remonstrances are promptly made, a similar course may be immediately followed in the case of the other harbours of the Confederate States.

I am to request that you will state to the Liverpool Shipowners' Association that the attention of Her Majesty's Government was at once attracted by the rumours which obtained currency some weeks ago, of such a course as that to which you refer being contemplated by the Government of the United States, and on the 20th of December Her Majesty's Minister at Washington was informed of the view taken of it by Her Majesty's Government.

Lord Lyons was told that such a cruel plan would seem to imply despair of the restoration of the Union, the professed object of the war. For it never could be the wish of the United States' Government to destroy cities from which their own country was to derive a portion of its riches and prosperity. Such a plan could only be adopted as a measure of revenge and of irremediable injury against an enemy.

Lord Lyons was further told that, even as a scheme of embittered and sanguinary war, such a measure would not be justifiable. It would be a plot against the commerce of all maritime nations, and against the free intercourse of the Southern States of America with the civilized world.

Lord Lyons was desired to speak in this sense to Mr. Seward, who, it was hoped, would disavow the alleged project. Now, however, that the project seems to have been carried into effect at Charleston, Lord Lyons will be instructed to make a further representation to Mr. Seward, with a view to prevent similar acts of destruction in other ports.

I am, &c.
(Signed)   E. HAMMOND.

No. 143.

Earl Russell to Lord Lyons.

My Lord,   *Foreign Office, January* 16, 1862.

I INSTRUCTED your Excellency in my despatch of the 20th of December to speak to Mr. Seward on the subject of a plan reported to be in the contemplation of the Government of the United States for blocking up the entrance into Charleston harbour by sinking ships laden with stones.

I had hoped that Mr. Seward would have promptly disavowed any such project; but it unfortunately appears that it has been actually carried into effect.

The observations which I instructed your Lordship in that despatch to address to Mr. Seward will have conveyed to him in some measure the impression which such a course of proceeding could not fail to make in this country, and in all other countries having commercial intercourse with America.

I inclose a copy of a representation which I have received from the Shipowners' Association of Liverpool, together with a copy of my reply.*

I have further to instruct your Lordship to observe to Mr. Seward, with reference as well to the destruction of the entrance into Charleston Harbour, which seems to have been effected, as to similar operations said to be in contemplation against other harbours in the so-styled Confederate States, that the object of war is peace, and the purposes of peace are mutual goodwill and advantageous commercial intercourse; but this barbarous proceeding deprives war of its legitimate objects, by stripping peace of its natural fruits.

The present contest between the North and South must end either in the conquest of the South by the North, or a separation by mutual agreement. In the first case this operation is suicidal, by taking away from what will in that case be a part of the territory of the Union advantages which the bounty of Heaven has bestowed; in the latter case, this proceeding will have implanted undying hatred in the breasts of those who being close neighbours ought to be also firm friends.

I am, &c.
(Signed)   RUSSELL.

No. 144.

Earl Russell to Lord Lyons.

My Lord,   *Foreign Office, January* 16, 1862.

I HAVE to acquaint your Lordship that Her Majesty's Government have learned with satisfaction that, as reported in your despatch of the 31st of December, the Government of the United States have released the three British subjects captured in the British schooner "Adeline," of Nassau, for breach of blockade, from the obligation so improperly imposed upon them by the Commander of the United States' steamer of war "Connecticut," "not to again embark in a like enterprise or interfere with the legitimate object of the United States' Government in suppressing the wicked and causeless rebellion now unhappily existing in this once happy and prosperous country."

I am, &c.
(Signed)   RUSSELL.

No. 145.

Earl Russell to Lord Lyons.

My Lord,   *Foreign Office, January* 17, 1862.

I HAVE received your Lordship's despatch of the 2nd instant, relating to the obstruction of the entrance to ports in the Southern States by sinking stones. My despatches of the 20th ultimo and of the 16th instant will have instructed your Lordship as to the language which you should hold to Mr. Seward on this subject.

I am, &c.
(Signed)   RUSSELL.

---

* Nos. 141 and 142.

No. 146.

Earl Russell to Lord Lyons.

My Lord,   Foreign Office, January 17, 1862.

I HAVE received your Lordship's despatch of the 31st of December, reporting that you had been informed by Mr. Seward that the two American citizens who had been taken out of the British vessel "Eugenia Smith" by the Commander of the United States' cruizer "Santiago de Cuba" had been set at liberty, and allowed to return to Norfolk, in Virginia; and I have to acquaint your Lordship that Her Majesty's Government have received this information with much satisfaction.

                   I am, &c.
                 (Signed)   RUSSELL.

No. 147.

Earl Russell to Lord Lyons.

My Lord,   Foreign Office, January 17, 1862.

I HAVE to acquaint your Lordship that Her Majesty's Government receive with satisfaction the apologies so promptly tendered by the United States' Government and by Commodore Paulding, as reported in your despatch of the 31st of December, for the unseemly proceedings of the prize-master on board the British schooner "James Campbell" in bringing that vessel into New York with the flag of the United States flying over the British flag.

                   I am, &c.
                 (Signed)   RUSSELL.

No. 148.

Lord Lyons to Earl Russell.—(Received January 20.)

(Extract.)   Washington, January 4, 1862.

I HAVE the honour to inclose a copy of a letter addressed to Mr. Harris, one of the Senators for the State of New York, and which has been printed in the "New York Tribune" newspaper. It contains a strong argument against treating the Southern privateersmen as pirates.

It may be hoped that in this, as in other respects, the Government of the United States will perceive the advantage and propriety of dealing with the facts of the present civil war as they exist in reality. For a long time it refused to exchange prisoners taken on shore, lest by so doing it should be held to admit that the contest with the South had reached the dimensions of a war; a system, however, of exchanging such prisoners has been gradually set on foot. Consistency would seem to require that prisoners taken at sea should be treated in the same manner. Already retaliatory measures have been taken by the Southern Government, in consequence of the imprisonment and trial, in the North, of captured privateersmen; and further retaliation on the South, in revenge for this, has been loudly called for in the United States' Congress and elsewhere.

Inclosure in No. 148.

Extract from the "New York Tribune" of January 3, 1862.

ARE THE SOUTHERN PRIVATEERSMEN PIRATES?

Letter of Judge Daly to the Hon. Ira Harris.

Dear Sir,   New York, December 21, 1861.

IN compliance with your request at our conversation in Washington, I will put in writing the reasons why the Southern privateersmen should be regarded as prisoners of war and not as pirates.

Privateering is a lawful mode of warfare except among those nations who by Treaty stipulate that they will not, as between themselves, resort to it. Pirates are the general enemies of all mankind, *hostis humani generis*, but privateersmen act under and are subject to the authority of the nation or power by whom they are commissioned. They enter into certain securities that they will respect the rights of neutrals; their vessel is liable to seizure and condemnation if they act illegally, and they wage war only against the Power with which the authority that commissioned them is at war. A privateer does no more than is done by a man-of-war, namely, seize the vessel of the enemy, the prize or booty being distributed as a reward among the captors. The only difference between them is, that the vessel of war is the property of the Government, manned and maintained by it, while the other is a private enterprize, undertaken for the same general purpose, and giving guarantees that it will be conducted according to the established usages of war. In short, one is a public, the other a private vessel of war, neither of which acquires any right to a prize taken until the lawfulness of the capture is declared by a competent Court, under whose direction the thing taken can be condemned and sold, and the proceeds distributed in such proportions as the Court considers equitable. The Government of the United States declined to become a party to the International Treaty of Paris in 1856, and therefore the whole people of the United States, as well those who are maintaining the Government as those who are in rebellion against it, have never agreed to dispense with privateering. It is not our interest to do so. We are a maritime people, with a large extent of sea-coast, which while it leaves us greatly exposed to attacks by sea, at the same time affords facilities that render privateering to us one of our most effective arms in warfare. This was the case in our contest with England in 1812, and should a war now grow out of the affair of the "Trent," privateering would be indispensable to enable us to cope with so formidable a Power as that of Great Britain.

A great deal has been written against this mode of warfare, but nations, like individuals, act upon the instinct of self-preservation, and avail themselves of the natural defences which grow out of their situation; and a system, therefore, which enables us to keep a small navy in peace, and improvise a large one in war, will never be relinquished, because nations who have everything to lose or little to gain by its continuance desire that it should be generally abolished. Being, then, a legitimate mode of making war, what is the difference between the Southern soldier who takes up arms against the Government of the United States upon land, and the Southern privateersman who does the same upon the water? Practically there is none; and if one should be held and exchanged as a prisoner of war, the other is equally entitled to the privilege. The Court before which the crew of the "Jefferson Davis" were convicted as pirates held that they could not be regarded as privateers upon the ground that they were not acting under the authority of an independent State with the recognized rights of sovereignty. This objection applies equally to the man-of-war's men in the Southern fleets, and to every soldier in the Southern army, none of whom are acting under the authority of a recognized Government. The Constitution defines treason to be the levying of war against the United States, and the giving of aid and comfort to its enemies. All of them are engaged in doing this; and although the Southern privateersmen may fall specifically under the provisions of the Act defining piracy, the guilt of the one is precisely the same as that of the other. The question then arises—as there is in point of fact no difference between them—is every seaman or soldier that shall be taken in arms against the Government to be hung as a traitor or a pirate? If the matter is to be left to the Courts, conviction and the sentence of death must follow in every instance. In the case of the "Jefferson Davis," the Court said that during civil war, in which hostilities are prosecuted on an extended scale, persons in arms against the established Government, captured by its naval or military forces, are often treated not as traitors or pirates, but according to the humane usages of war. They are detained as prisoners until exchanged or discharged on parole, or, if surrendered to the civil authorities and convicted, they are respited or pardoned; but the Court said this was a matter with which courts and juries had nothing to do; that it was purely a question of governmental policy, depending upon the decision of the Executive or Legislative Department of the Government, and not upon its judicial organ.

If this view be correct, the disposition of this matter rests exclusively with the Government, and its decision must be pronounced sooner or later, as every day increases the complication and difficulties growing out of the present state of things. Are the Courts to go on? Is the Government prepared to say that every man in arms against the United States upon the land or upon the water is to be tried and executed as a traitor or pirate, either upon the ground that it is right, or upon the supposition that it will prove an effective means for suppressing the rebellion? That policy was tried by the Duke of

Alva in the revolt of the seven Provinces of the Netherlands, and 18,000 persons by his order suffered death upon the scaffold; the result being a more desperate resistance, the sympathy of surrounding nations, and the ultimate independence of the Dutch. Neither the Constitution of the United States nor the Act against piracy was framed in view of any such state of things as that which now exists. The civil war which now prevails is in its magnitude beyond anything previously known in history. The revolting States hold possession of a large portion of the territory of the Union, embracing a great extent of sea-coast, and including some of our principal cities and harbours. They hold forcible possession of it by means of an army estimated at 300,000 men, and are practically exercising over it all the power and authority of Government. They claim to have separated from the United States, to have founded a Government of their own, and are in armed resistance to maintain it. To reduce them to obedience, and to recover that of which they hold forcible possession, it has been necessary for us to resort to military means of more than corresponding magnitude, until the combatants on both sides have reached the prodigious number of 1,000,000 of men. The principal nations of Europe, recognizing this state of things, have conceded to the rebellious States the rights of belligerents—a course of which we have no reason to complain, as we did precisely the same thing towards the States of South America in their revolt against the Government of Spain. It is natural that we should have hesitated to consider the Southern States in the light of belligerents before the rebellion had expanded to its present proportions; but now we cannot, if we would, shut our eyes to the fact that war, and war upon a more extensive scale than usually takes place between contending nations, actually exists. It is now, and it will be continued to be, carried on upon both sides by a resort to all the means and appliances known to modern warfare, and unless we are to fall back into the barbarism of the middle ages we must observe in its conduct those humane usages in the treatment and exchange of prisoners which modern civilization has shown to be equally the dictates of humanity and policy. For every seaman that we have arrested as a pirate, they have incarcerated a Northern soldier, to be dealt with exactly as we do with the privateersmen. We have convicted as pirates four of the crew of the "Jefferson Davis," and there are others in New York awaiting trial. Are those men to be executed? If they are, then by that act we deliberately consign to death a number of our own officers and soldiers, the most of whom owe their captivity and present peril to the heroic courage with which they stood by their colours in a day of disastrous flight and panic. If such a course is to be pursued, it will not be very encouraging for the soldier now in arms for the maintenance of the Union to know that what may be asked of him is to fight upon one side with the risk of being hanged upon the other, and in face of the enemy, with his line broken, instead of rallying again, he may, in view of the possibility of a halter, deem it prudent to retire before the double danger. If, on the other hand, we convict these men as criminals and pause there, then the crime of which we have declared them to be guilty is not followed by its necessary consequence, the proper punishment. There is no terror inspired and no check interposed by such a procedure, for the plainest man in the South knows that the motive which restrains us from going further is the fact that the execution of these men as pirates seals the doom of a corresponding number of our own people; that the account is exactly balanced; that, with ample means of retaliation, they have the power to prevent, or if mutual blood is to be shed in this way, we and not they will have commenced it. By such a course, nothing is effected except to keep our own officers and soldiers in the cells of Southern prisons, subject to that mental torture produced by the uncertainty of their fate, which with the majority of men is more difficult to bear than the certainty of death itself, and oblige them to endure, in the ill-provided and badly-conducted prisons in which they are confined, sufferings, the sickening details of which are constantly before us in their published letters to their friends. "I little thought," writes the gallant Colonel Cogswell of the regular service, "when I faced the storm of bullets at Edward's Ferry, and escaped a soldier's death upon the field, that it was only to be left by my country to die upon a gallows." And the nature of their sufferings will be understood when it is told that the noble-hearted and self-sacrificing Colonel Corcoran was handcuffed and placed in a solitary cell with a chain attached to the floor, until the mental excitement produced by the ignominious treatment, combining with a susceptible constitution and the infectious character of the locality, brought on an attack of typhoid fever. Shall this state of things continue to exist? Let us take counsel of our common sense. These men are treated as criminals because, while we give to the Southern soldier the rights of war (for numerous exchanges of soldiers have taken place), we convict the Southern mariner of a crime punishable with death. Is there any reason, even upon the grounds of policy, for making this distinction? We have, by the blockade of the whole Southern coast, cut the privateersman off from bringing his prize into the ports of the South for adjudication, and the ports of all neutral nations being closed against him for such a purpose, he is deprived of means of making lawful prize, and must eventually convert his vessel into a ship of war, or degenerate into a pirate by unlawful acts which will make him amenable to the tribunal of every civilized nation. The comparative injury that may be done to our commerce by the few privateers which it will be now in the power of the rebellious States to maintain upon the ocean is as nothing compared to the disastrous and lasting consequences to the whole nation, to its industry, its commerce, and its future, that would grow out of making this war one of retaliatory vengeance. We have the fruitful experience of history to admonish us that in such acts are sown the seeds of the dissolution of nations, and especially of Republics. By acceding to the rebellious States the rights of belligerents, at least to the extent of exchanging prisoners, whether privateersmen, men-of-war's-men, or soldiers, we do not concede to them the rights of sovereignty. There is a well-defined distinction between the two recognized by the United States' Court in the case of Rose v. Himley (4 Cranch, 241). One may exist without the other, and by exchanging prisoners, therefore, we concede nothing and admit nothing, except what everybody knows, that actual war exists, and that as a Christian people we mean to carry it on according to the usages of civilized nations.

The existing embarrassment is easily overcome; further prosecutions can be stopped, and in respect to the privateersmen who have been convicted, the President, acting upon the suggestion of the Court that tried them, can, by the exercise of the pardoning power, relieve them from their position as criminals and place them in that of prisoners of war.

In conclusion, we are not to forget that we are carrying on this war for the restoration of the Union, and that every act of aggression not essential to military success will but separate more widely the two sections from each other, and increase the difficulty of cementing us again in one nationality. We are to remember that the people of the South, whose infirmity it has been to have very extravagant ideas of their own superiority, and whose contempt of the people of the North has been in proportion to their want of information respecting them, have been hurried into their present position by the professional politicians and large landed proprietors to whom they have hitherto been accustomed to confide the management of their public affairs; that, though prone to commit outrageous acts when under the influence of excitement, they are, upon the whole, a kindly and affectionate people, and have, when not blinded by passion, a very keen perception of their own interest; that there are throughout the South thousands of loyal hearts paralyzed by the excitement by which they are surrounded, who still cling to the flag of their fathers, and await the delivering stroke of our armies. Relying on our superior naval and military strength, and the settled determination of our people that this nation shall not be dismembered, we can, as the Swiss Cantons recently did in a similar crisis, put down this rebellion. That great duty imposes upon us all the exigencies of war. War, when conducted in accordance with the strictest usages of humanity, is, as all who have shared in the recent battles know, a sufficiently bloody business, and if we are to add to its horrors by hanging up all who fall into our hands as traitors or pirates, we leave to the South no alternative but resistance to the last extremity; and should we ultimately triumph, we would have entailed upon us, as the consequences of such a policy, the bitter inheritance of maintaining a Government by force over a people conquered but not subdued.

Very truly yours,
(Signed) CHARLES P. DALY.

No. 149.

Lord Lyons to Earl Russell.—(Received January 20.)

My Lord, *Washington, January 4, 1862.*

THE President of the United States received the Diplomatic Body on New Year's day. I was present at the reception with the whole of Her Majesty's Legation.

I called afterwards, according to custom, upon each of the members of the Cabinet, at his own house.

I was received with great cordiality by the President and the Cabinet.

I have, &c.
(Signed) LYONS.

No. 150.

Lord Lyons to Earl Russell.—(Received January 23.)

My Lord, *Washington, January 9, 1862.*

WITH reference to my despatch of the 31st ultimo, I have the honour to transmit to your Lordship copies of two notes and their inclosures, which have been addressed to me by the State Department, with respect to the unseemly position in which the British flag was placed on board the captured schooner "James Campbell," in New York harbour.

I have also the honour to inclose a copy of a note which I have written to Mr. Seward in reply.

The occurrence seems to have been caused solely by the ignorance of the prize-master in charge of the "James Campbell," and reparation for the apparent disrespect to the flag was made immediately and spontaneously by the superior naval authority on the spot. Such being the case, I have expressed to Mr. Seward my thanks for the measures taken to do away with the unpleasant impression which was produced by the error of the prize-master.

I have, &c.
(Signed) LYONS.

Inclosure 1 in No. 150.

Mr. F. Seward to Lord Lyons.

My Lord, *Washington, January 3, 1862.*

REFERRING to your private note of the 30th ultimo, in which, among other cases, mention is made of the improper manner in which the British flag was placed on board of the schooner "James Campbell," captured on a charge of breach of blockade, and to my reply, I now have the honour to inclose to you, for your information, the copy of a letter just received from the Secretary of the Navy on the subject.

I avail, &c.
(Signed) F. W. SEWARD.

Inclosure 2 in No. 150.

Mr. Welles to Mr. Seward.

Sir, *Navy Department, January 2, 1862.*

I HAVE the honour to acknowledge the receipt of your note of the 31st ultimo, relating to the circumstance of the prize-schooner "James Campbell" having been taken into the port of New York with the British flag flying under that of the United States. The fact adverted to was reported to the Department under date of the 27th ultimo by the Commandant of the New York Navy-yard, who stated that the prize-master of the schooner kept the British flag in that position until ordered to haul it down by the authorities of the yard. The Commandant of the yard, as soon as he became aware of the circumstance, expressed his regret to Her Britannic Majesty's Consul, Mr. Archibald, and informed him that the prize-master should be reported to the Department.

I have called on Acting-Master John Baker, who had charge of the prize, for an explanation of the reasons for the act, which has not yet been received.

I have, &c.
(Signed) GIDEON WELLES.

Inclosure 3 in No. 150.

Mr. Seward to Lord Lyons.

My Lord, *Department of State, Washington, January 8, 1862.*

ADVERTING to my note to you of the 3rd instant relative to the improper position in which the British flag was placed on board the schooner "James Campbell," captured on a charge of breach of blockade, I now have the honour to inclose to you, for your information, a copy of a further communication just received from the Secretary of the Navy on that subject.

I have, &c.
(Signed)   W. H. SEWARD.

Inclosure 4 in No. 150.

Mr. Welles to Mr. Seward.

Sir,   *Navy Department, January* 7, 1862.

REFERRING to my letter of the 2nd instant, I have the honour to transmit herewith an extract from a communication received from Acting-Master John Baker, in explanation of his conduct in taking the prize schooner "James Campbell" into New York, with the British flag flying under the American.

I have, &c.
(Signed)   GIDEON WELLES.

Inclosure 5 in No. 150.

Mr. Baker to Flag Officer Paulding.

(Extract.)   *New York, January* 3, 1862.

I RECEIVED your order to-day stating for me to make a written statement, and explain the reason for hoisting the English flag under the American. Commodore, not being acquainted with the customs of fetching in prizes, I was under the impression that I was right. My intention was to do right, but it was not done for any bad purpose in intention to insult the English flag in any way whatever. I was wrong for so doing, and truly hope the Department will forgive me.

Inclosure 6 in No. 150.

Lord Lyons to Mr. Seward.

Sir,   *Washington, January* 9, 1862.

I HAVE the honour to acknowledge the receipt of the notes from the State Department of the 3rd and 8th instant, relative to the unseemly position in which the British flag was placed on board the captured vessel "John Campbell," in New York harbour.

No sooner did the superior naval authorities of the United States at New York perceive the position in which the flag was placed, than they ordered it to be removed. Commander Paulding, moreover, immediately wrote to Her Majesty's Consul to express his regret at the occurrence. He was, besides, so good as to address a letter to the Commander of Her Majesty's ship "Racer," disavowing, in behalf of the Government of the United States, any intention to show disrespect to the British flag. Finally, it appears from the report of the prize-master, of which you have now done me the honour to send me a copy, that he acted from ignorance, and without any intention to slight the flag.

Under these circumstances, it only remains for me to express my thanks for the prompt measures which have been taken by the United States' authorities to do away with the unpleasant impression which was produced by the error of the prize-master.

I have, &c.
(Signed)   LYONS.

No. 151.

Lord Lyons to Earl Russell.—(*Received January* 23.)

My Lord,   *Washington, January* 9, 1862.

WITH reference to my despatches of the 31st ultimo and of the 2nd instant, I have the honour to transmit to your Lordship copies of a note and its inclosures which I have received from Mr. Seward on the subject of the engagement exacted from some of the crew of the schooner "Adeline" as a condition of their being set at liberty.

The letter from Commander Woodhall to the Secretary of the Navy (Inclosure No. 3), shows how necessary it was that instructions should be given to the naval officers of the United States with regard to the treatment of the crews of vessels captured for breach of blockade.

I have, &c.
(Signed) LYONS.

Inclosure 1 in No. 151.

Mr. Seward to Lord Lyons.

My Lord, *Washington, January 7,* 1862.

WITH reference to your private note of the 30th ultimo, in which mention is made of the imprisonment of three of the crew of the schooner "Adeline," and of the oath exacted from them as a condition of their release, and to my reply, I now have the honour to inclose to you, for your information, the copy of a communication of the 4th instant, addressed to this Department by the Secretary of the Navy on the subject.

I avail, &c.
(Signed) WILLIAM H. SEWARD.

Inclosure 2 in No. 151.

Mr. Welles to Mr. Seward.

Sir, *Navy Department, January* 4, 1862.

I HAVE had the honour to receive your communication of the 31st ultimo in reference to the conditional release of three of the crew of the schooner "Adeline," captured for a breach of the blockade by Commander Maxwell Woodhall, of the United States' steamer "Connecticut."

Commander Woodhall has been informed that, in your opinion, the requirement exacted by him is not warranted by public law, and that the three alleged British subjects in question are, consequently, to be considered as absolved from the obligation required of them. I have also given instructions to the flag-officers of the blockading squadrons, so that a similar condition for the release of persons found on board of prizes, or vessels charged with a breach of the blockade, may not in future be exacted.

I transmit herewith for your information an extract from a report of Commander Woodhall in relation to the release of the parties, &c.

I am, &c.
(Signed) GIDEON WELLES.

Inclosure 3 in No. 151.

Commander Woodhall, U.S.N., to Mr. Welles.

(Extract.) *Brooklyn Navy Yard, December* 17, 1861.

AMONG the persons found on board the schooner "Adeline" (one of the above prizes), was a citizen of Georgia, Captain Hardee, commanding a company of Artillery, now located in one of the forts near Savannah. He was connected with the "Adeline" as her supercargo, and, by his own acknowledgment, a bearer of despatches from Messrs. Mason and Slidell, which documents he threw overboard a few moments before we boarded the schooner. I understand also that he is the nephew of Colonel Hardee, late of the United States' army, now a General of the rebel forces. He is of an influential family, who, doubtless, will use great exertion to obtain his release or exchange. Under these circumstances, I determined to bring him north, and place him in charge of the United States' Marshal at New York, to await the further orders of the Government.

It was also my desire to bring with me the captain of the "Adeline," her pilot, and mate, "old offenders," having, by their own admission, and other evidence, satisfactorily proved that they had run the blockade several times before; but as they were claimed as

British subjects by Her Britannic Majesty's Vice-Consul at Key West, I did, by advice (though not by my own judgment) of Judge Marvin, conclude to liberate them; first, however, causing the said Consul to furnish me their written personal obligation under oath, not to again embark in a like enterprise, or interfere with the legitimate object of the United States' Government in suppressing the rebellion.

No. 152.

Earl Russell to Lord Lyons.

My Lord,   *Foreign Office, January* 24, 1862.

I HAVE received your Lordship's despatch of the 4th instant, inclosing a copy of Judge Daly's published letter on the question whether the Southern privateersmen can be regarded as pirates, and Her Majesty's Government are glad to find that that pretension has been so successfully combated. There can be no doubt that men embarked on board a man-of-war or privateer having a commission, or of which the Commander has a commission from the so-called President Davis, should be treated in the same way as officers and soldiers similarly commissioned for operations on land.

Your Lordship will observe to Mr. Seward that an insurrection extending over nine States in space, and ten months in duration, can only be considered as a civil war, and that persons taken prisoners on either side should be regarded as prisoners of war. Reason, humanity, and the practice of nations, require that this should be the case.

                        I am, &c.
                 (Signed)   RUSSELL.

No. 153.

Lord Lyons to Earl Russell.—(Received January 27.)

My Lord,   *Washington, January* 14, 1862.

THREE days ago, in obedience to your Lordship's orders, I spoke to Mr. Seward in the sense of your Lordship's despatch of the 20th ultimo, on the subject of the plan adopted by this Government of obstructing the entrance of some of the harbours in the Southern States by sinking vessels laden with stones in the channels.

Mr. Seward observed, that it was altogether a mistake to suppose that this plan had been devised with a view to injure the harbours permanently. It was, he said, simply a temporary military measure, adopted to aid the blockade. The Government of the United States had, last spring, with a navy very little prepared for so extensive an operation, undertaken to blockade upwards of 3,000 miles of coast. The Secretary of the Navy had reported that he could stop up the "large holes" by means of his ships, but that he could not stop up the "small ones." It had been found necessary, therefore, to close some of the numerous small inlets by sinking vessels in the channels. It would be the duty of the Government of the United States to remove all these obstructions as soon as the Union was restored. It was well understood that this was an obligation incumbent on the Federal Government. At the end of the war with Great Britain that Government had been called upon to remove a vessel which had been sunk in the harbour of Savannah, and had recognized the obligation, and removed the vessel accordingly. Moreover, the United States were now engaged in a civil war with the South. He was not prepared to say that, as an operation in war, it was unjustifiable to destroy permanently the harbours of the enemy. But nothing of the kind had been done on the present occasion. Vessels had been sunk by the rebels to prevent the access to their ports of the cruizers of the United States: the same measure had been adopted by the United States, in order to make the blockade complete. When the war was ended, the removal of all these obstructions would be a mere matter of expense; there would be no great difficulty in removing them effectually. Besides, as had already been done in the case of Port Royal, the United States would open better harbours than those which they closed.

I asked Mr. Seward whether the principal entrance to Charleston harbour had not been recently closed altogether by vessels sunk by order of this Government; and I observed to him that the opening of a new port, thirty or forty miles off, would hardly console the people of the large town of Charleston for the destruction of their own harbour.

Mr. Seward said that the best proof he could give me that the harbour of Charleston
                                      T

had not been rendered inaccessible, was that, in spite of the sunken vessels and of the blockading squadron, a British steamer laden with contraband of war had just succeeded in getting in.

I have, &c.
(Signed) LYONS.

No. 154.

Lord Lyons to Earl Russell.—(Received January 27.)

My Lord, *Washington, January* 14, 1862.

IN obedience to the instruction contained in your Lordship's despatch of the 27th ultimo, I delivered to Mr. Seward, on the 11th instant, a copy of your Lordship's despatch of the 22nd November last, relative to the arbitrary arrests of British subjects.

I have the honour to inclose a copy of a note dated yesterday, which I have just received from Mr. Seward, and which contains comments on your Lordship's despatch.

I have also the honour to inclose a copy of a short note in which I have informed Mr. Seward in reply that I shall transmit to your Lordship a copy of his communication.

I have, &c.
(Signed) LYONS.

Inclosure 1 in No. 154.

Mr. Seward to Lord Lyons.

My Lord, *Washington, January* 13, 1862.

YOU have kindly left with me a copy of an instruction which you had received from Earl Russell, dated on the 22nd of November last.

I have great pleasure in stating to you, for the information of his Lordship, that the President frankly and unhesitatingly accepts the explanations given by Earl Russell of what was the meaning of the British Government in the views which, at their instance, you had heretofore submitted to me concerning the right of the President to suspend the *habeas corpus* in time of insurrection, without waiting for direct authority from Congress.

I have to regret, however, that while the misapprehension which has existed upon this one point is thus generously removed by Earl Russell, he deems it necessary to persist in the opinion that the President's proceeding, under a suspension of the *habeas corpus*, in the case of William Patrick, was wanton and capricious, and that it had not been rendered necessary by the exigencies of the civil war.

As Government must proceed always upon information, and often with great promptness and energy, it could hardly be possible to avoid the commission of occasional errors in the exercise of precautionary power to repress insurrection, manifesting itself more or less formidably in every State of the American Union. I cannot but think that a prompt correction of the error in such a case, such a correction as was made in the case of Mr. Patrick, is all that could reasonably be required by persons willing to deliberate carefully and anxious to interpret the action of the Government with candour and impartiality, as I am sure Earl Russell is.

I cheerfully consent to leave Earl Russell's protest on the record where it will lie side by side with the decisions of this Government, which show that during a civil war, now of nine months' duration, no complaint of any kind has been denied a hearing, not one person has been pressed into the land or naval service, not one disloyal citizen or resident, however guilty of treason or conspiracy, has forfeited his life except in battle, not one has been detained a day in confinement who could and would give reliable pledges of his forbearance from evil designs, nor indeed has one person who could or would give no such pledges been detained a day beyond the period when the danger which he was engaged in producing had safely passed away.

Happily, it is not the judgment of even great and good men like Earl Russell, pronounced in the excitement of the hour, and possibly subject to the influences of disturbing events, which determine the characters of States. From such judgments we cheerfully appeal to that of history, confident that it records no instance in which any Government or people has practised moderation in civil war equal to that which thus far has distinguished this Government and the American people.

I avail, &c.
(Signed) WILLIAM H. SEWARD.

Inclosure 2 in No. 154.

Lord Lyons to Mr. Seward.

Sir, *Washington, January* 14, 1862.

I HAVE the honour to acknowledge the receipt of the note which you were so good as to address to me yesterday, on the subject of the despatch from Earl Russell to me relative to the arrests of British subjects, of which I delivered a copy to you three days ago. I will to-day forward to Lord Russell a copy of the communication which you have thus been so good as to make to me.

I have, &c.
(Signed)   LYONS.

No. 155.

Lord Lyons to Earl Russell.—(Received January 27.)

(Extract.) *Washington, January* 14, 1862.

MR. SEWARD said that he was desirous that the United States should, in the present war, offer to the world an example of leniency towards the enemy and regard for the interests of neutrals, such as had never before been seen. He proceeded to enlarge upon the moderation hitherto displayed by this Government; on its having abstained from shedding the blood of traitors or inflicting any severe punishments upon them; on its having adopted the mild form of a blockade for closing the Southern ports, and on other similar topics. He went on to say that he hoped to be able to give still another proof of moderation. He was occupied in devising a plan for reopening correspondence by letter with the South. Of course what was conceded to one foreign nation must be conceded to all; and what was conceded to foreigners must be equally conceded to American citizens. He thought it might be possible to establish at some point a special office to which letters to and from the Southern States should be sent, and from which such as, on examination, should prove to be unobjectionable might be forwarded. He had not, however, had time to consider the matter maturely, nor had he yet submitted it to the President or the Cabinet.

Without entering into details, I endeavoured to impress upon Mr. Seward the great advantage of removing the irritation against the United States, and the general dissatisfaction which the interruption of the correspondence kept up in Europe. I said that, rightly or wrongly, the loss, the inconvenience, and the distress of mind occasioned by the interruption, could not but alienate the sympathies of Europe from the Government whose regulations were the cause of them.

No. 156.

Earl Russell to Lord Lyons.

My Lord, *Foreign Office, February* 1, 1862.

I INCLOSE, for your information, and for communication to Her Majesty's Consuls in the Northern and Southern States, copies of the "Gazette" of last evening, containing a copy of a letter which I have addressed to the Lords Commissioners of the Admiralty, to the several Secretaries of State, and to the Lords Commissioners of Her Majesty's Treasury, signifying the Queen's pleasure with regard to the rules which Her Majesty, with the view of preserving a strict neutrality, has commanded to be observed in all ports, harbours, roadsteads, and waters within Her Majesty's territorial jurisdiction during the continuance of the existing hostilities between the United States and the States calling themselves the Confederate States of North America.

I am, &c.
(Signed)   RUSSELL.

Inclosure in No. 156.

Earl Russell to the Lords Commissioners of the Admiralty.

My Lords,   *Foreign Office, January* 31, 1862.

HER Majesty being fully determined to observe the duties of neutrality during the existing hostilities between the United States and the States calling themselves the Confederate States of America, and being, moreover, resolved to prevent, as far as possible, the use of Her Majesty's harbours, ports, and coasts, and the waters within Her Majesty's territorial jurisdiction, in aid of the warlike purposes of either belligerent, has commanded me to communicate to your Lordships, for your guidance, the following rules, which are to be treated and enforced as Her Majesty's orders and directions.

Her Majesty is pleased further to command that these rules shall be put in force in the United Kingdom, and in the Channel Islands, on and after Thursday the 6th day of February next, and in Her Majesty's territories and possessions beyond the seas six days after the day when the Governor or other chief authority of each of such territories or possessions respectively shall have notified and published the same, stating in such notification that the said rules are to be obeyed by all persons within the same territories and possessions.

1. During the continuance of the present hostilities between the Government of the United States of North America and the States calling themselves the Confederate States of America, or until Her Majesty shall otherwise order, no ships of war or privateers belonging to either of the belligerents shall be permitted to enter or remain in the port of Nassau, or in any other port, roadstead, or waters of the Bahama Islands, except by special leave of the Lieutenant-Governor of the Bahama Islands, or in case of stress of weather. If any such vessel should enter any such port, roadstead, or waters, by special leave, or under stress of weather, the authorities of the place shall require her to put to sea as soon as possible, without permitting her to take in any supplies beyond what may be necessary for her immediate use.

If at the time when this order is first notified in the Bahama Islands, there shall be any such vessel already within any port, roadstead, or waters of those islands, the Lieutenant-Governor shall give notice to such vessel to depart, and shall require her to put to sea within such time as he shall, under the circumstances, consider proper and reasonable. If there shall then be ships of war or privateers belonging to both the said belligerents within the territorial jurisdiction of Her Majesty, in or near the said port, roadstead or waters, the Lieutenant-Governor shall fix the order of time in which such vessels shall depart. No such vessel of either belligerent shall be permitted to put to sea until after the expiration of at least twenty-four hours from the time when the last preceding vessel of the other belligerent (whether the same shall be a ship of war, or privateer, or merchant-ship) which shall have left the same port, roadstead, or waters adjacent thereto, shall have passed beyond the territorial jurisdiction of Her Majesty.

2. During the continuance of the present hostilities between the Government of the United States of North America and the States calling themselves the Confederate States of America, all ships of war and privateers of either belligerent are prohibited from making use of any port or roadstead in the United Kingdom of Great Britain and Ireland, or in the Channel Islands, or in any of Her Majesty's Colonies, or Foreign Possessions, or Dependencies, or of any waters subject to the territorial jurisdiction of the British Crown, as a station or place of resort for any warlike purpose, or for the purpose of obtaining any facilities of warlike equipment; and no ship of war or privateer of either belligerent shall hereafter be permitted to sail out of or leave any port, roadstead, or waters subject to British jurisdiction, from which any vessel of the other belligerent (whether the same shall be a ship of war, a privateer, or a merchant-ship) shall have previously departed, until after the expiration of at least twenty-four hours from the departure of such last-mentioned vessel beyond the territorial jurisdiction of Her Majesty.

3. If any ship of war or privateer of either belligerent shall, after the time when this order shall be first notified and put in force in the United Kingdom and in the Channel Islands, and in the several Colonies, and Foreign Possessions, and Dependencies of Her Majesty respectively, enter any port, roadstead, or waters belonging to Her Majesty, either in the United Kingdom or in the Channel Islands, or in any of Her Majesty's Colonies, or Foreign Possessions, or Dependencies, such vessel shall be required to depart and to put to sea within twenty-four hours after her entrance into such port, roadstead, or waters, except in case of stress of weather, or of her requiring provisions or things necessary for the subsistence of her crew, or repairs, in either of which cases the authorities of the port, or of the nearest port (as the case may be), shall require her to put to sea as soon as possible

after the expiration of such period of twenty-four hours, without permitting her to take in supplies beyond what may be necessary for her immediate use; and no such vessel which may have been allowed to remain within British waters for the purpose of repair, shall continue in any such port, roadstead, or waters, for a longer period than twenty-four hours after her necessary repairs shall have been completed: Provided, nevertheless, that in all cases in which there shall be any vessels (whether ships of war, privateers, or merchant-ships) of both the said belligerent parties in the same port, roadstead, or waters within the territorial jurisdiction of Her Majesty, there shall be an interval of not less than twenty-four hours between the departure therefrom of any such vessel (whether a ship of war, a privateer, or a merchant-ship) of the one belligerent, and the subsequent departure therefrom of any ship of war or privateer of the other belligerent; and the times hereby limited for the departure of such ships of war and privateers respectively shall always, in case of necessity, be extended so far as may be requisite for giving effect to this proviso, but not further or otherwise.

4. No ship of war or privateer of either belligerent shall hereafter be permitted, while in any port, roadstead, or waters subject to the territorial jurisdiction of Her Majesty, to take in any supplies except provisions and such other things as may be requisite for the subsistence of her crew; and except so much coal only as may be sufficient to carry such vessel to the nearest port of her own country, or to some nearer destination; and no coal shall be again supplied to any such ship of war or privateer, in the same or any other port, roadstead, or waters subject to the territorial jurisdiction of Her Majesty, without special permission, until after the expiration of three months from the time when such coal may have been last supplied to her within British waters as aforesaid.

I have, &c.
(Signed) RUSSELL.

NORTH AMERICA.

No. 1.

CORRESPONDENCE relating to the Civil War in the United States of North America.

Presented to both Houses of Parliament by Command of Her Majesty. 1862.

www.ingramcontent.com/pod-product-compliance
Lightning Source LLC
Chambersburg PA
CBHW030344170426
43202CB00010B/1229